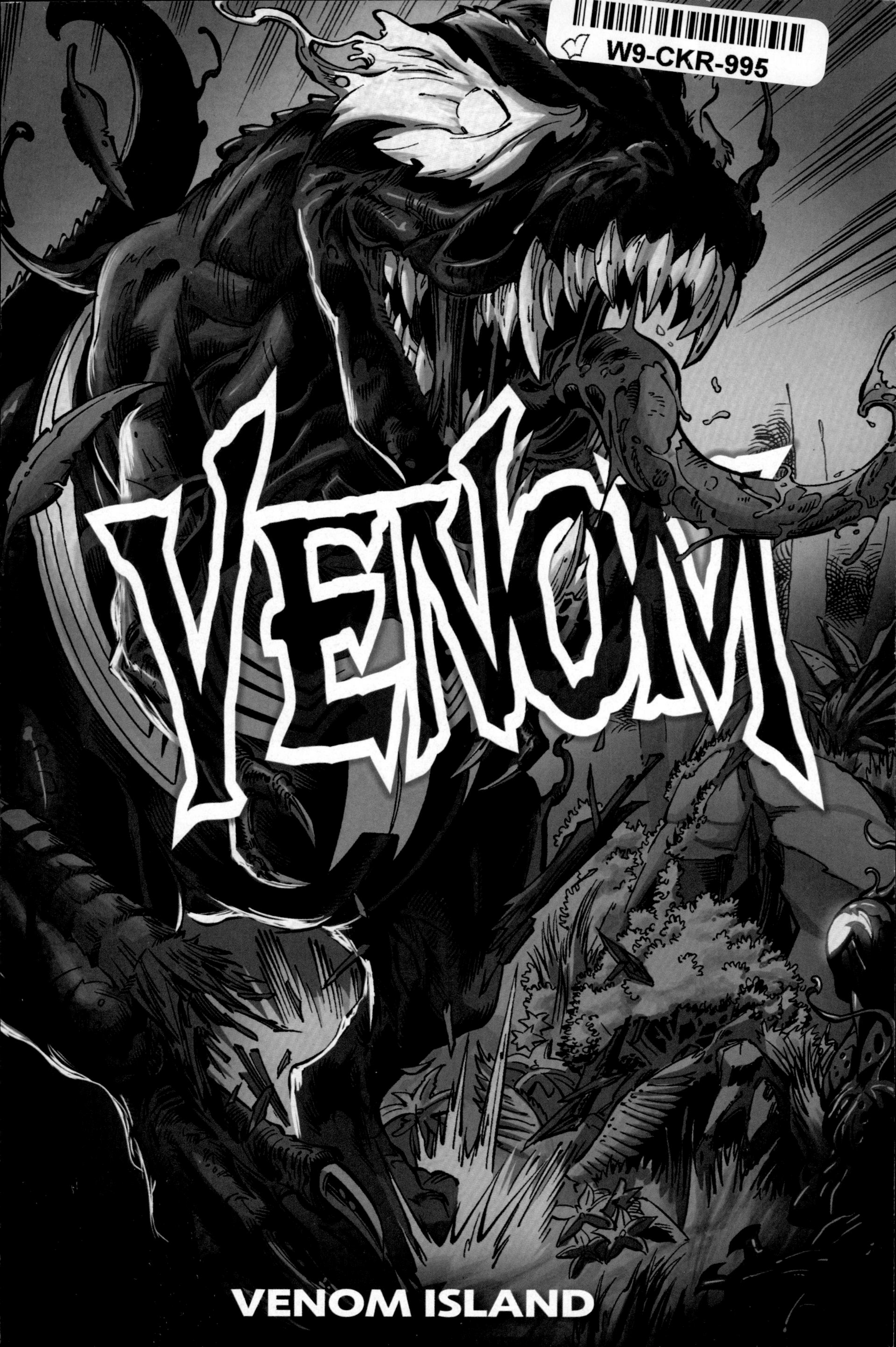
VENOM
VENOM ISLAND

DISGRACED REPORTER EDDIE BROCK STUMBLED UPON AN AGGRESSIVE ALIEN ORGANISM CALLED A SYMBIOTE DURING ONE OF THE LOWEST POINTS OF HIS LIFE. THE TWO WERE JOINED AND USED THEIR COMBINED LUST FOR VIOLENCE TO MAKE THEIR CITY SAFER AS THE LETHAL PROTECTOR, VENOM.

RECENTLY, THE BLOODTHIRSTY SERIAL KILLER NAMED CARNAGE RETURNED, HOPING TO SLAUGHTER ANYONE WITH SYMBIOTE DNA IN THE BODIES TO FREE THE SYMBIOTE GOD KNULL FROM HIS PRISON AT THE HEART OF THE PLANET KLYNTAR.

BUT WHEN EDDIE BROCK'S SON, DYLAN, GOT CAUGHT IN CARNAGE'S PATH, VENOM THREW CAUTION TO THE WIND AND ABSORBED CARNAGE'S SYMBIOTE.

HE SAVED DYLAN, BUT SET KNULL FREE IN THE PROCESS. NOW, KNULL IS EN ROUTE TO EARTH—AND NOBODY BUT EDDIE BROCK KNOWS...

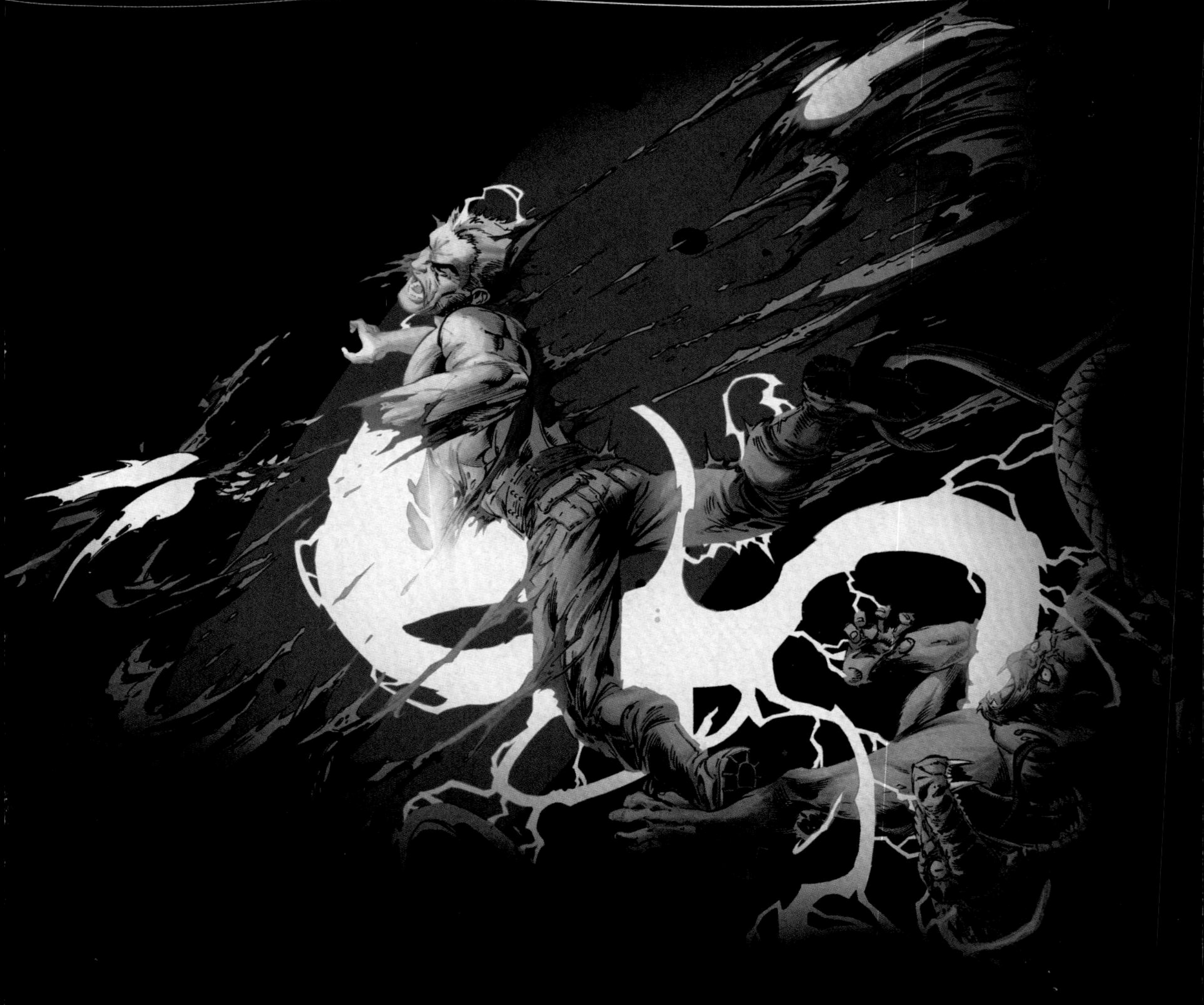

COLLECTION EDITOR MARK D. BEAZLEY • ASSISTANT MANAGING EDITOR MAIA LOY • ASSISTANT MANAGING EDITOR LISA MONTALBANO
SENIOR EDITOR, SPECIAL PROJECTS JENNIFER GRÜNWALD • VP PRODUCTION & SPECIAL PROJECTS JEFF YOUNGQUIST
BOOK DESIGNERS SALENA MAHINA WITH JAY BOWEN & ANTHONY GAMBINO
SVP PRINT, SALES & MARKETING DAVID GABRIEL • EDITOR IN CHIEF C.B. CEBULSKI

VENOM BY DONNY CATES VOL. 4: VENOM ISLAND. Contains material originally published in magazine form as VENOM (2018) #21-25. First printing 2020. ISBN 978-1-302-92020-3. Published by MARVEL WORLDWIDE, INC., a subsidiary of MARVEL ENTERTAINMENT, LLC. OFFICE OF PUBLICATION: 1290 Avenue of the Americas, New York, NY 10104. **Printed in Canada.** KEVIN FEIGE, Chief Creative Officer; DAN BUCKLEY, President, Marvel Entertainment; JOHN NEE, Publisher; JOE QUESADA, EVP & Creative Director; TOM BREVOORT, SVP of Publishing; DAVID BOGART, Associate Publisher & SVP of Talent Affairs; Publishing & Partnership; DAVID GABRIEL, VP of Print & Digital Publishing; JEFF YOUNGQUIST, VP of Production & Special Projects; DAN CARR, Executive Director of Publishing Technology; ALEX MORALES, Director of Publishing Operations; DAN EDINGTON, Managing Editor; SUSAN CRESPI, Production Manager; STAN LEE, Chairman Emeritus. For information regarding advertising in Marvel Comics or on Marvel.com, please contact Vit DeBellis, Custom Solutions & Integrated Advertising Manager, at vdebellis@marvel.com. For Marvel subscription inquiries, please call 888-511-5480. **Manufactured between 5/29/2020 and 6/30/2020 by SOLISCO PRINTERS, SCOTT, QC, CANADA.**

10 9 8 7 6 5 4 3 2 1

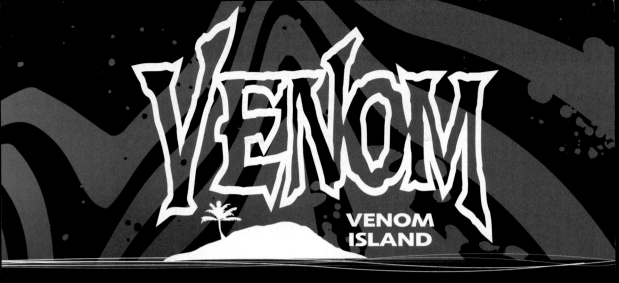

VENOM

VENOM ISLAND

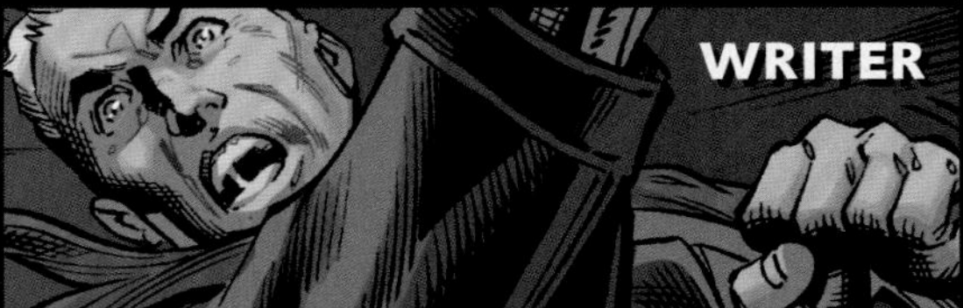

WRITER **DONNY CATES**

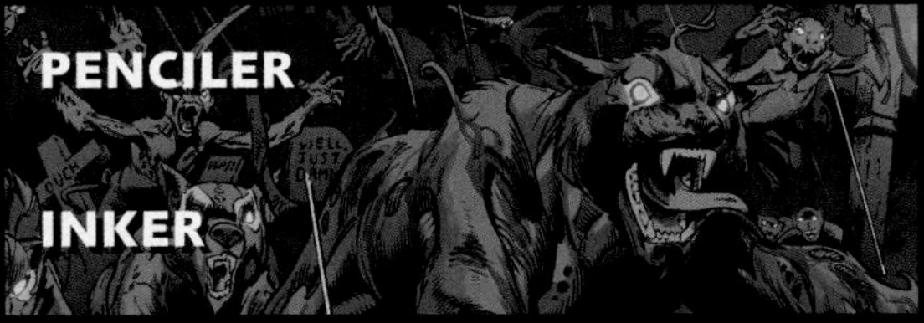

PENCILER **MARK BAGLEY**

INKER **ANDY OWENS**

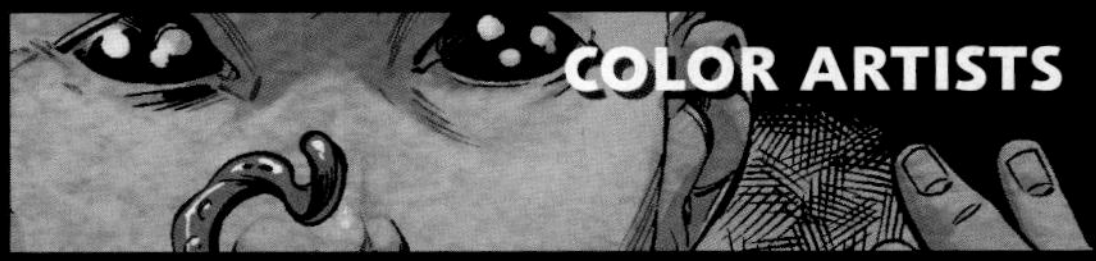

COLOR ARTISTS **FRANK MARTIN** WITH **ERICK ARCINIEGA** (#21-#22)

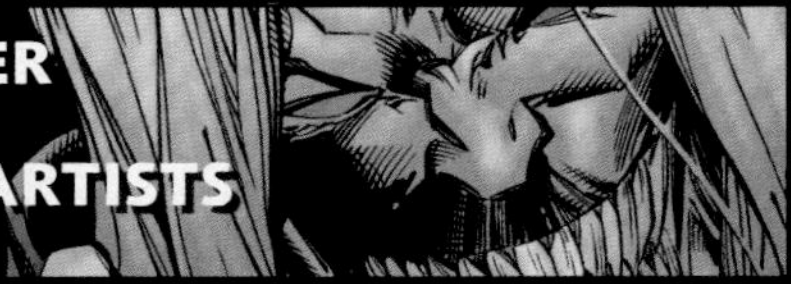

LETTERER **VC's CLAYTON COWLES**

COVER ARTISTS **MARK BAGLEY, ANDY OWENS & JASON KEITH** (#21-#24) AND **RYAN STEGMAN, JP MAYER & FRANK MARTIN** (#25)

VENOM **FLASHBACK:** WRITER **DAVID MICHELINIE** PENCILER **RON LIM** INKER **JP MAYER** COLOR ARTIST **ERICK ARCINIEGA** LETTERER **VC's CLAYTON COWLES**

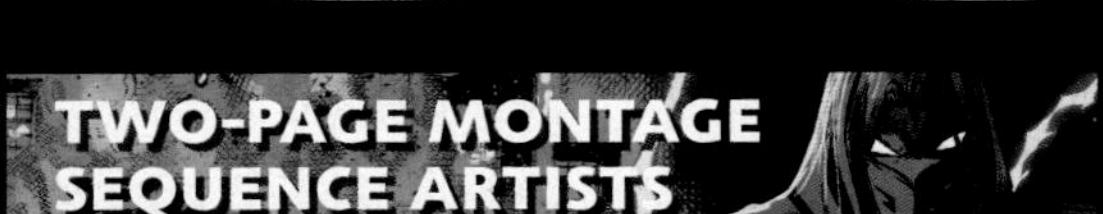

TWO-PAGE MONTAGE SEQUENCE ARTISTS **RYAN STEGMAN, JP MAYER & FRANK MARTIN**

DANNY KHAZEM **ASSISTANT EDITOR**

DEVIN LEWIS **EDITOR**

NICK LOWE **EXECUTIVE EDITOR**

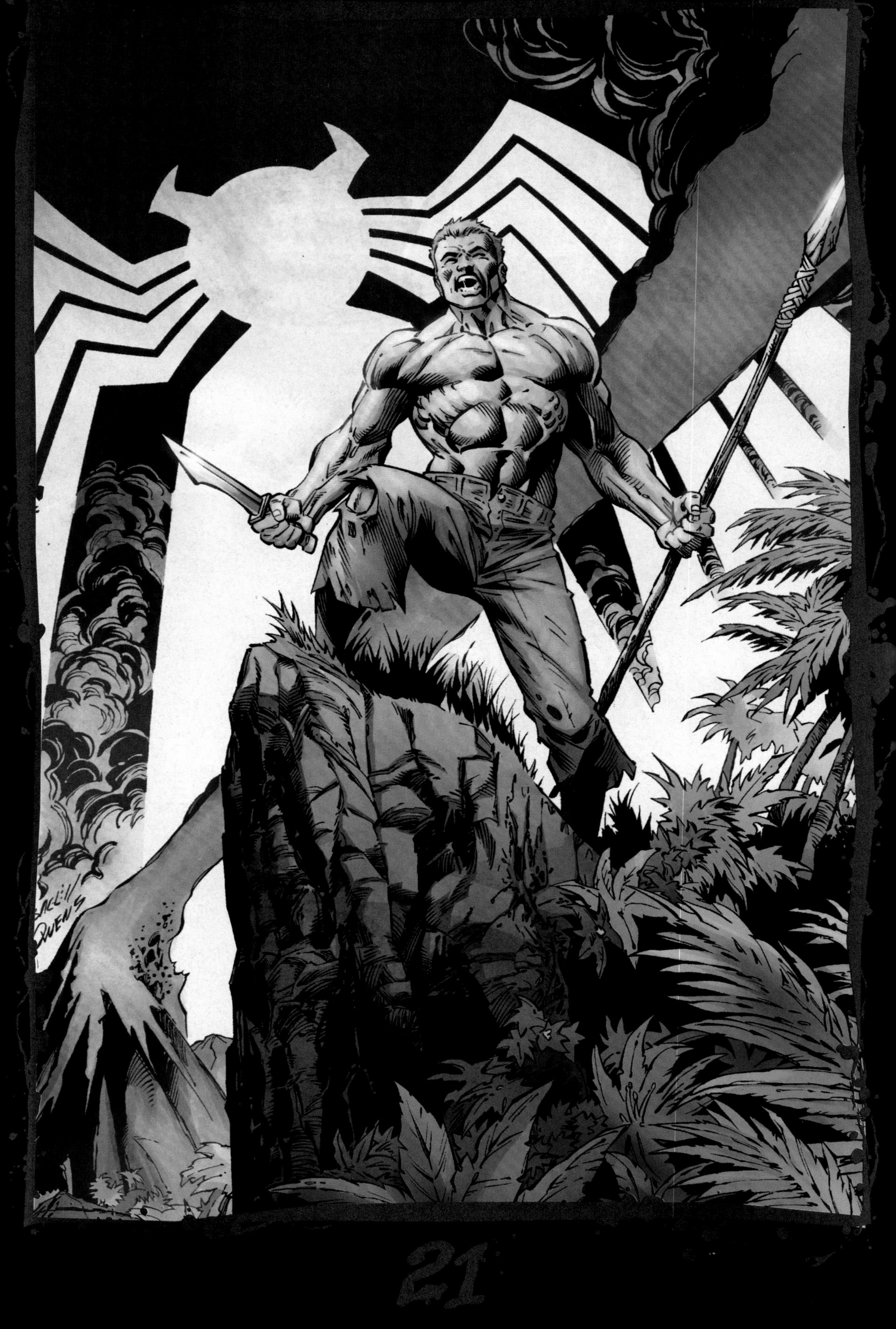

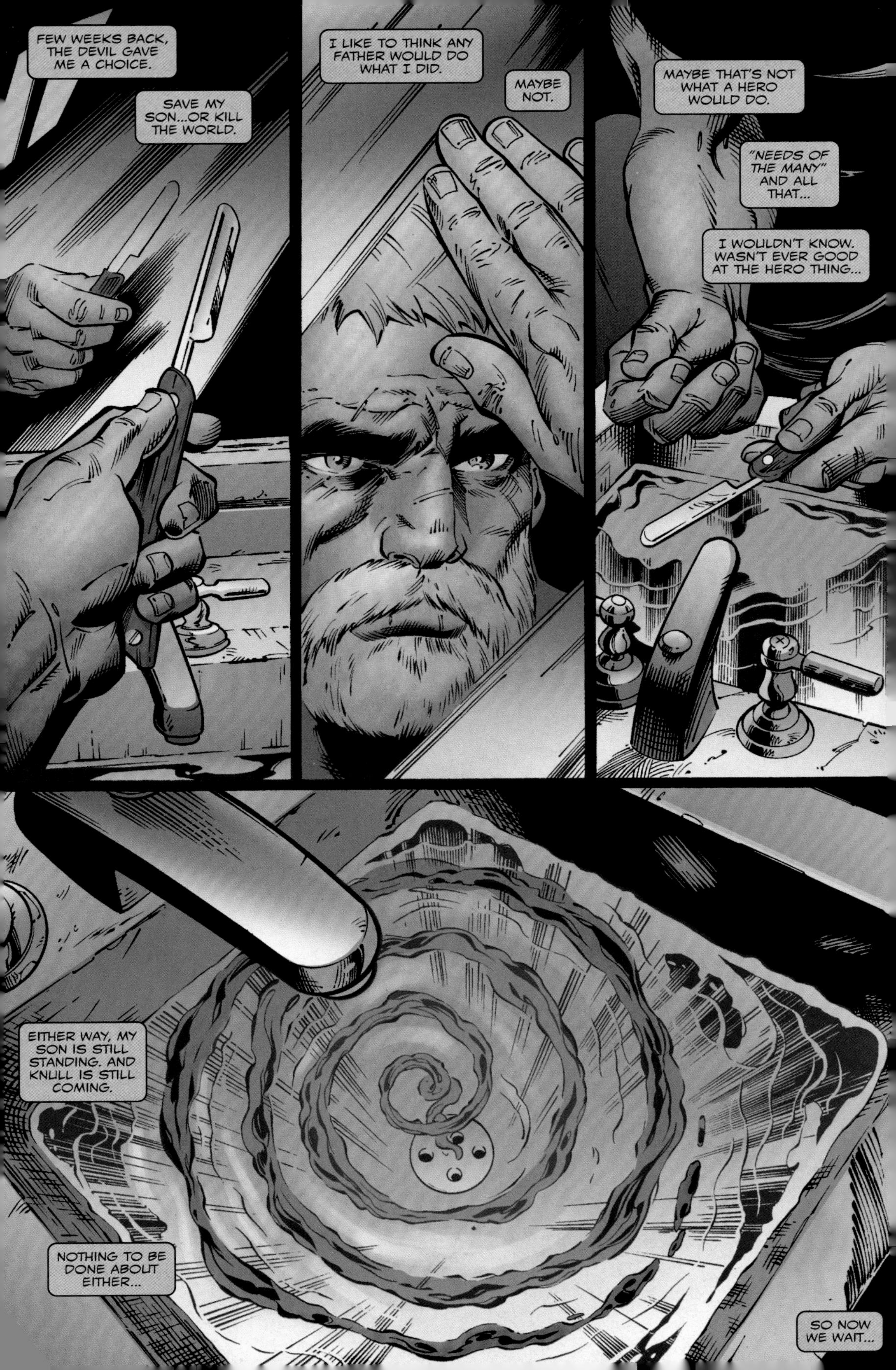
FEW WEEKS BACK, THE DEVIL GAVE ME A CHOICE.
SAVE MY SON...OR KILL THE WORLD.
I LIKE TO THINK ANY FATHER WOULD DO WHAT I DID.
MAYBE NOT.
MAYBE THAT'S NOT WHAT A HERO WOULD DO.
"NEEDS OF THE MANY" AND ALL THAT...
I WOULDN'T KNOW. WASN'T EVER GOOD AT THE HERO THING...
EITHER WAY, MY SON IS STILL STANDING. AND KNULL IS STILL COMING.
NOTHING TO BE DONE ABOUT EITHER...
SO NOW WE WAIT...

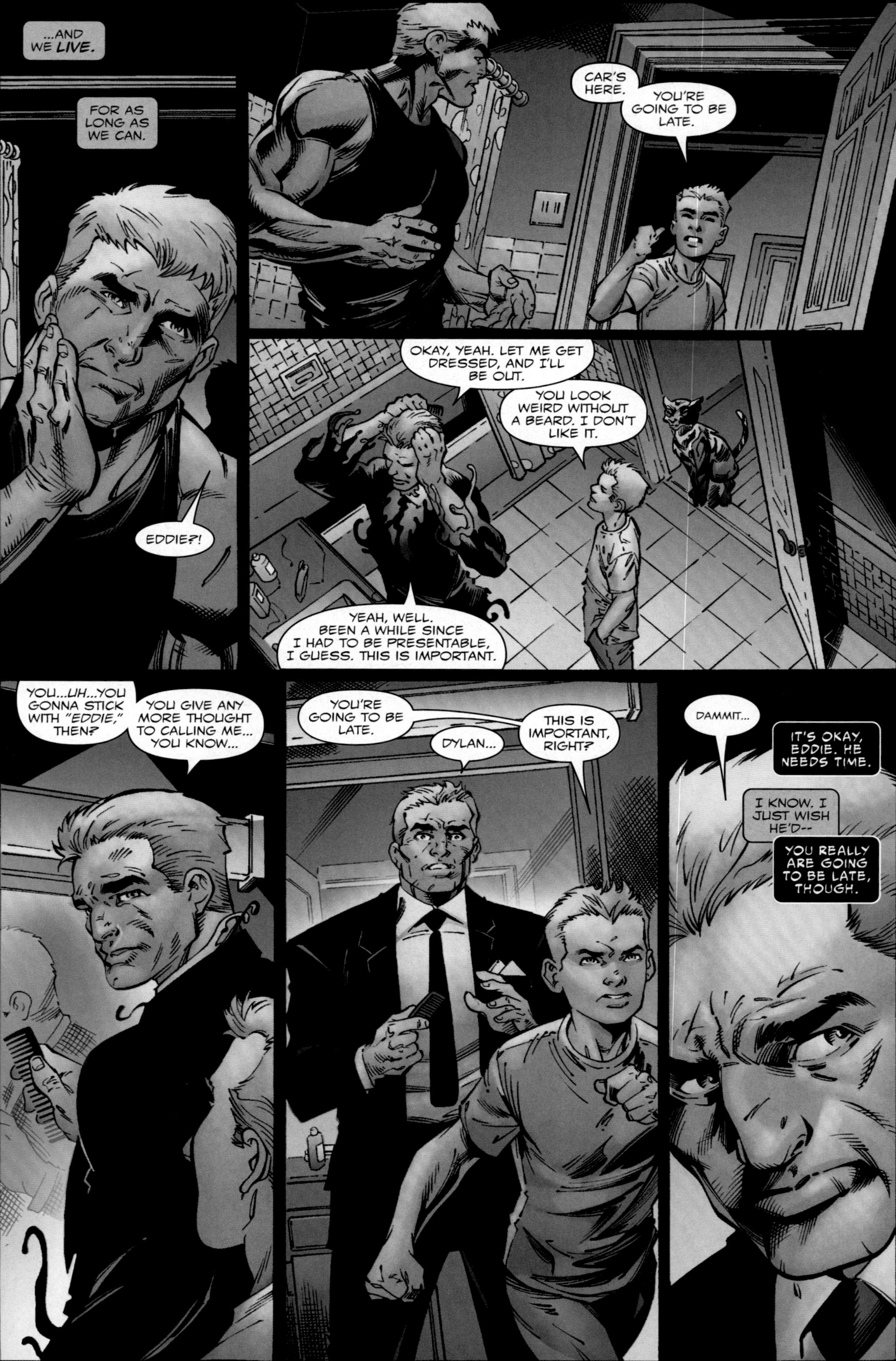
...AND WE LIVE.
FOR AS LONG AS WE CAN.
CAR'S HERE.
YOU'RE GOING TO BE LATE.
EDDIE?!
OKAY, YEAH. LET ME GET DRESSED, AND I'LL BE OUT.
YOU LOOK WEIRD WITHOUT A BEARD. I DON'T LIKE IT.
YEAH, WELL. BEEN A WHILE SINCE I HAD TO BE PRESENTABLE, I GUESS. THIS IS IMPORTANT.
YOU...UH...YOU GONNA STICK WITH "EDDIE," THEN?
YOU GIVE ANY MORE THOUGHT TO CALLING ME... YOU KNOW...
YOU'RE GOING TO BE LATE.
DYLAN...
THIS IS IMPORTANT, RIGHT?
DAMMIT...
IT'S OKAY, EDDIE. HE NEEDS TIME.
I KNOW. I JUST WISH HE'D--
YOU REALLY ARE GOING TO BE LATE, THOUGH.

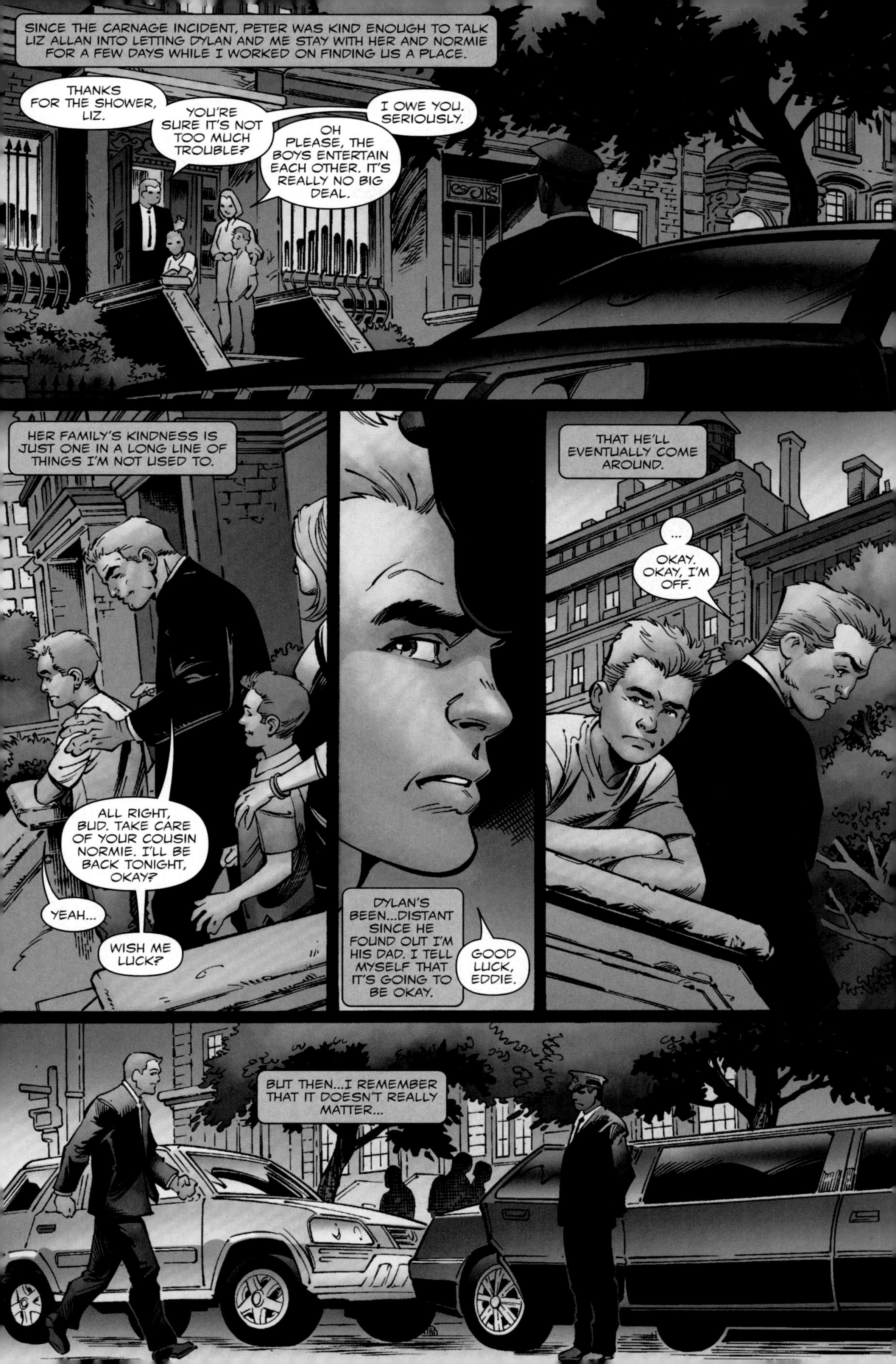
SINCE THE CARNAGE INCIDENT, PETER WAS KIND ENOUGH TO TALK LIZ ALLAN INTO LETTING DYLAN AND ME STAY WITH HER AND NORMIE FOR A FEW DAYS WHILE I WORKED ON FINDING US A PLACE.
THANKS FOR THE SHOWER, LIZ.
YOU'RE SURE IT'S NOT TOO MUCH TROUBLE?
I OWE YOU. SERIOUSLY.
OH PLEASE, THE BOYS ENTERTAIN EACH OTHER. IT'S REALLY NO BIG DEAL.
HER FAMILY'S KINDNESS IS JUST ONE IN A LONG LINE OF THINGS I'M NOT USED TO.
ALL RIGHT, BUD. TAKE CARE OF YOUR COUSIN NORMIE. I'LL BE BACK TONIGHT, OKAY?
YEAH...
WISH ME LUCK?
DYLAN'S BEEN...DISTANT SINCE HE FOUND OUT I'M HIS DAD. I TELL MYSELF THAT IT'S GOING TO BE OKAY.
GOOD LUCK, EDDIE.
THAT HE'LL EVENTUALLY COME AROUND.
...
OKAY. OKAY, I'M OFF.
BUT THEN...I REMEMBER THAT IT DOESN'T REALLY MATTER...

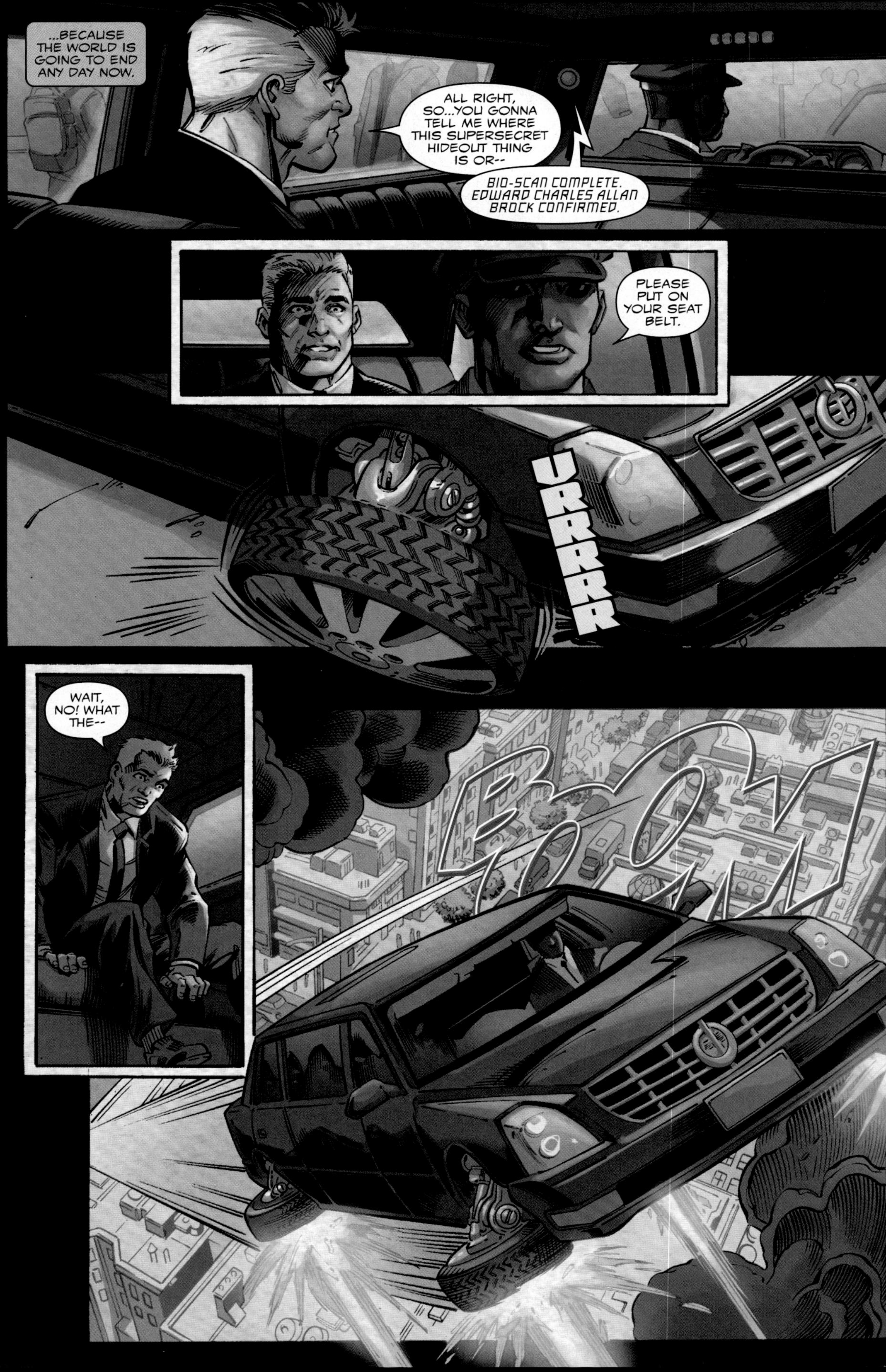
...BECAUSE THE WORLD IS GOING TO END ANY DAY NOW.
ALL RIGHT, SO...YOU GONNA TELL ME WHERE THIS SUPERSECRET HIDEOUT THING IS OR--
BIO-SCAN COMPLETE. EDWARD CHARLES ALLAN BROCK CONFIRMED.
PLEASE PUT ON YOUR SEAT BELT.
URRRRR
WAIT, NO! WHAT THE--
BOOM

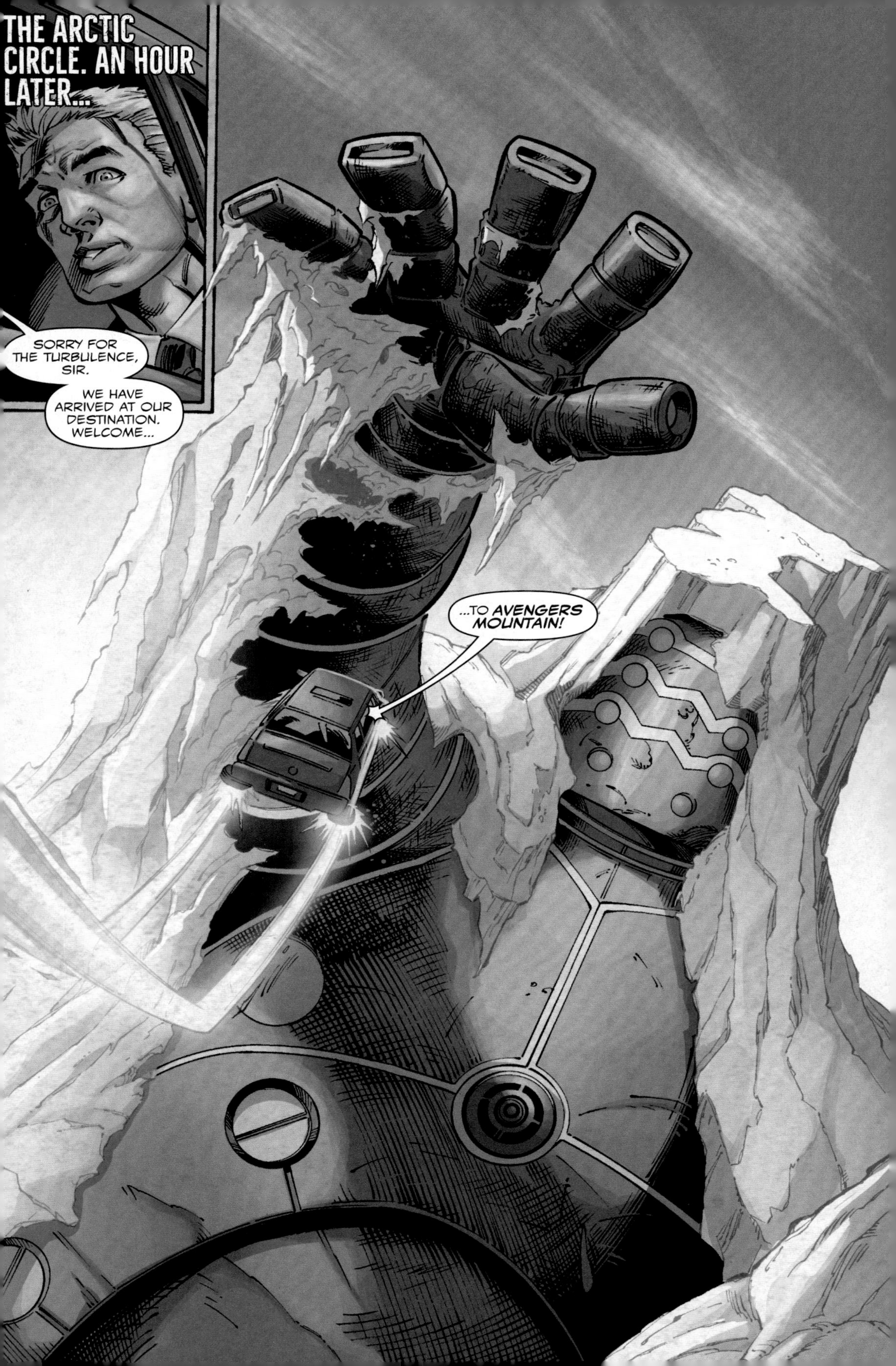
THE ARCTIC CIRCLE. AN HOUR LATER...
SORRY FOR THE TURBULENCE, SIR.
WE HAVE ARRIVED AT OUR DESTINATION. WELCOME...
...TO AVENGERS MOUNTAIN!

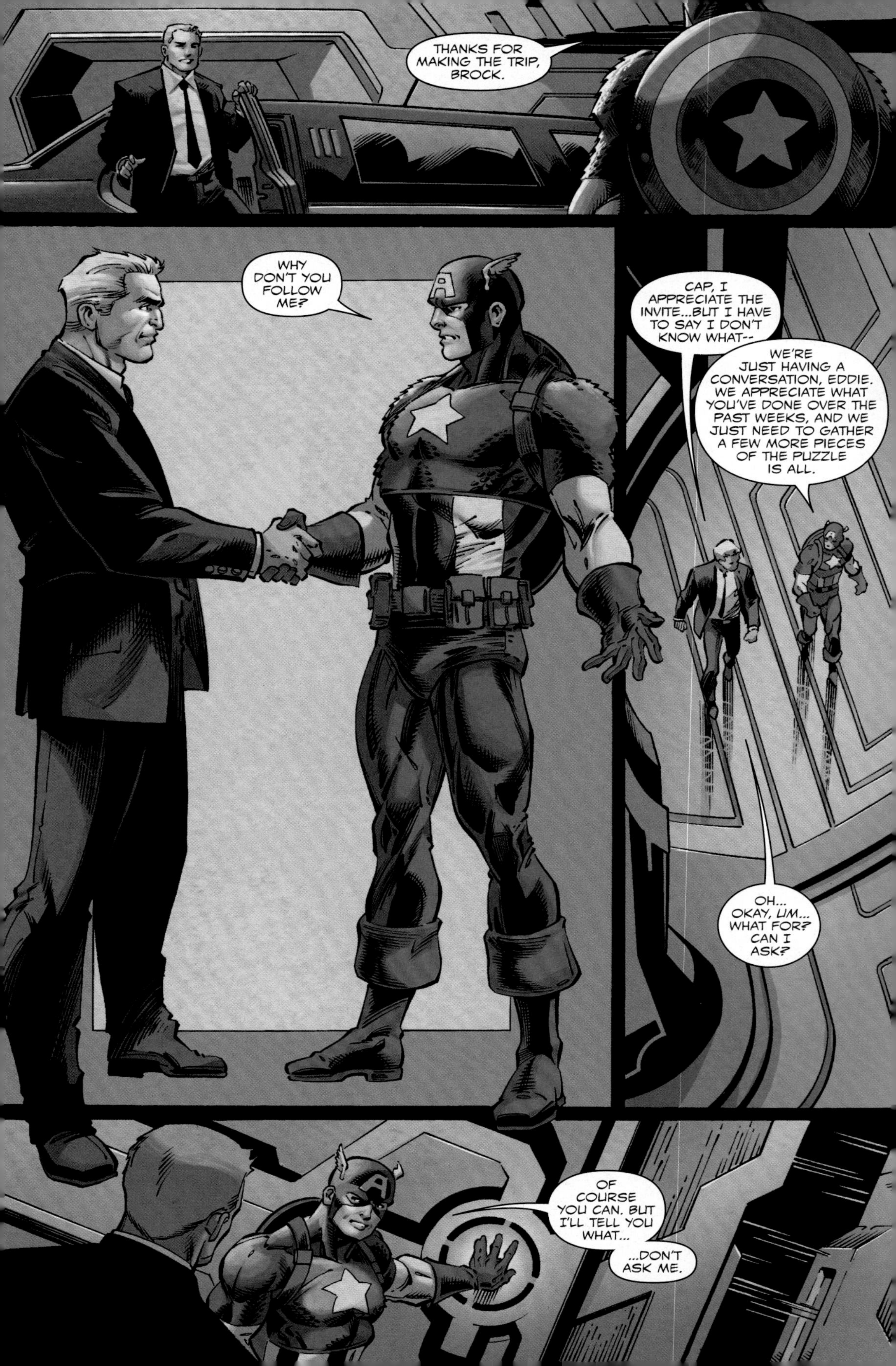
THANKS FOR MAKING THE TRIP, BROCK.
WHY DON'T YOU FOLLOW ME?
CAP, I APPRECIATE THE INVITE...BUT I HAVE TO SAY I DON'T KNOW WHAT--
WE'RE JUST HAVING A CONVERSATION, EDDIE. WE APPRECIATE WHAT YOU'VE DONE OVER THE PAST WEEKS, AND WE JUST NEED TO GATHER A FEW MORE PIECES OF THE PUZZLE IS ALL.
OH... OKAY, UM... WHAT FOR? CAN I ASK?
OF COURSE YOU CAN. BUT I'LL TELL YOU WHAT...
...DON'T ASK ME.

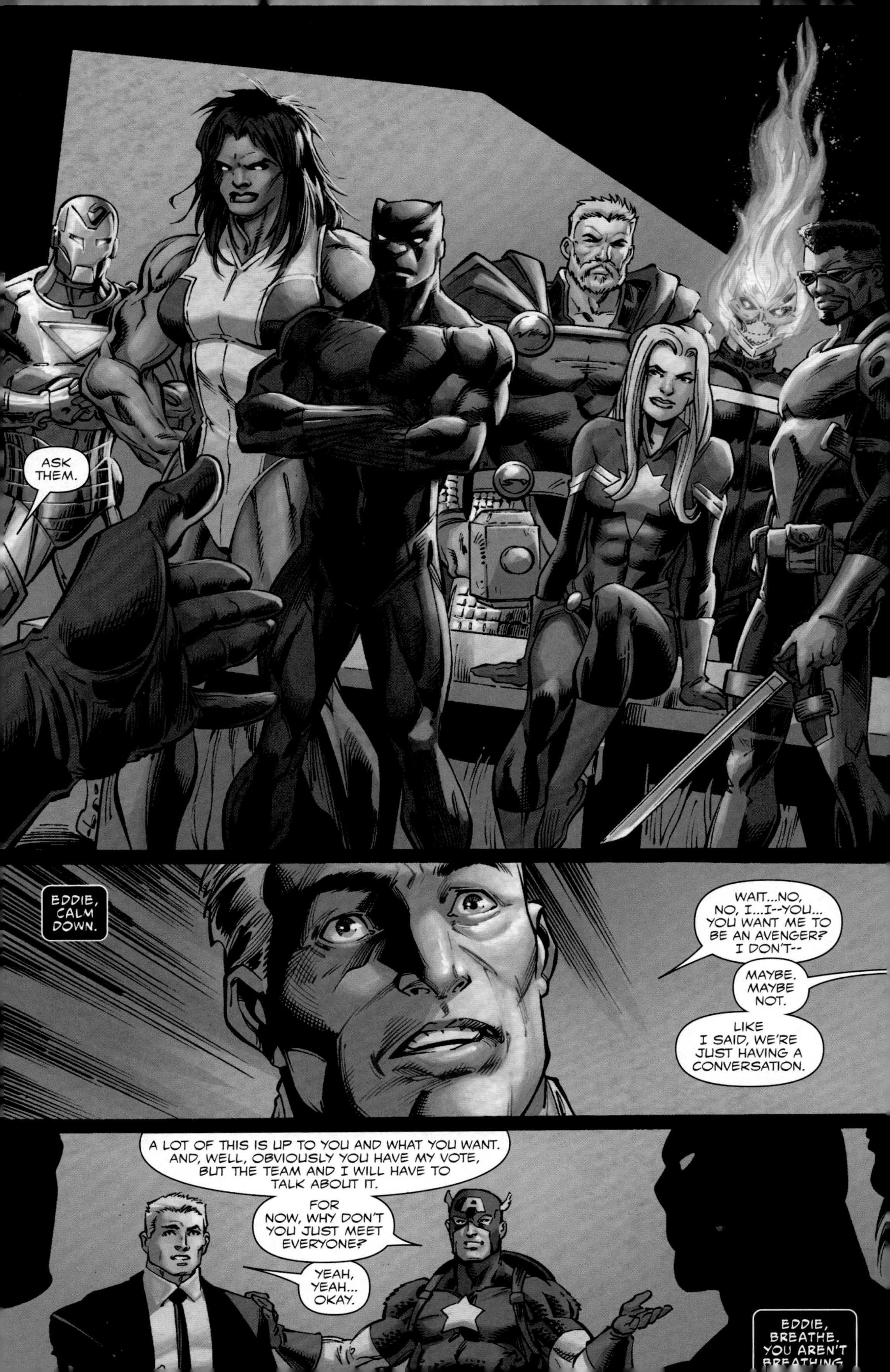
ASK THEM.
EDDIE, CALM DOWN.
WAIT...NO, NO, I...I--YOU... YOU WANT ME TO BE AN AVENGER? I DON'T--
MAYBE. MAYBE NOT.
LIKE I SAID, WE'RE JUST HAVING A CONVERSATION.
A LOT OF THIS IS UP TO YOU AND WHAT YOU WANT. AND, WELL, OBVIOUSLY YOU HAVE MY VOTE, BUT THE TEAM AND I WILL HAVE TO TALK ABOUT IT.
FOR NOW, WHY DON'T YOU JUST MEET EVERYONE?
YEAH, YEAH... OKAY.
EDDIE, BREATHE. YOU AREN'T

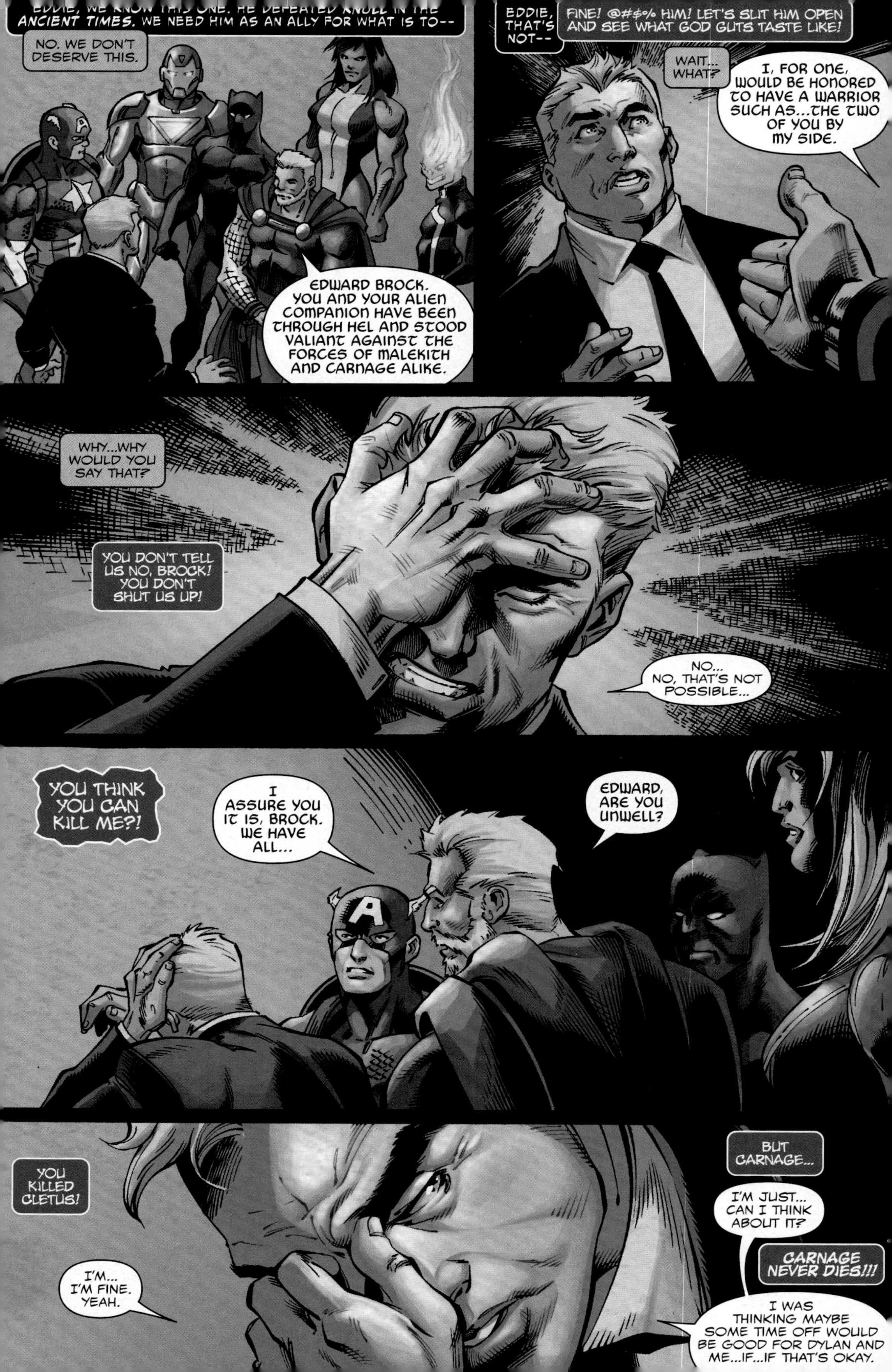
EDDIE, WE KNOW THIS ONE. HE DEFEATED KNULL IN THE ANCIENT TIMES. WE NEED HIM AS AN ALLY FOR WHAT IS TO--
NO. WE DON'T DESERVE THIS.
EDWARD BROCK. YOU AND YOUR ALIEN COMPANION HAVE BEEN THROUGH HEL AND STOOD VALIANT AGAINST THE FORCES OF MALEKITH AND CARNAGE ALIKE.
EDDIE, THAT'S NOT--
FINE! @#$% HIM! LET'S SLIT HIM OPEN AND SEE WHAT GOD GUTS TASTE LIKE!
WAIT... WHAT?
I, FOR ONE, WOULD BE HONORED TO HAVE A WARRIOR SUCH AS...THE TWO OF YOU BY MY SIDE.
WHY...WHY WOULD YOU SAY THAT?
YOU DON'T TELL US NO, BROCK! YOU DON'T SHUT US UP!
NO... NO, THAT'S NOT POSSIBLE...
YOU THINK YOU CAN KILL ME?!
I ASSURE YOU IT IS, BROCK. WE HAVE ALL...
EDWARD, ARE YOU UNWELL?
YOU KILLED CLETUS!
I'M... I'M FINE. YEAH.
BUT CARNAGE...
I'M JUST... CAN I THINK ABOUT IT?
CARNAGE NEVER DIES!!!
I WAS THINKING MAYBE SOME TIME OFF WOULD BE GOOD FOR DYLAN AND ME...IF...IF THAT'S OKAY.

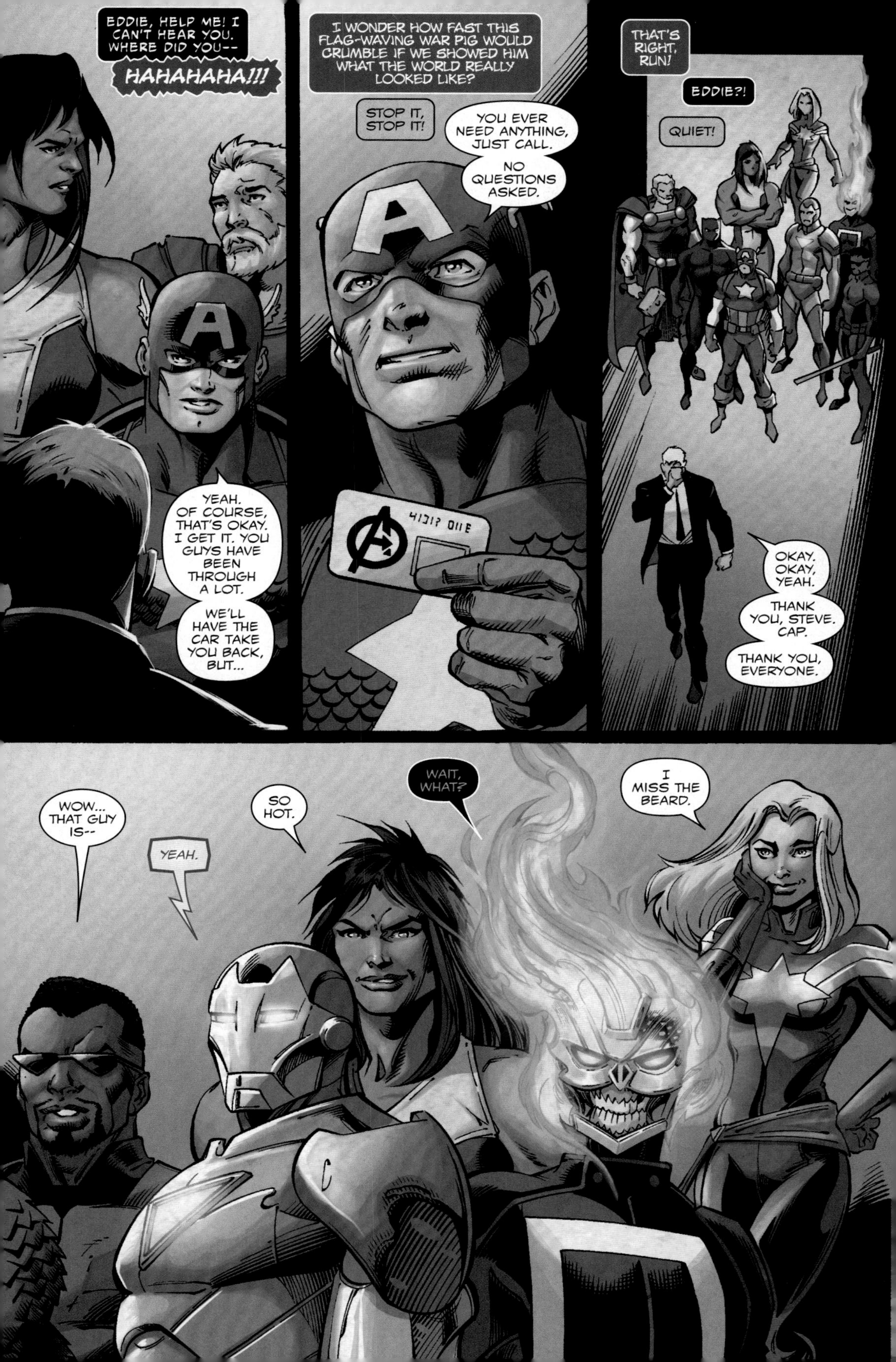
EDDIE, HELP ME! I CAN'T HEAR YOU. WHERE DID YOU--
HAHAHAHA!!!
YEAH. OF COURSE, THAT'S OKAY. I GET IT. YOU GUYS HAVE BEEN THROUGH A LOT.
WE'LL HAVE THE CAR TAKE YOU BACK, BUT...
I WONDER HOW FAST THIS FLAG-WAVING WAR PIG WOULD CRUMBLE IF WE SHOWED HIM WHAT THE WORLD REALLY LOOKED LIKE?
STOP IT, STOP IT!
YOU EVER NEED ANYTHING, JUST CALL.
NO QUESTIONS ASKED.
THAT'S RIGHT, RUN!
EDDIE?!
QUIET!
OKAY. OKAY, YEAH.
THANK YOU, STEVE. CAP.
THANK YOU, EVERYONE.
WOW... THAT GUY IS--
YEAH.
SO HOT.
WAIT, WHAT?
I MISS THE BEARD.

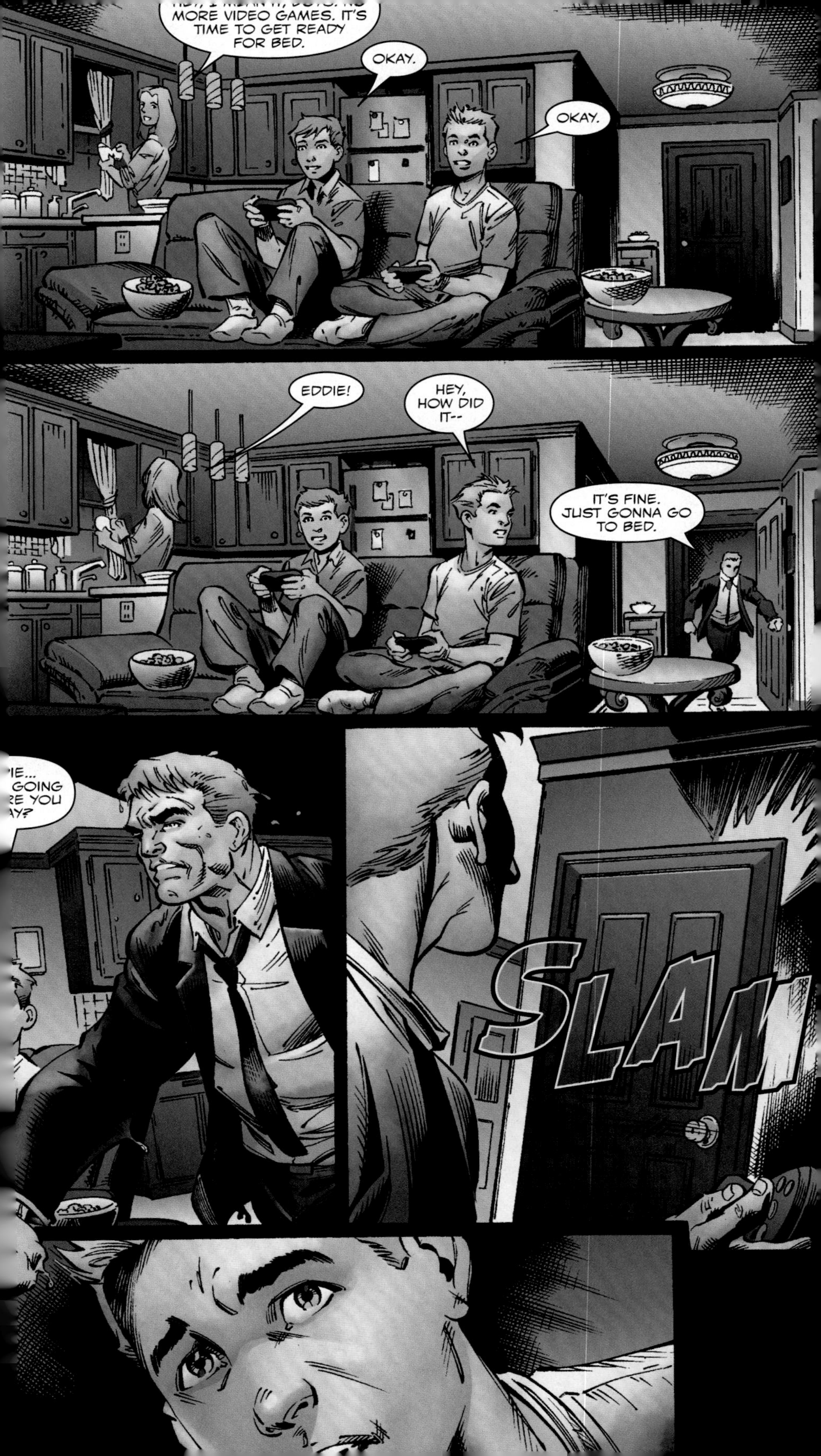

MORE VIDEO GAMES. IT'S
TIME TO GET READY
FOR BED.
OKAY.
OKAY.
EDDIE!
HEY,
HOW DID
IT--
IT'S FINE.
JUST GONNA GO
TO BED.
GOING
SLAM

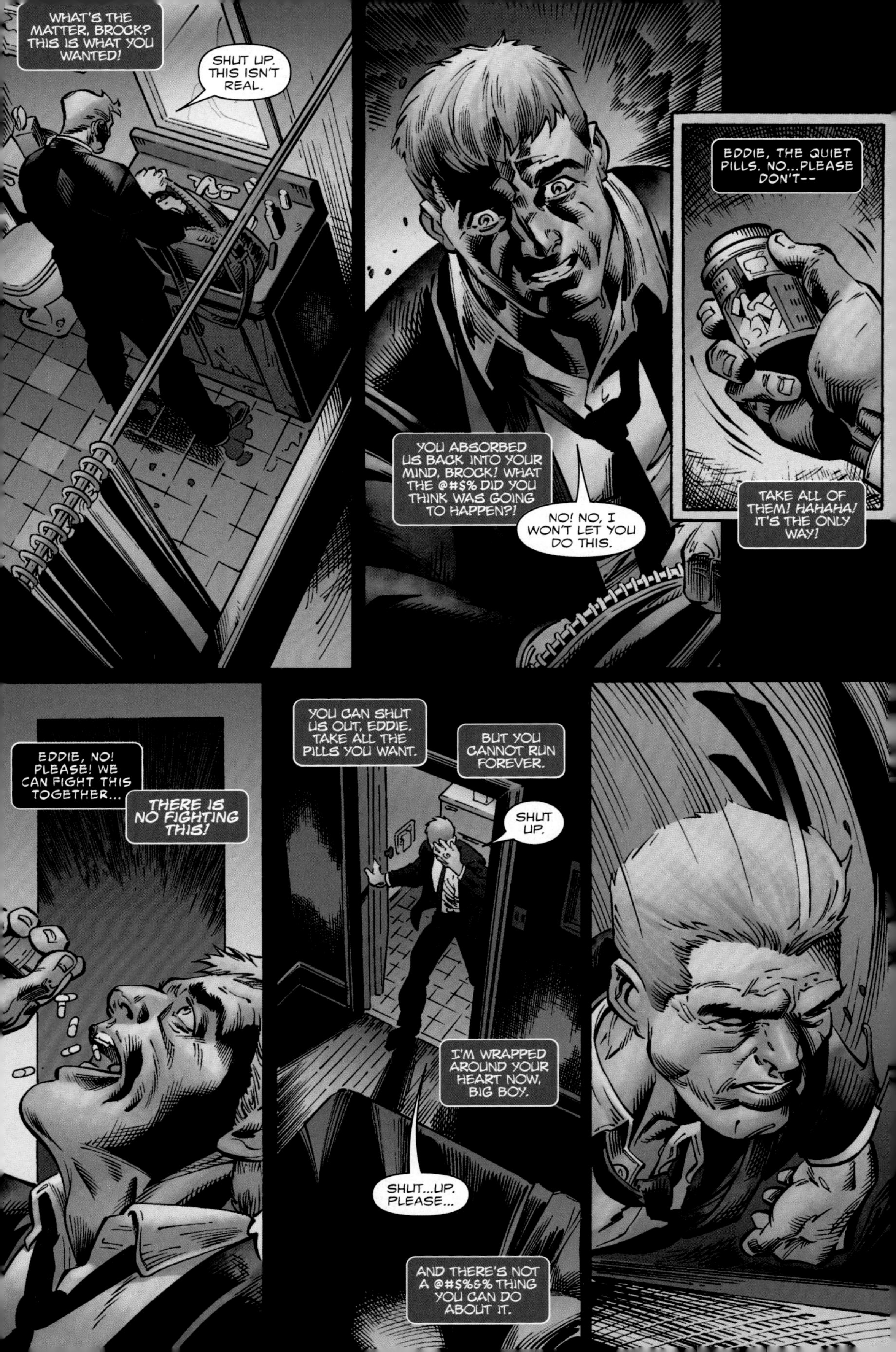
WHAT'S THE MATTER, BROCK? THIS IS WHAT YOU WANTED!
SHUT UP. THIS ISN'T REAL.
YOU ABSORBED US BACK INTO YOUR MIND, BROCK! WHAT THE @#$% DID YOU THINK WAS GOING TO HAPPEN?!
NO! NO, I WON'T LET YOU DO THIS.
EDDIE, THE QUIET PILLS. NO...PLEASE DON'T--
TAKE ALL OF THEM! HAHAHA! IT'S THE ONLY WAY!
EDDIE, NO! PLEASE! WE CAN FIGHT THIS TOGETHER...
THERE IS NO FIGHTING THIS!
YOU CAN SHUT US OUT, EDDIE. TAKE ALL THE PILLS YOU WANT.
BUT YOU CANNOT RUN FOREVER.
SHUT UP.
I'M WRAPPED AROUND YOUR HEART NOW, BIG BOY.
SHUT...UP. PLEASE...
AND THERE'S NOT A @#$%&% THING YOU CAN DO ABOUT IT.

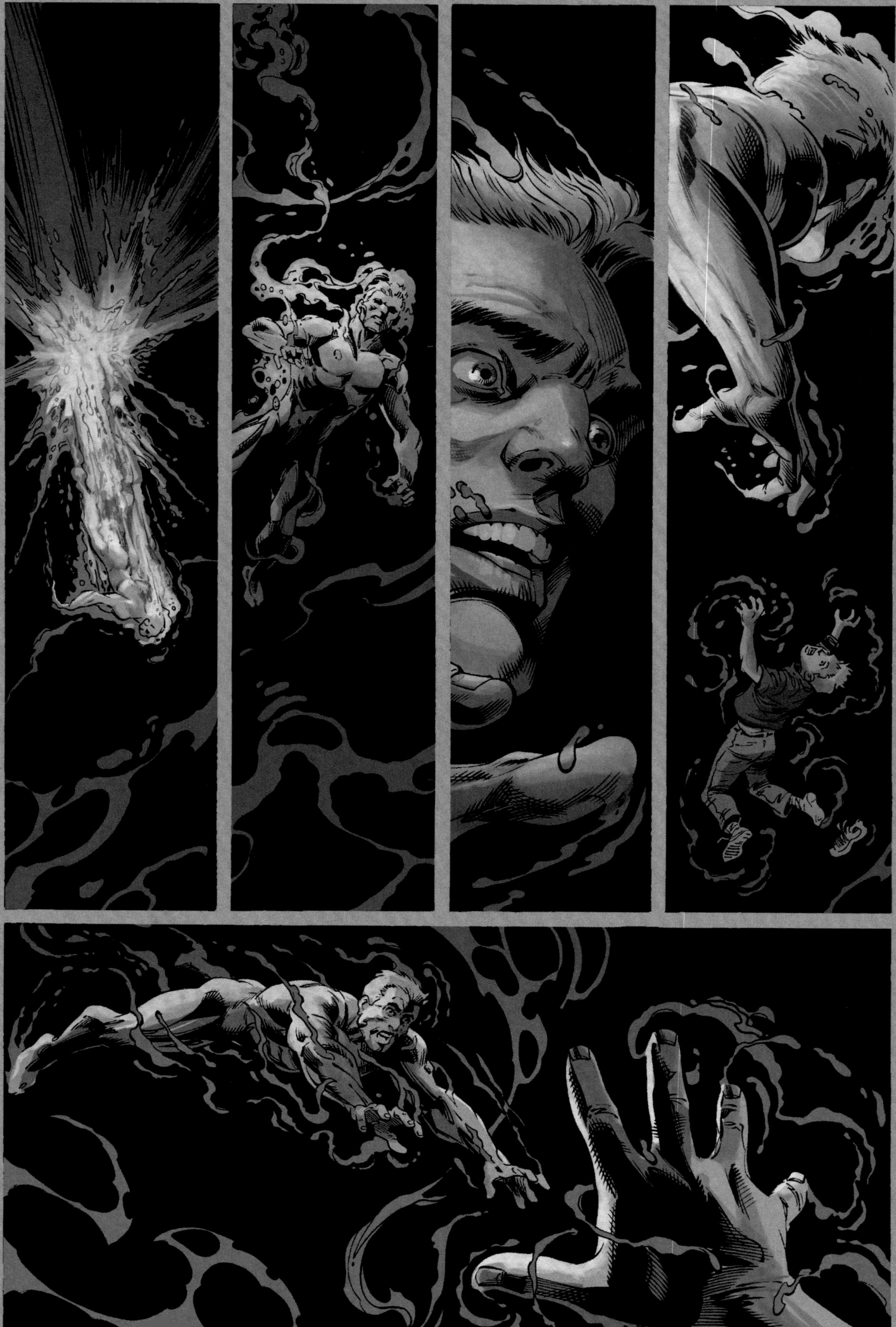

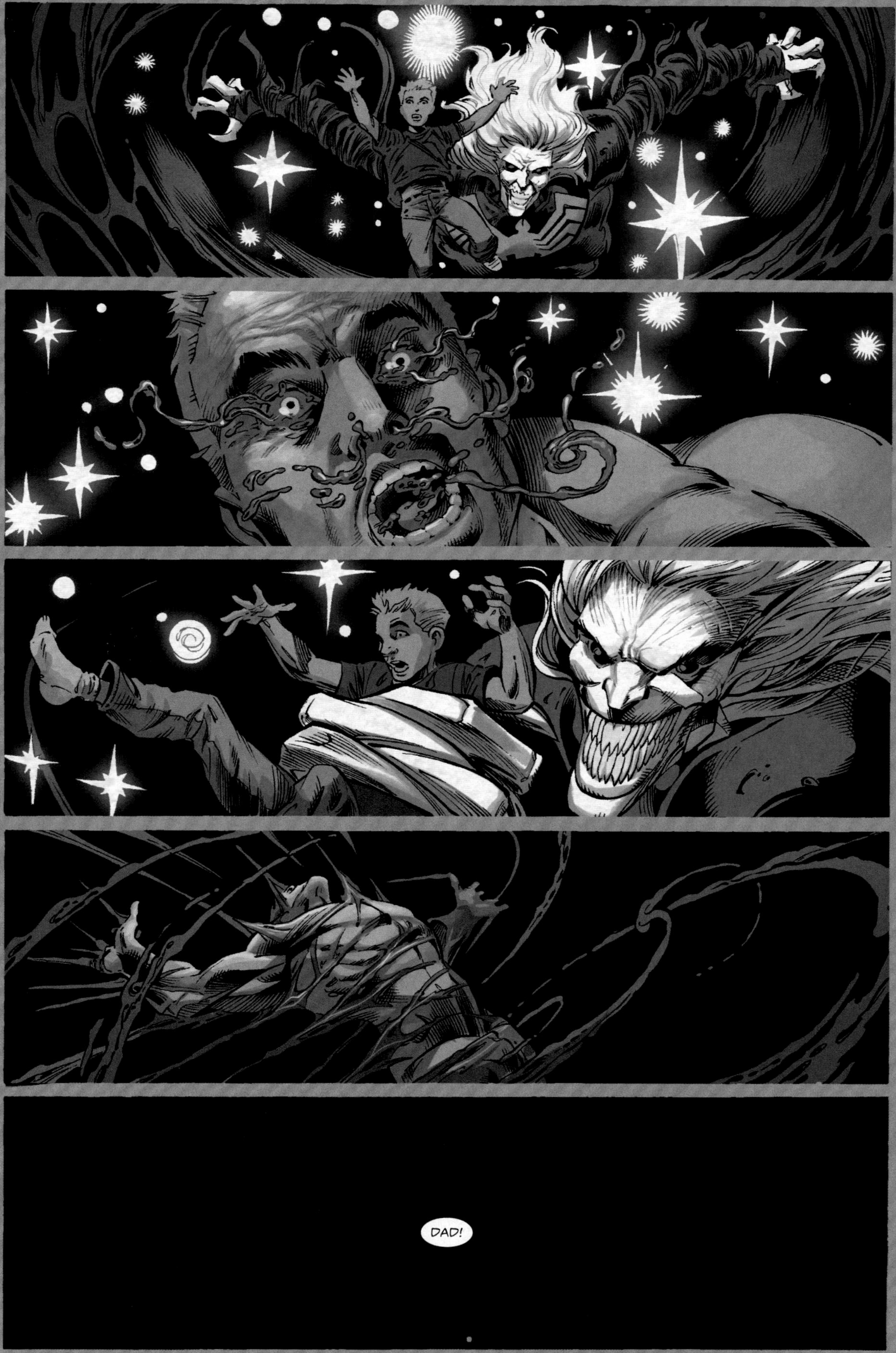
DAD!

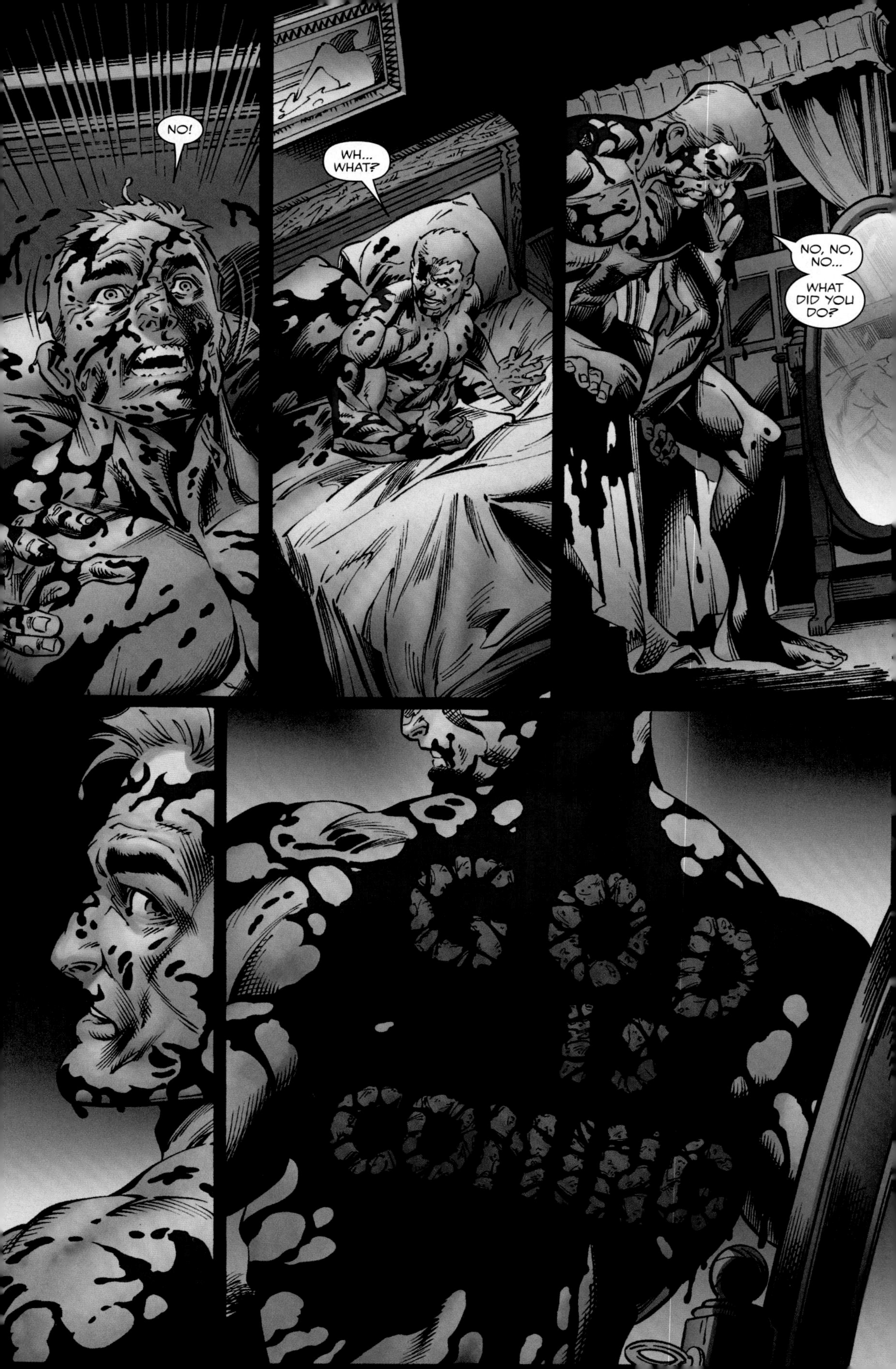
NO!
WH... WHAT?
NO, NO, NO...
WHAT DID YOU DO?

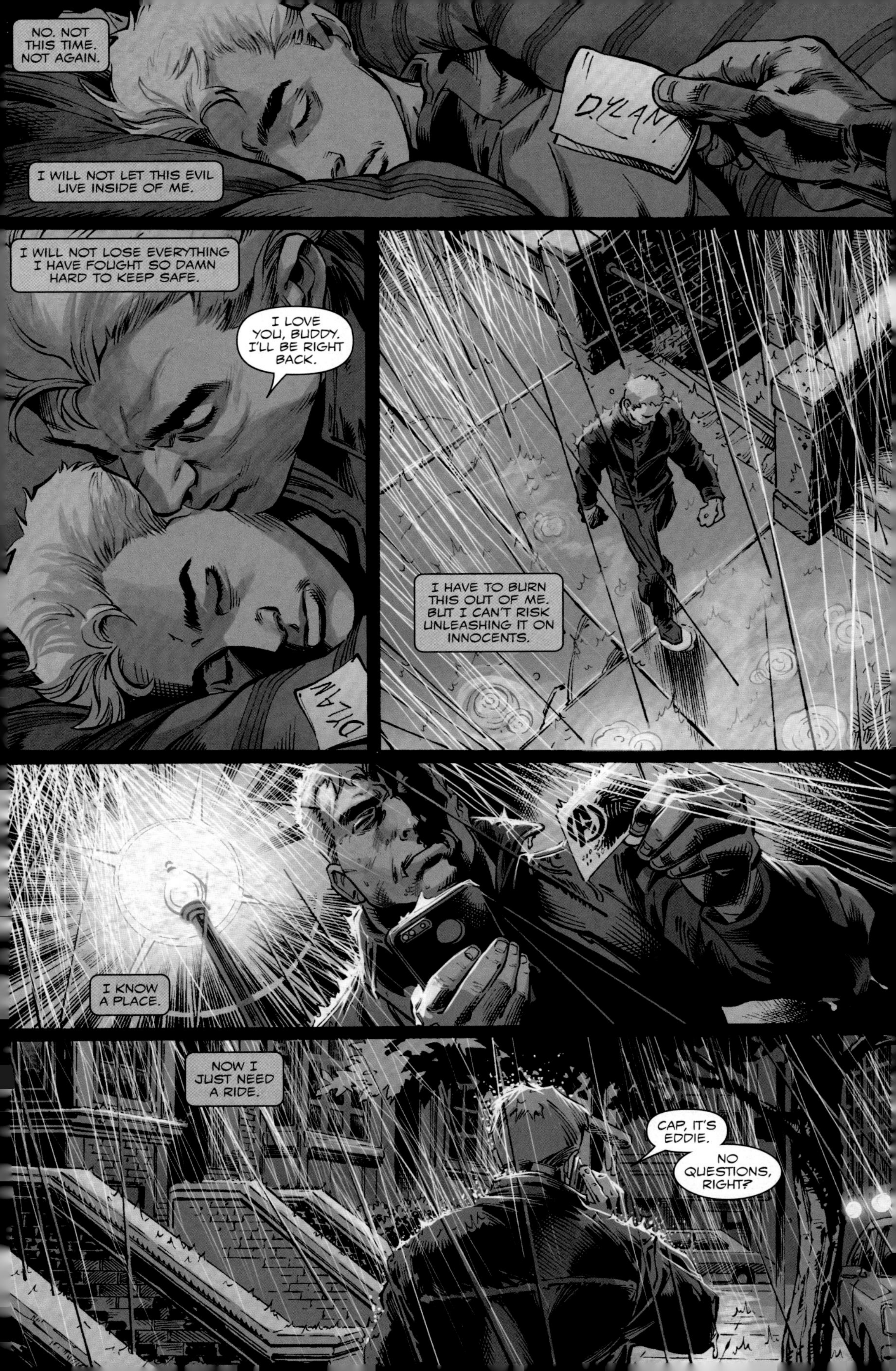
NO. NOT THIS TIME. NOT AGAIN.
DYLAN!
I WILL NOT LET THIS EVIL LIVE INSIDE OF ME.
I WILL NOT LOSE EVERYTHING I HAVE FOUGHT SO DAMN HARD TO KEEP SAFE.
I LOVE YOU, BUDDY. I'LL BE RIGHT BACK.
DYLAN
I HAVE TO BURN THIS OUT OF ME. BUT I CAN'T RISK UNLEASHING IT ON INNOCENTS.
I KNOW A PLACE.
NOW I JUST NEED A RIDE.
CAP, IT'S EDDIE.
NO QUESTIONS, RIGHT?

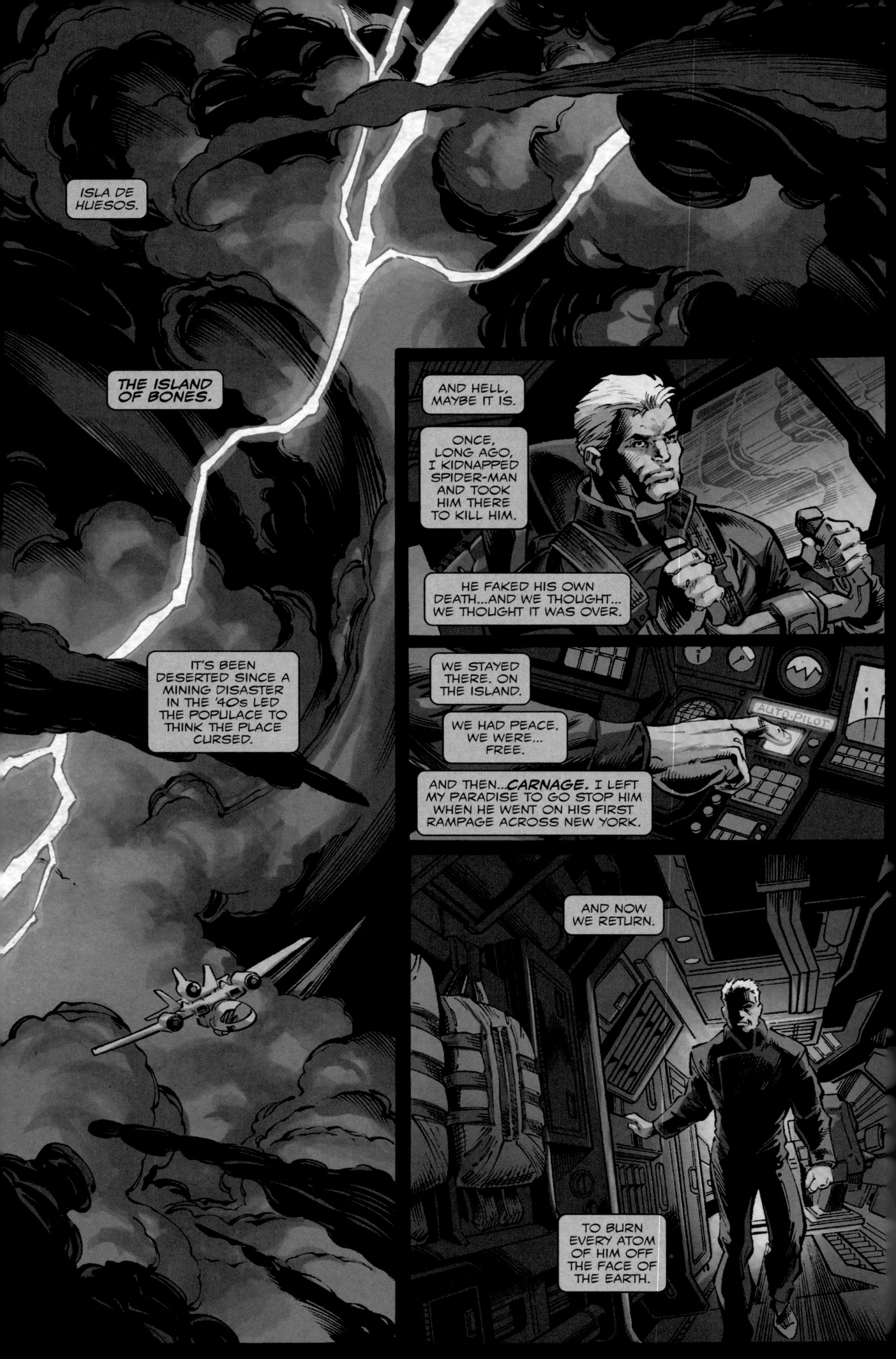
ISLA DE HUESOS.
THE ISLAND OF BONES.
IT'S BEEN DESERTED SINCE A MINING DISASTER IN THE '40s LED THE POPULACE TO THINK THE PLACE CURSED.
AND HELL, MAYBE IT IS.
ONCE, LONG AGO, I KIDNAPPED SPIDER-MAN AND TOOK HIM THERE TO KILL HIM.
HE FAKED HIS OWN DEATH...AND WE THOUGHT... WE THOUGHT IT WAS OVER.
WE STAYED THERE. ON THE ISLAND.
AUTO-PILOT
WE HAD PEACE. WE WERE... FREE.
AND THEN...CARNAGE. I LEFT MY PARADISE TO GO STOP HIM WHEN HE WENT ON HIS FIRST RAMPAGE ACROSS NEW YORK.
AND NOW WE RETURN.
TO BURN EVERY ATOM OF HIM OFF THE FACE OF THE EARTH.

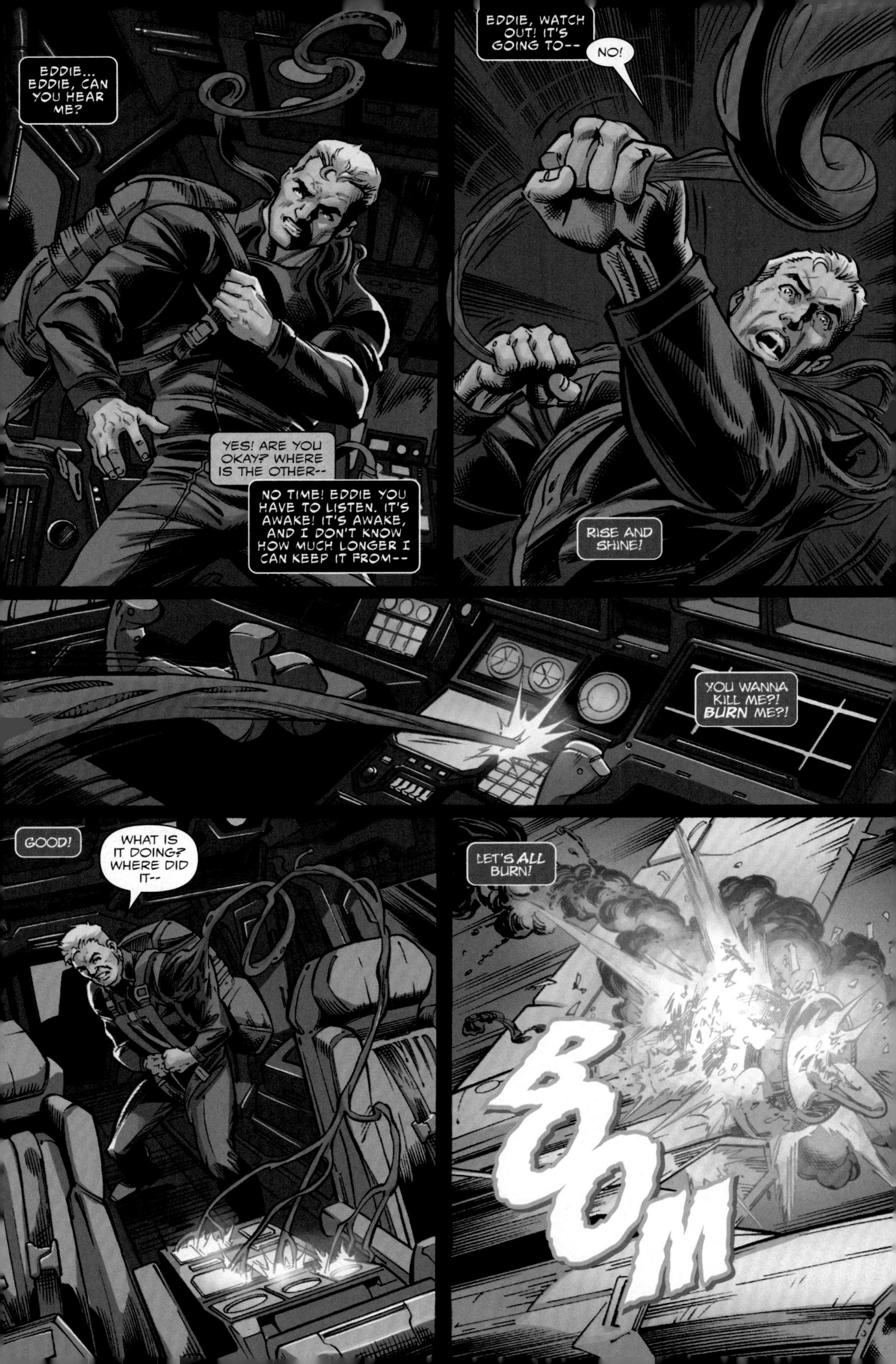
EDDIE... EDDIE, CAN YOU HEAR ME?
YES! ARE YOU OKAY? WHERE IS THE OTHER--
NO TIME! EDDIE YOU HAVE TO LISTEN. IT'S AWAKE! IT'S AWAKE, AND I DON'T KNOW HOW MUCH LONGER I CAN KEEP IT FROM--
EDDIE, WATCH OUT! IT'S GOING TO--
NO!
RISE AND SHINE!
YOU WANNA KILL ME?! BURN ME?!
GOOD!
WHAT IS IT DOING? WHERE DID IT--
LET'S ALL BURN!
BOOM

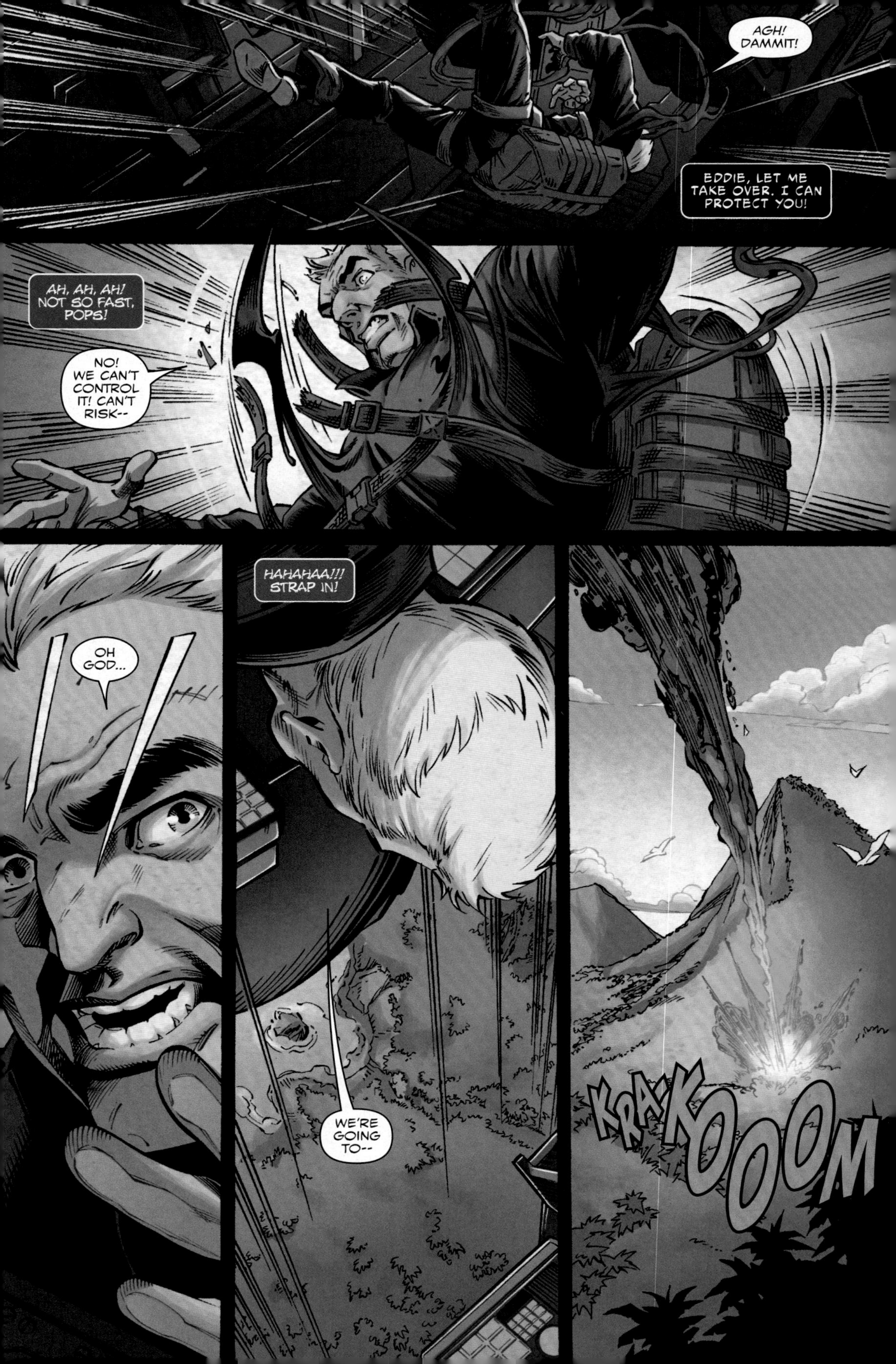
AGH! DAMMIT!
EDDIE, LET ME TAKE OVER. I CAN PROTECT YOU!
AH, AH, AH! NOT SO FAST, POPS!
NO! WE CAN'T CONTROL IT! CAN'T RISK--
OH GOD...
HAHAHAA!!! STRAP IN!
WE'RE GOING TO--
KRA-KOOOOM

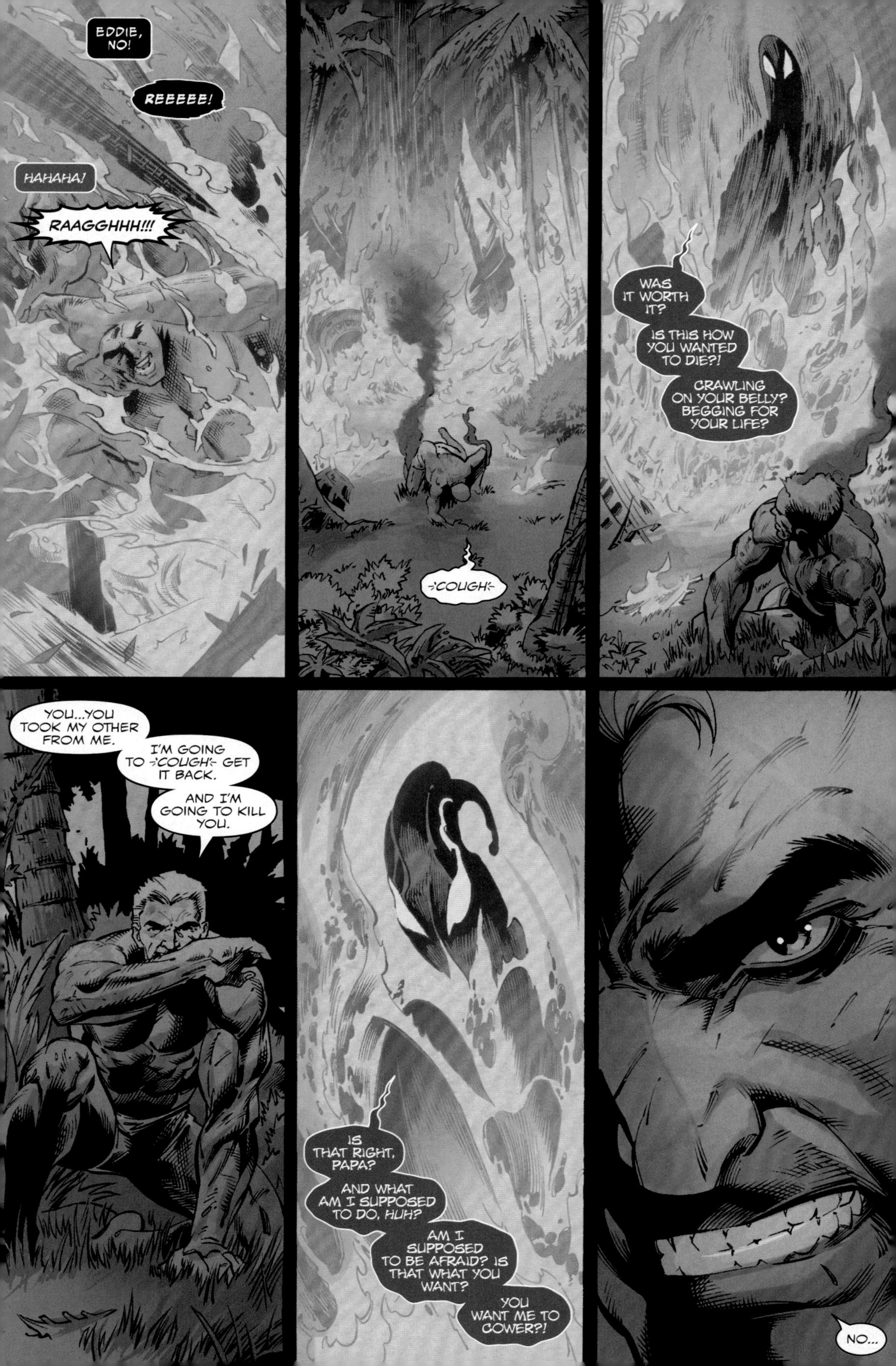
EDDIE, NO!
REEEEE!
HAHAHA!
RAAGGHHH!!!
-COUGH-
WAS IT WORTH IT?
IS THIS HOW YOU WANTED TO DIE?!
CRAWLING ON YOUR BELLY? BEGGING FOR YOUR LIFE?
YOU...YOU TOOK MY OTHER FROM ME.
I'M GOING TO -COUGH- GET IT BACK.
AND I'M GOING TO KILL YOU.
IS THAT RIGHT, PAPA?
AND WHAT AM I SUPPOSED TO DO, HUH?
AM I SUPPOSED TO BE AFRAID? IS THAT WHAT YOU WANT?
YOU WANT ME TO COWER?!
NO...

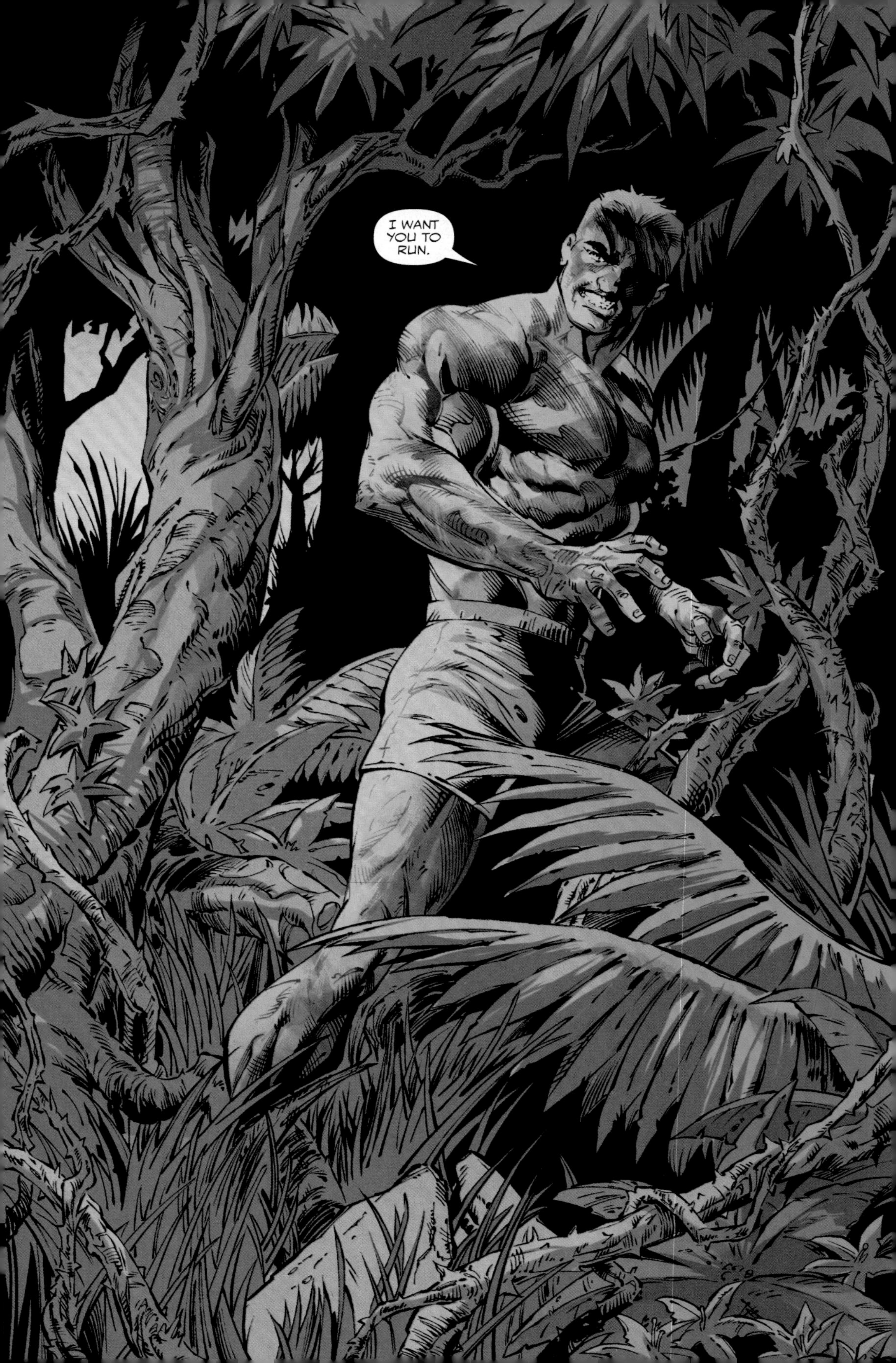
I WANT YOU TO RUN.

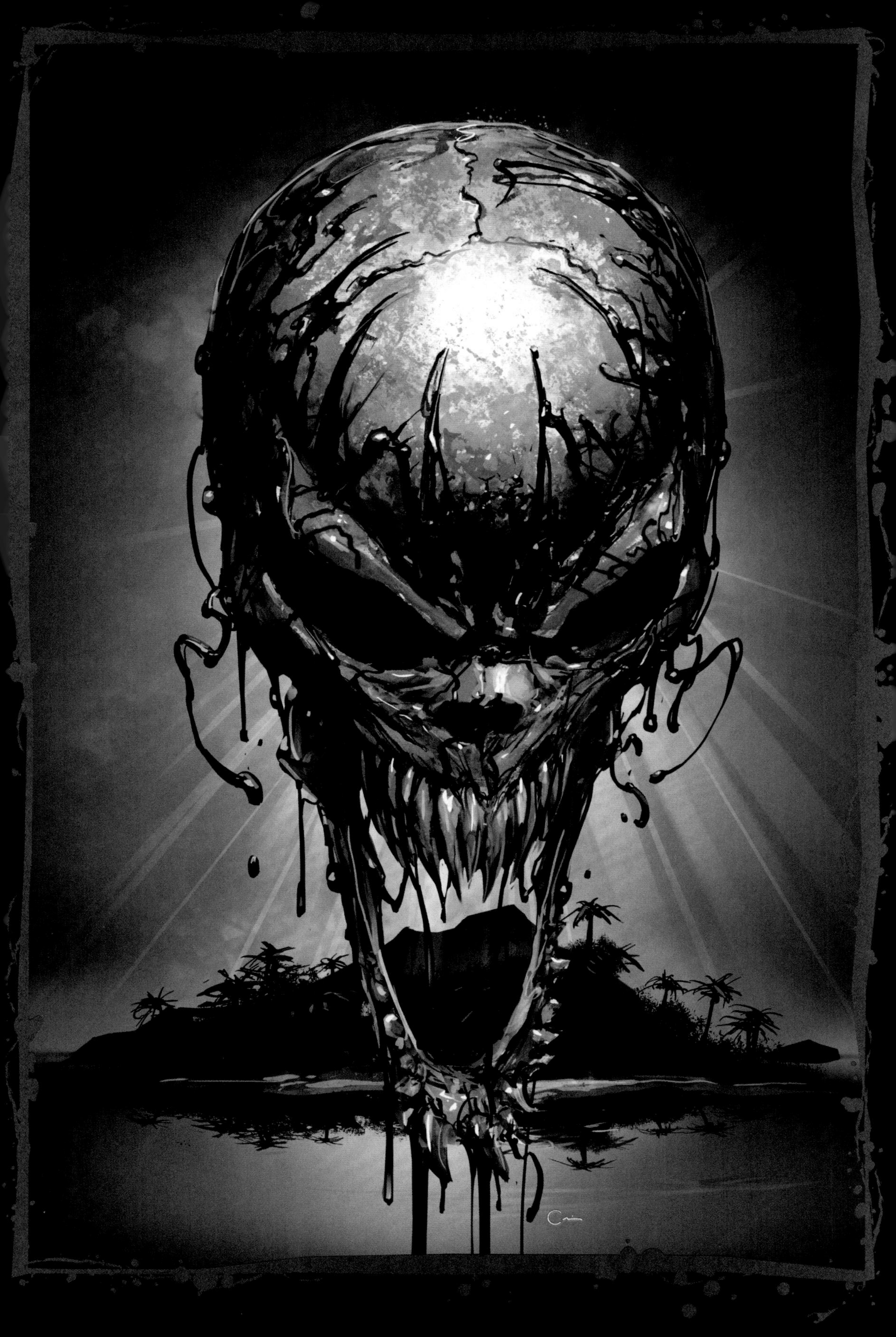

#21 VARIANT BY **CLAYTON CRAIN**

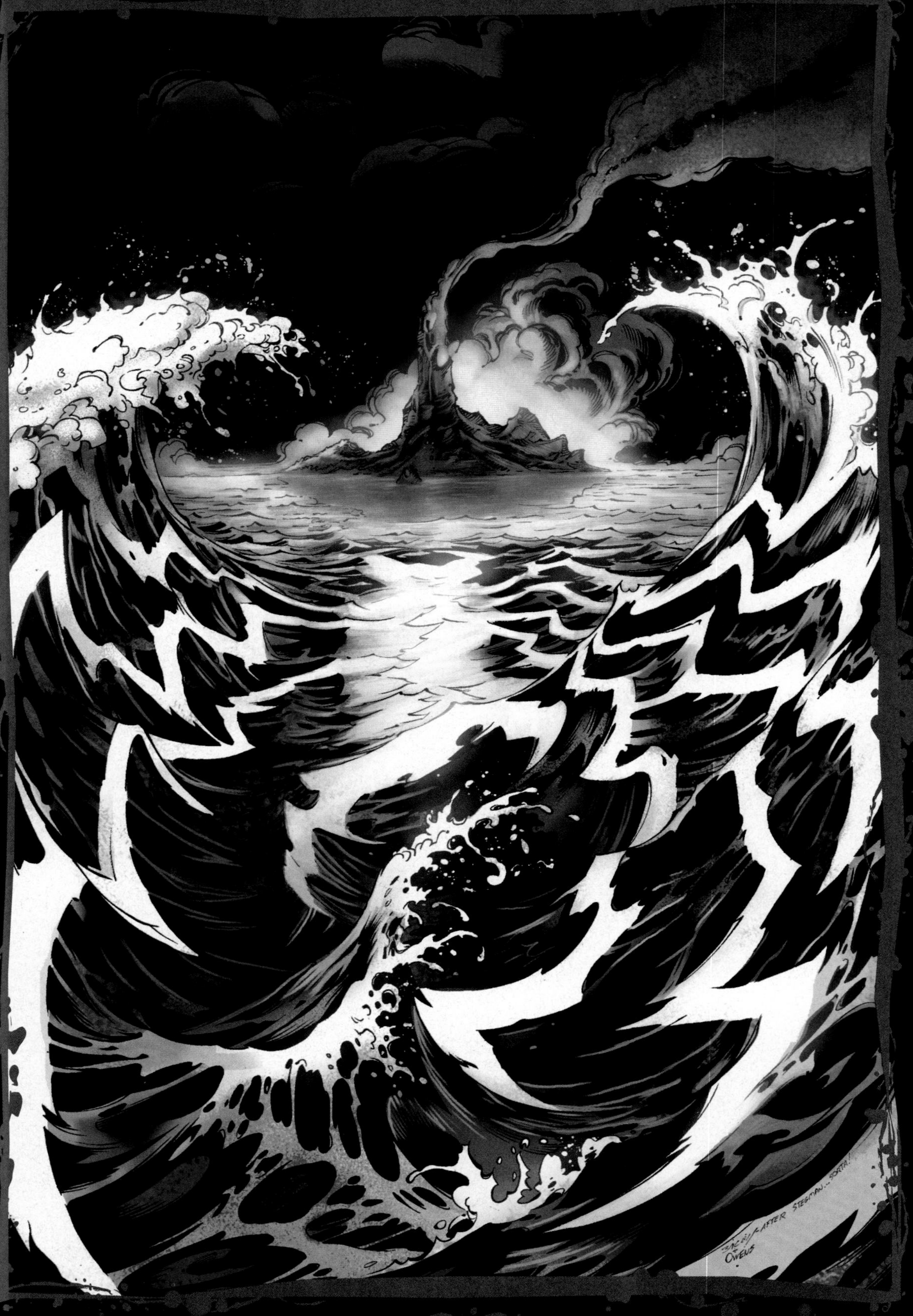
AFTER STEGMAN... SORTA!
OWENS

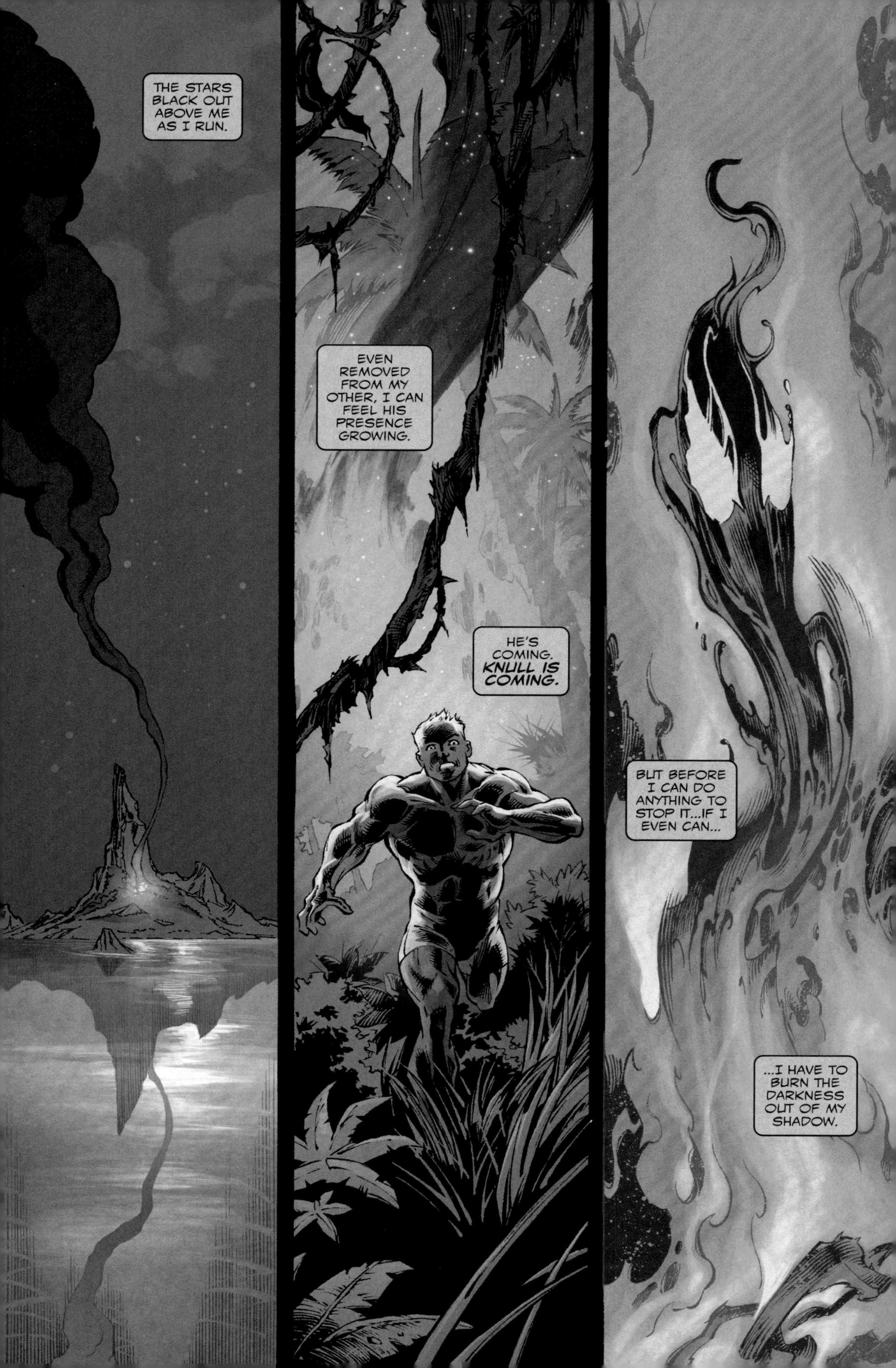
THE STARS BLACK OUT ABOVE ME AS I RUN.
EVEN REMOVED FROM MY OTHER, I CAN FEEL HIS PRESENCE GROWING.
HE'S COMING. **KNULL IS COMING.**
BUT BEFORE I CAN DO ANYTHING TO STOP IT...IF I EVEN CAN...
...I HAVE TO BURN THE DARKNESS OUT OF MY SHADOW.

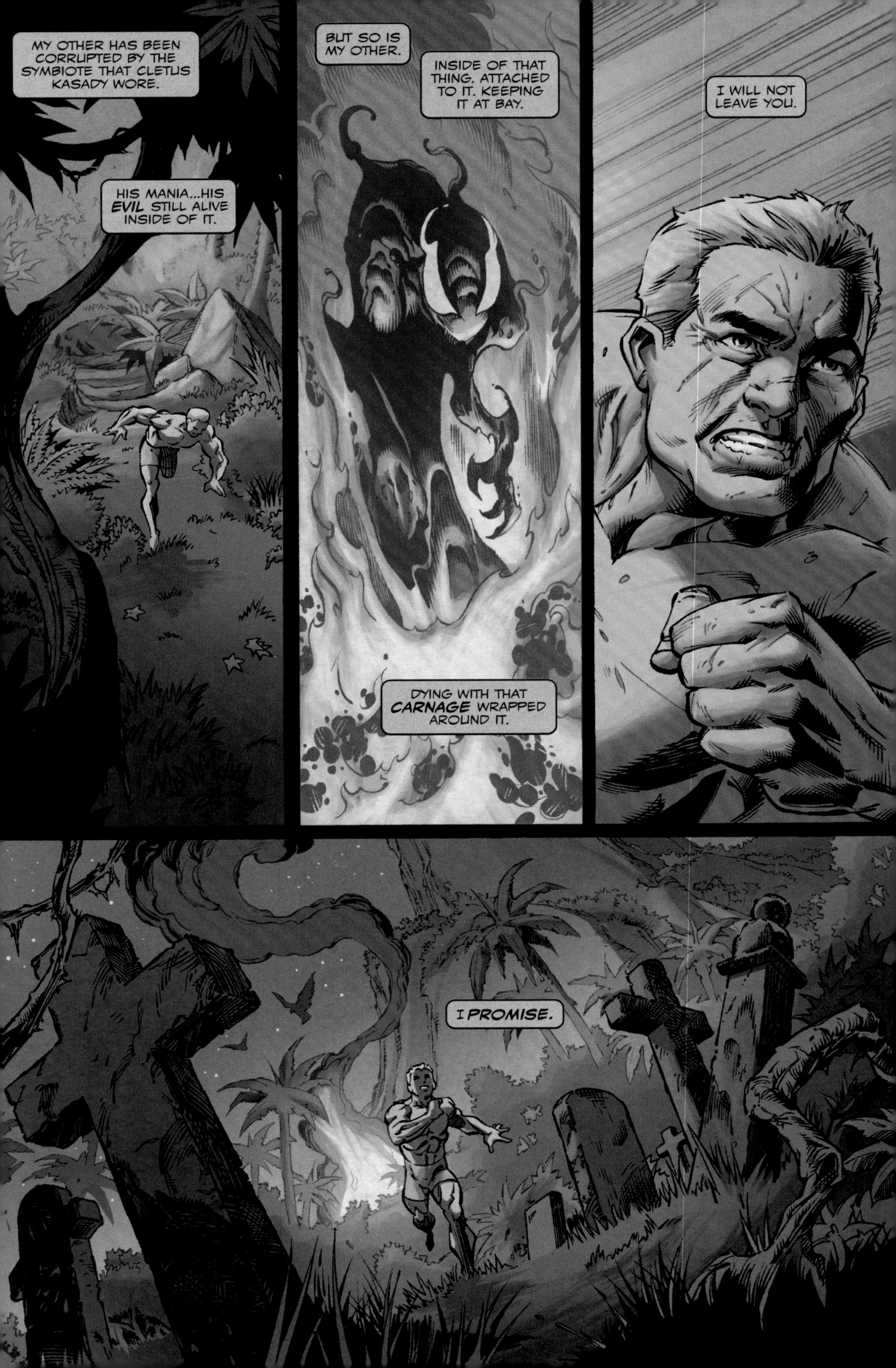

MY OTHER HAS BEEN CORRUPTED BY THE SYMBIOTE THAT CLETUS KASADY WORE.
HIS MANIA...HIS ***EVIL*** STILL ALIVE INSIDE OF IT.
BUT SO IS MY OTHER.
INSIDE OF THAT THING. ATTACHED TO IT. KEEPING IT AT BAY.
DYING WITH THAT ***CARNAGE*** WRAPPED AROUND IT.
I WILL NOT LEAVE YOU.
I ***PROMISE.***

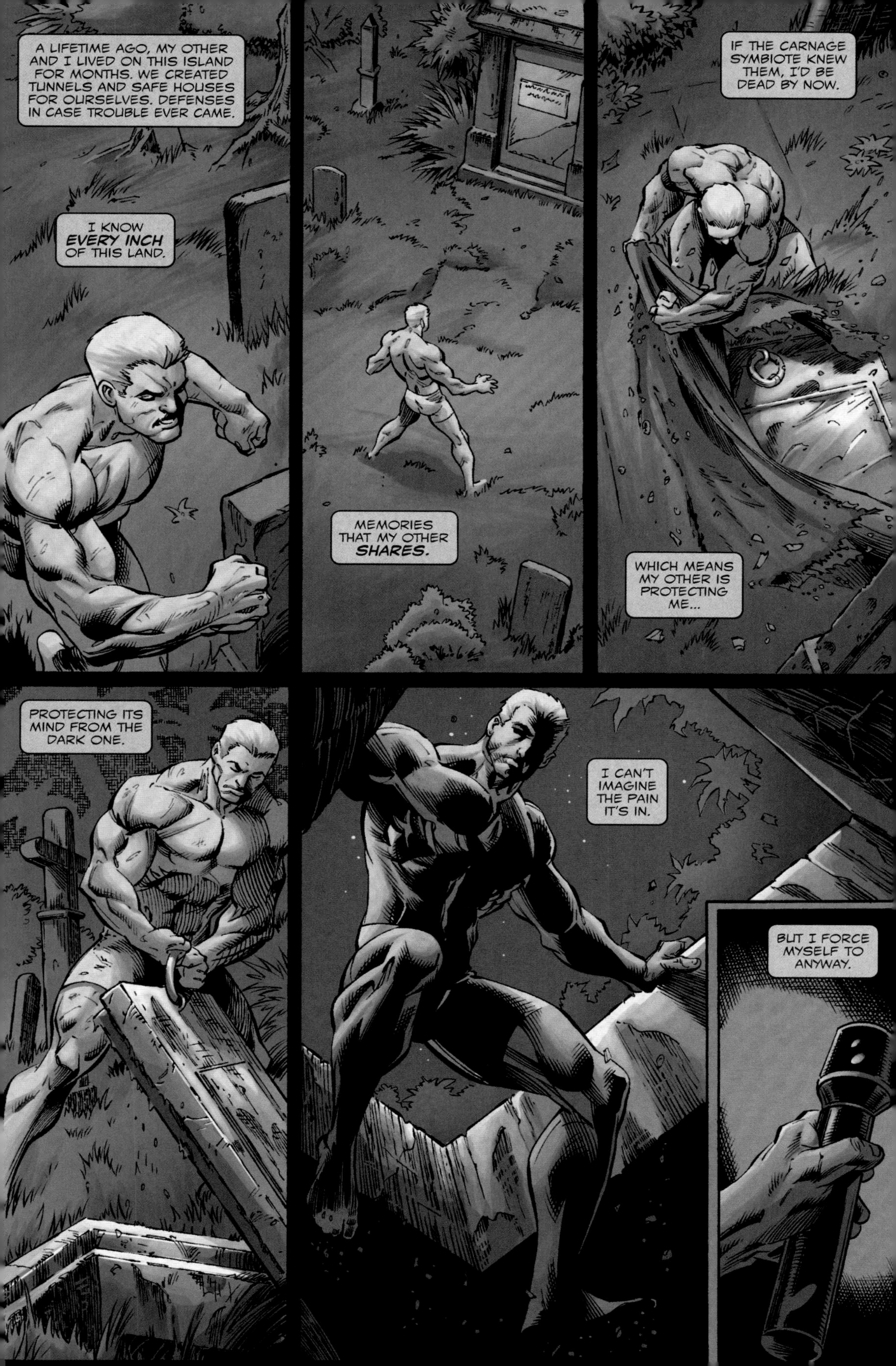
A LIFETIME AGO, MY OTHER AND I LIVED ON THIS ISLAND FOR MONTHS. WE CREATED TUNNELS AND SAFE HOUSES FOR OURSELVES. DEFENSES IN CASE TROUBLE EVER CAME.
I KNOW *EVERY INCH* OF THIS LAND.
MEMORIES THAT MY OTHER *SHARES.*
IF THE CARNAGE SYMBIOTE KNEW THEM, I'D BE DEAD BY NOW.
WHICH MEANS MY OTHER IS PROTECTING ME...
PROTECTING ITS MIND FROM THE DARK ONE.
I CAN'T IMAGINE THE PAIN IT'S IN.
BUT I FORCE MYSELF TO ANYWAY.

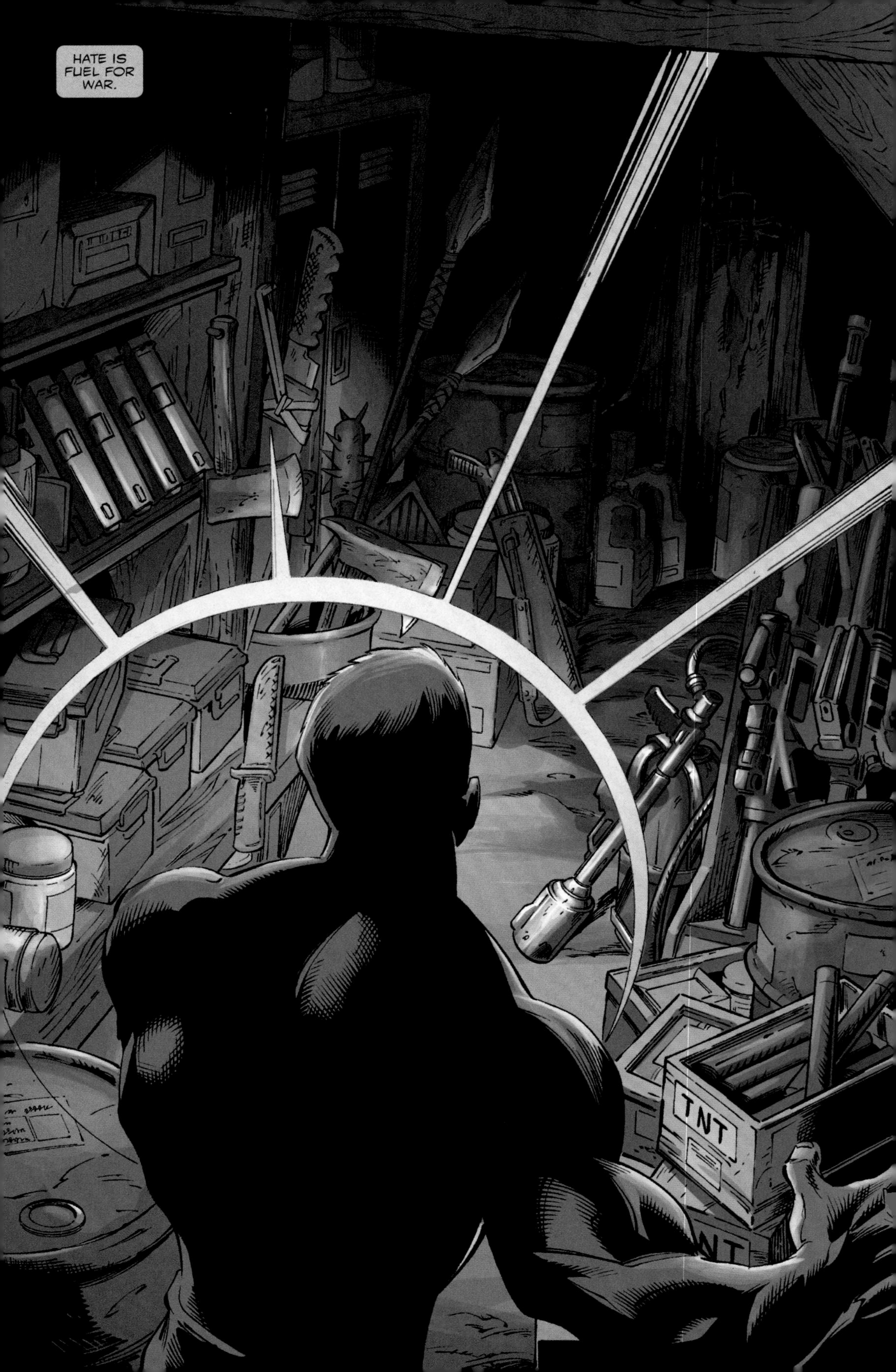
HATE IS FUEL FOR WAR.

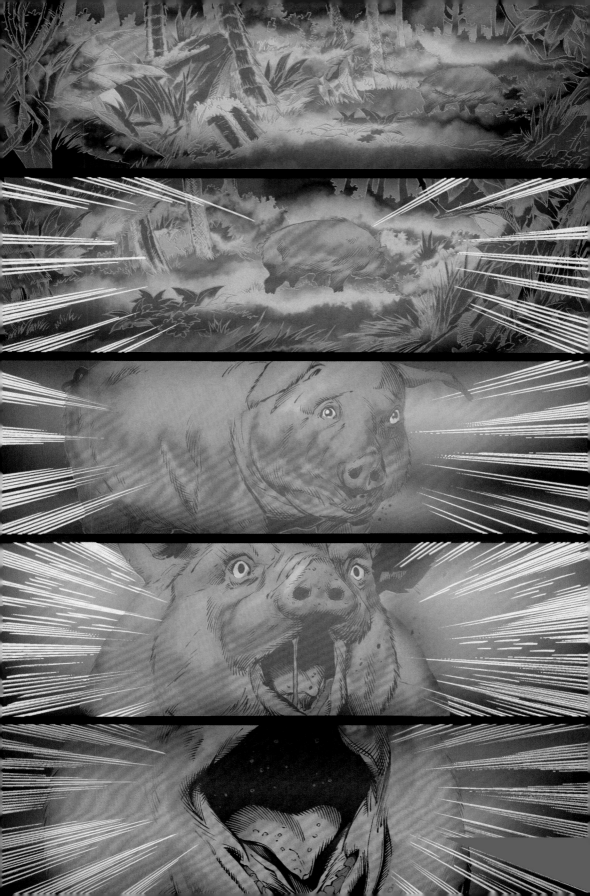

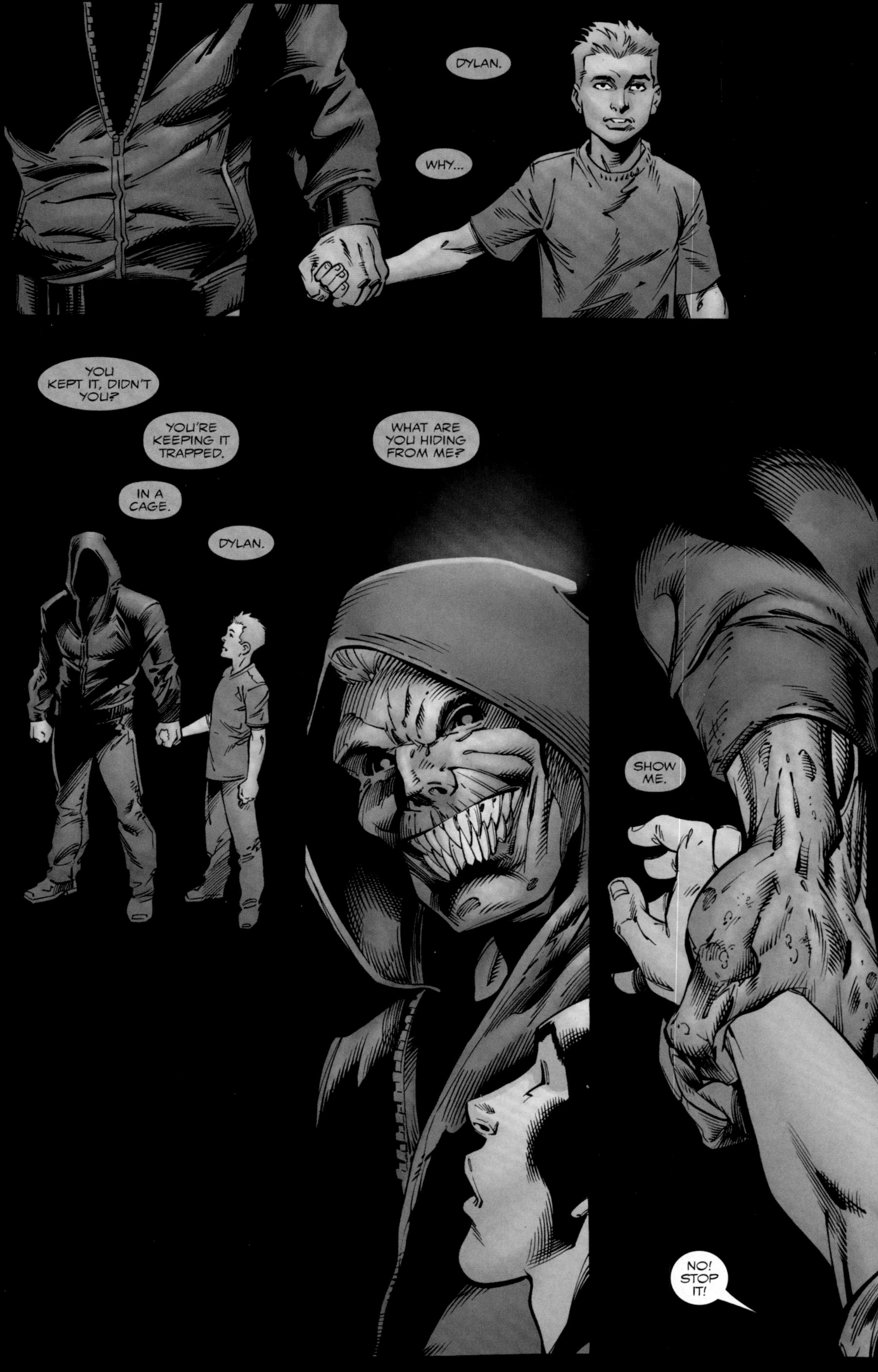
DYLAN.
WHY...
YOU KEPT IT, DIDN'T YOU?
YOU'RE KEEPING IT TRAPPED.
IN A CAGE.
DYLAN.
WHAT ARE YOU HIDING FROM ME?
SHOW ME.
NO! STOP IT!

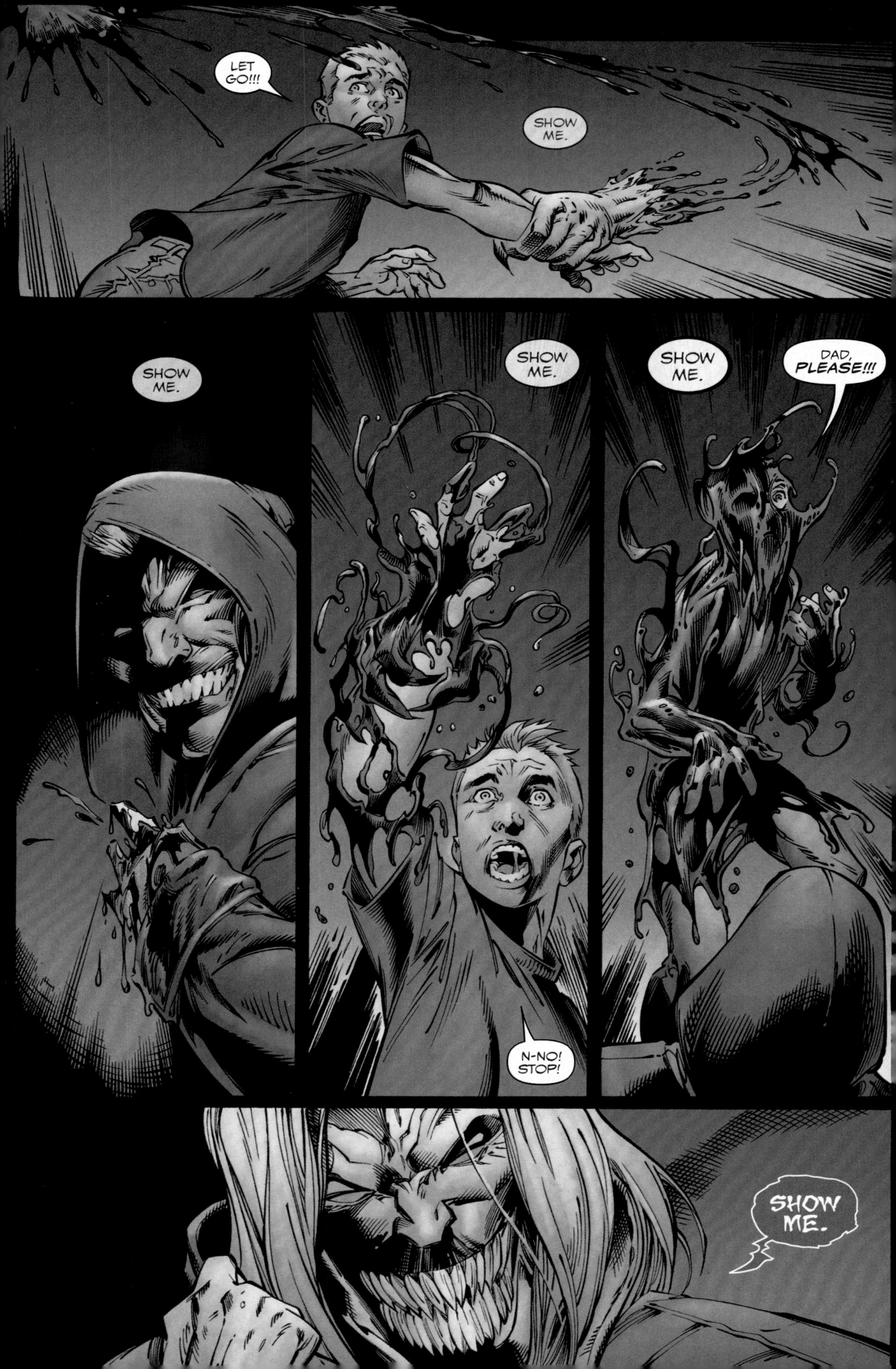
LET GO!!!
SHOW ME.
SHOW ME.
SHOW ME.
N-NO! STOP!
SHOW ME.
DAD, PLEASE!!!
SHOW ME.

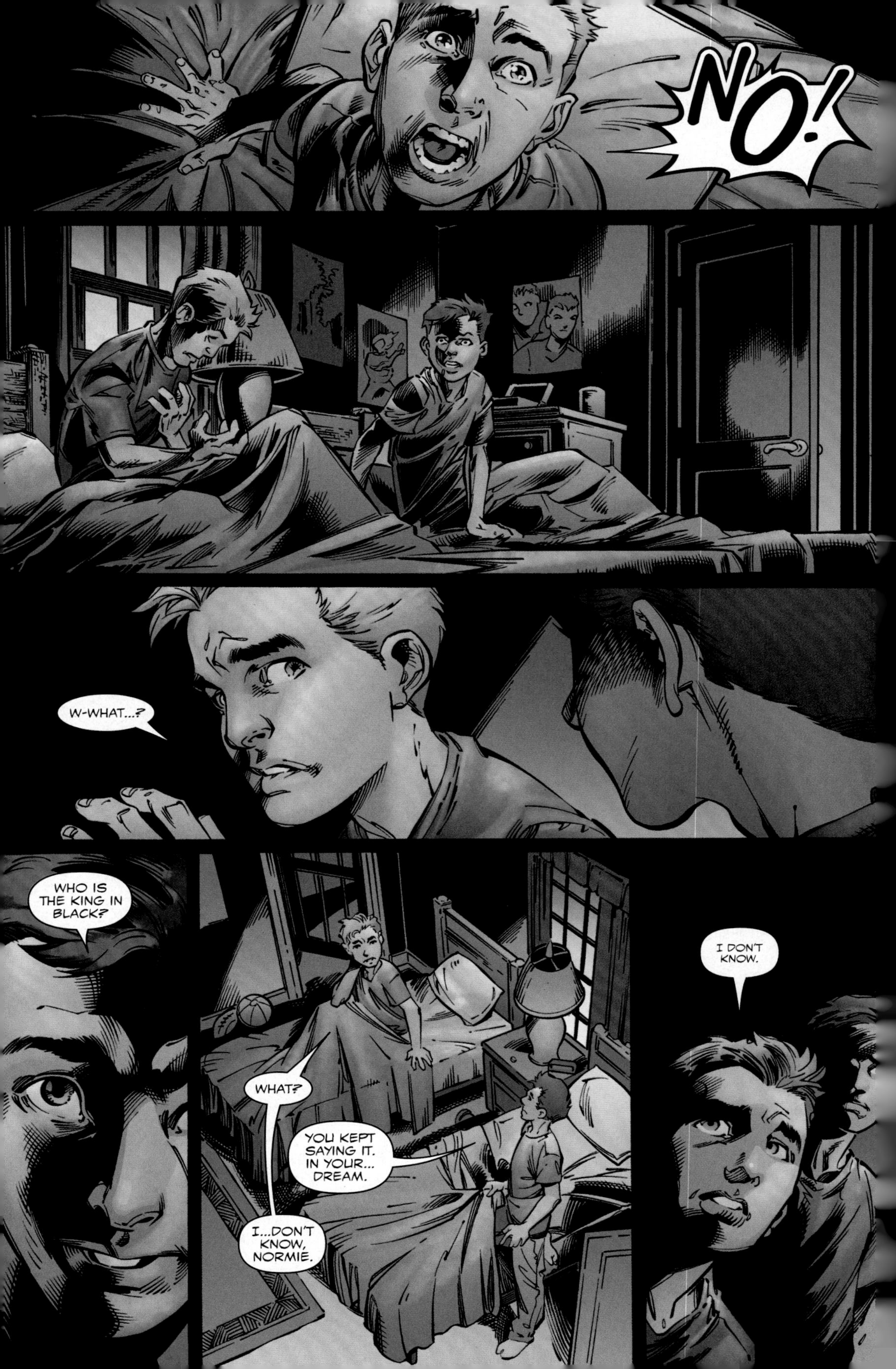
NO!
W-WHAT...?
WHO IS THE KING IN BLACK?
WHAT?
YOU KEPT SAYING IT. IN YOUR... DREAM.
I...DON'T KNOW, NORMIE.
I DON'T KNOW.

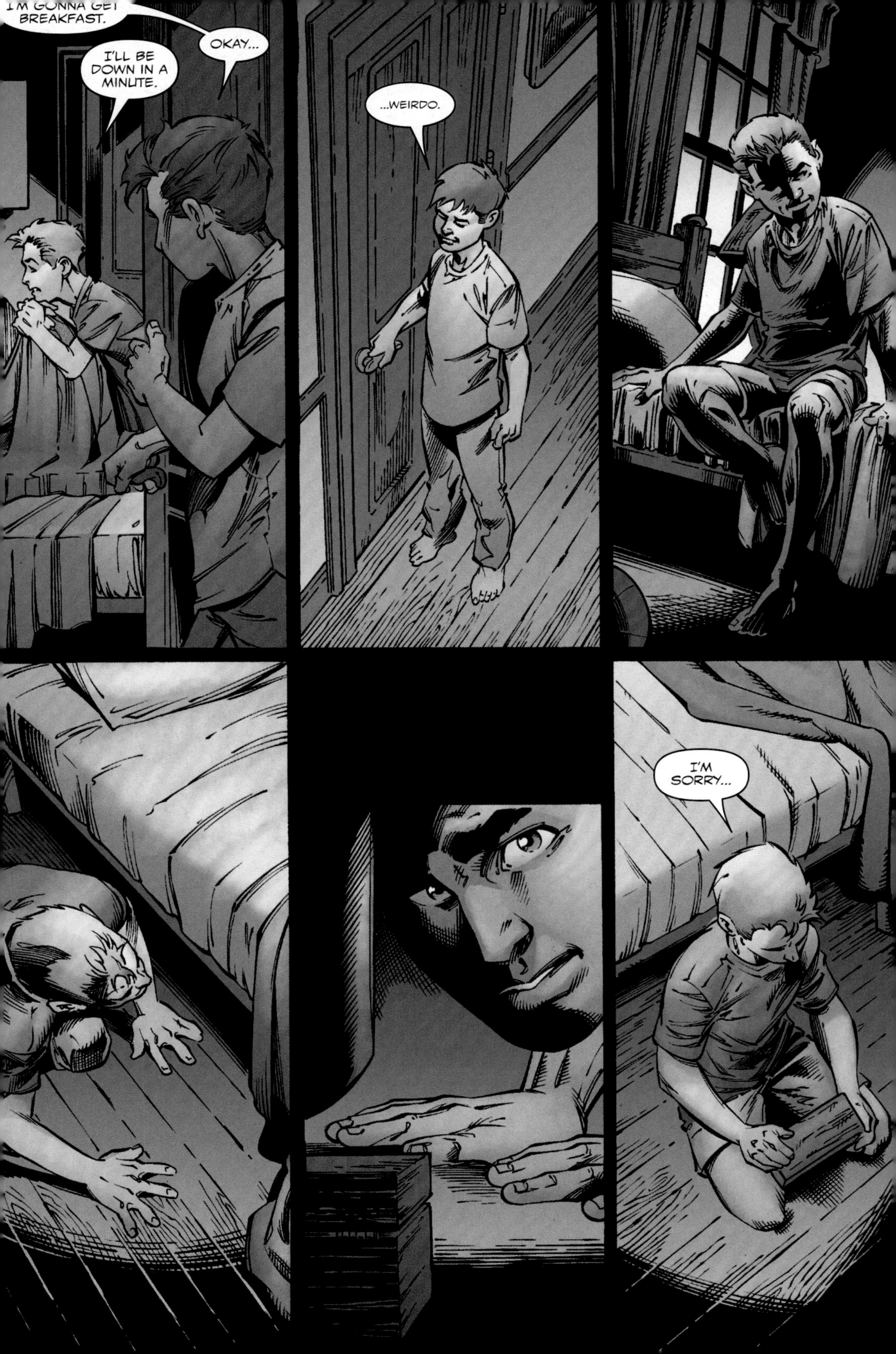
I'M GONNA GET BREAKFAST.
OKAY...
I'LL BE DOWN IN A MINUTE.
...WEIRDO.
I'M SORRY...

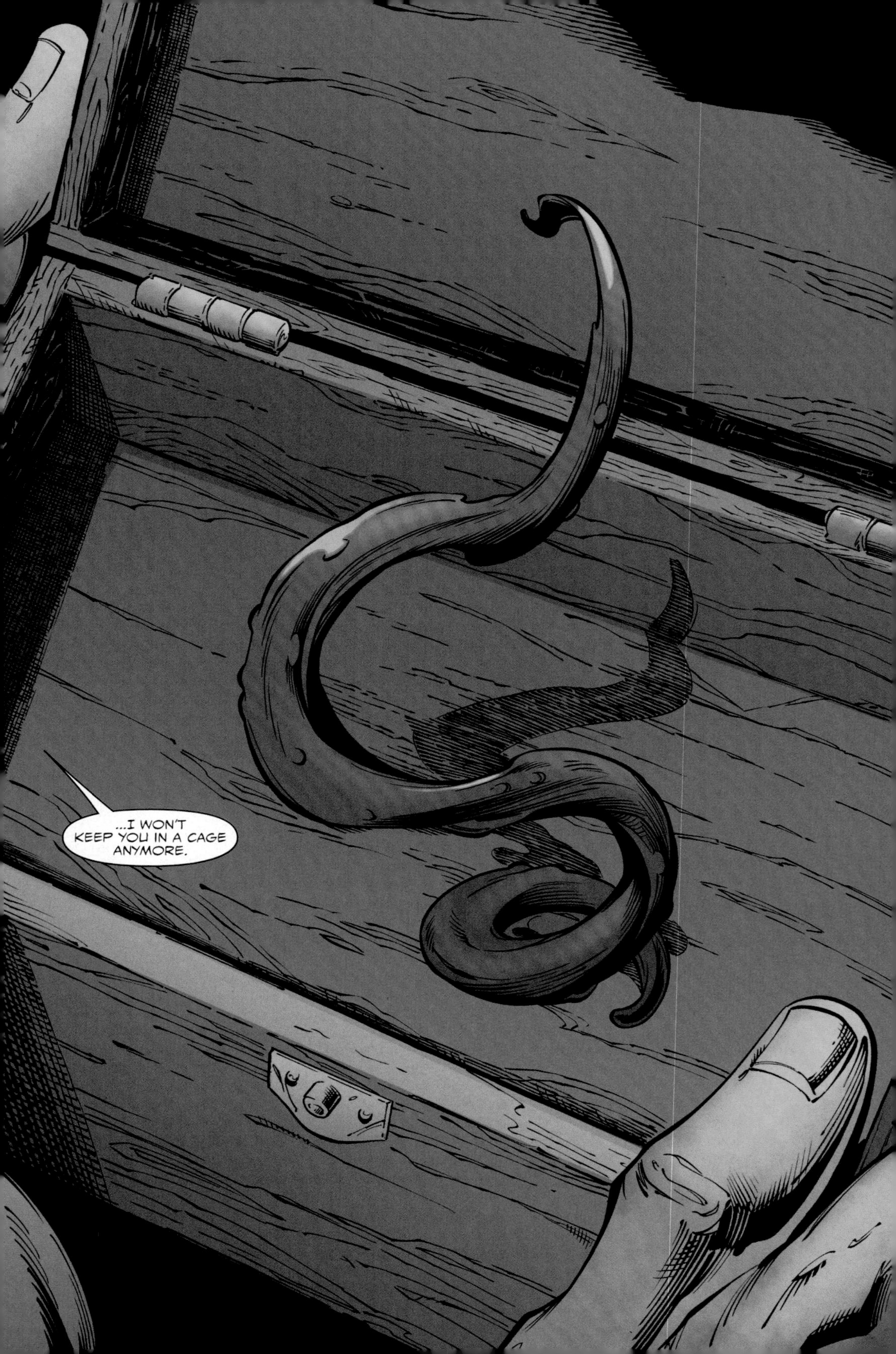
...I WON'T KEEP YOU IN A CAGE ANYMORE.

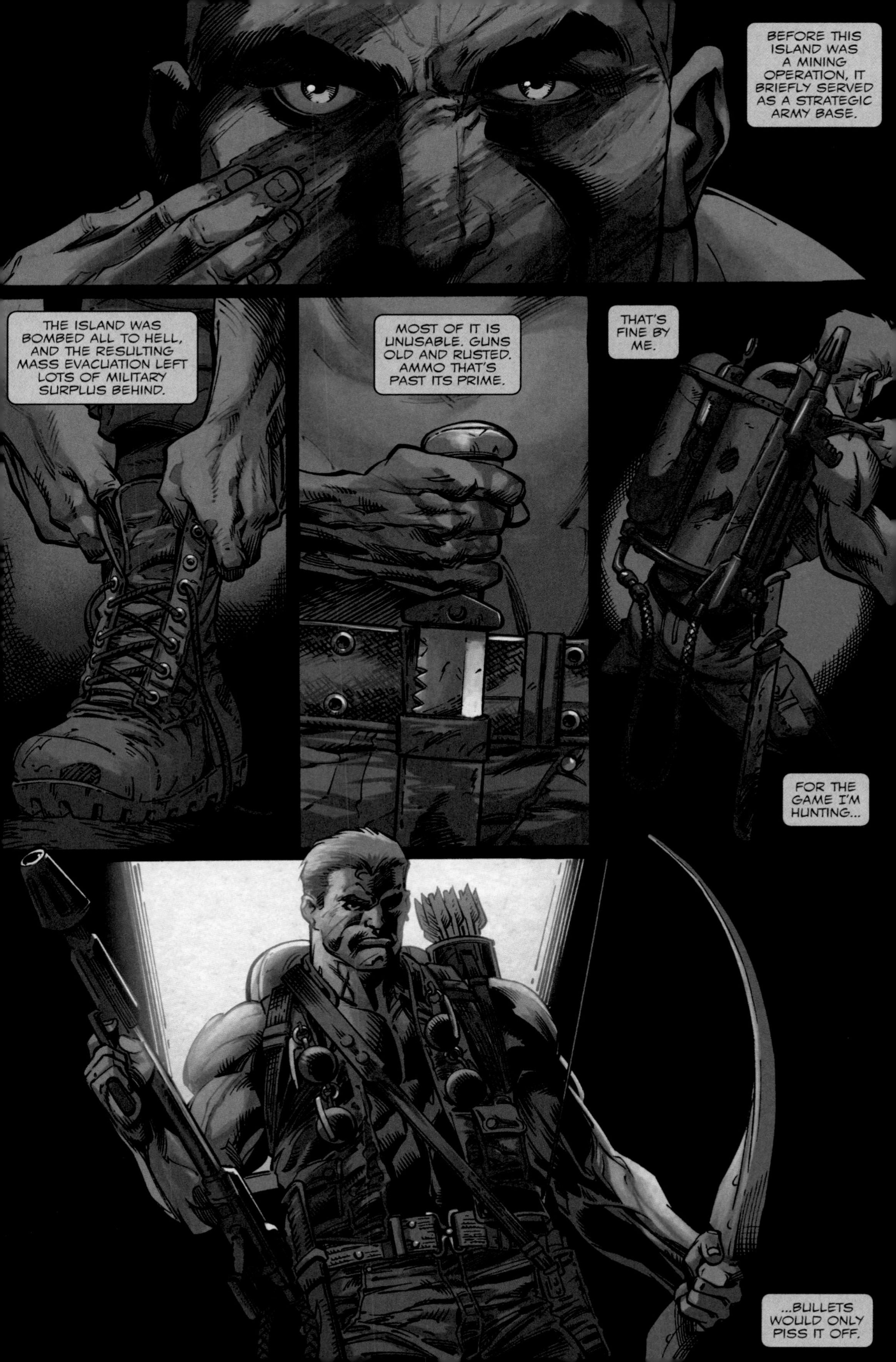
BEFORE THIS ISLAND WAS A MINING OPERATION, IT BRIEFLY SERVED AS A STRATEGIC ARMY BASE.
THE ISLAND WAS BOMBED ALL TO HELL, AND THE RESULTING MASS EVACUATION LEFT LOTS OF MILITARY SURPLUS BEHIND.
MOST OF IT IS UNUSABLE. GUNS OLD AND RUSTED. AMMO THAT'S PAST ITS PRIME.
THAT'S FINE BY ME.
FOR THE GAME I'M HUNTING...
...BULLETS WOULD ONLY PISS IT OFF.

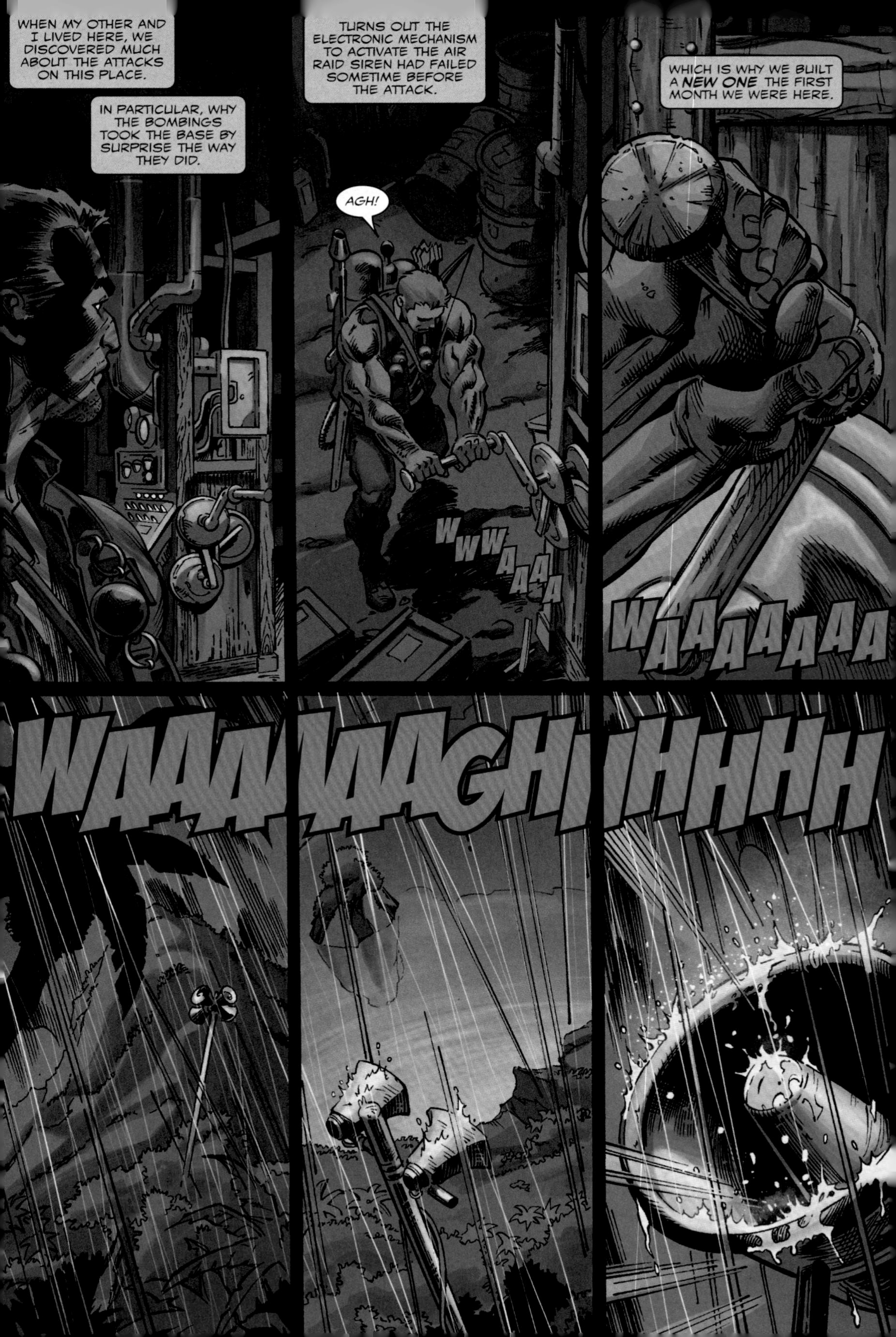
WHEN MY OTHER AND I LIVED HERE, WE DISCOVERED MUCH ABOUT THE ATTACKS ON THIS PLACE.
IN PARTICULAR, WHY THE BOMBINGS TOOK THE BASE BY SURPRISE THE WAY THEY DID.
TURNS OUT THE ELECTRONIC MECHANISM TO ACTIVATE THE AIR RAID SIREN HAD FAILED SOMETIME BEFORE THE ATTACK.
AGH!
WWWAAAA
WHICH IS WHY WE BUILT A NEW ONE THE FIRST MONTH WE WERE HERE.
WAAAAAAA
WAAAAAAAGHHHHHH

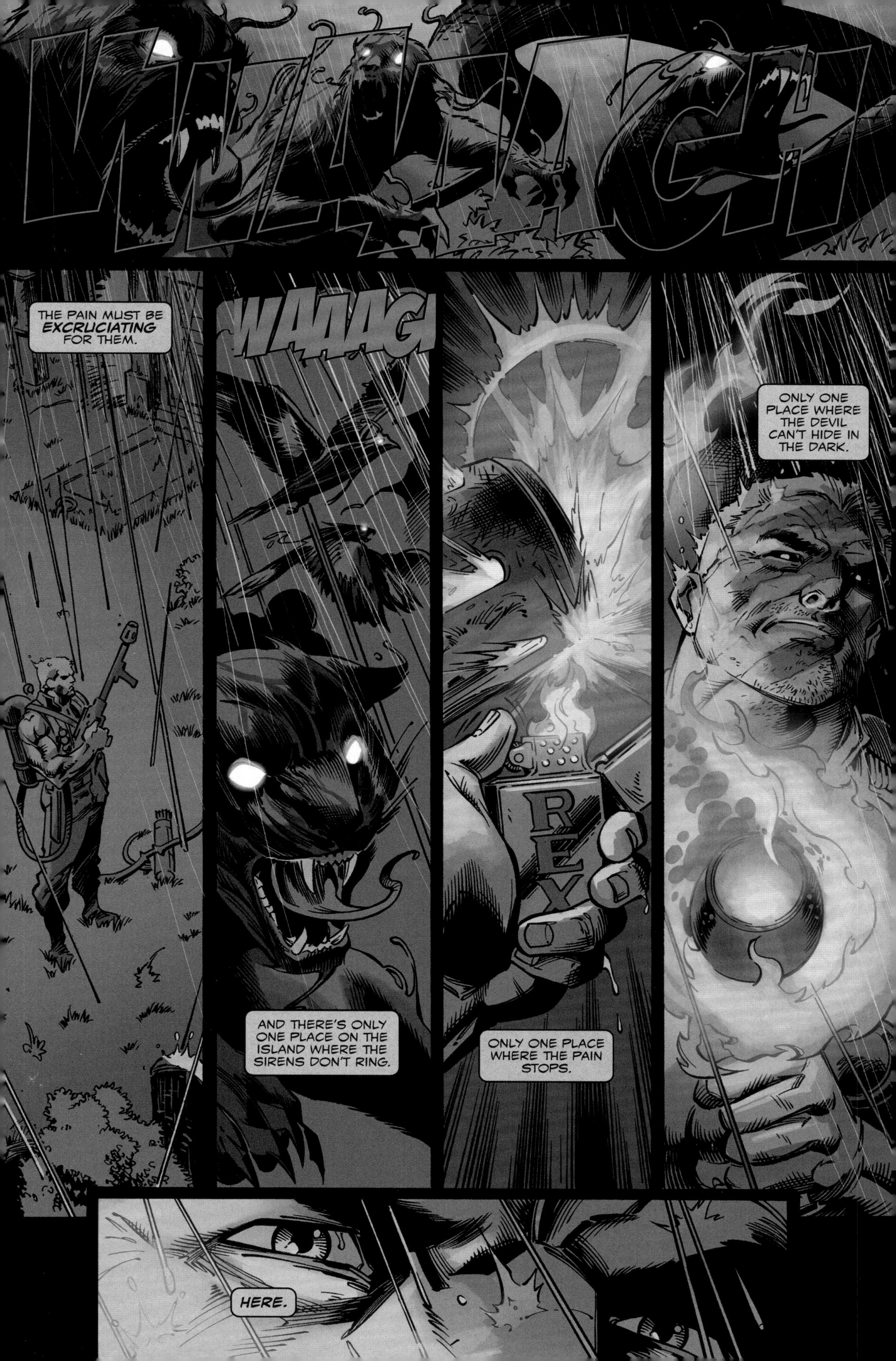
THE PAIN MUST BE *EXCRUCIATING* FOR THEM.
WAAAG
AND THERE'S ONLY ONE PLACE ON THE ISLAND WHERE THE SIRENS DON'T RING.
REX
ONLY ONE PLACE WHERE THE PAIN STOPS.
ONLY ONE PLACE WHERE THE DEVIL CAN'T HIDE IN THE DARK.
HERE.

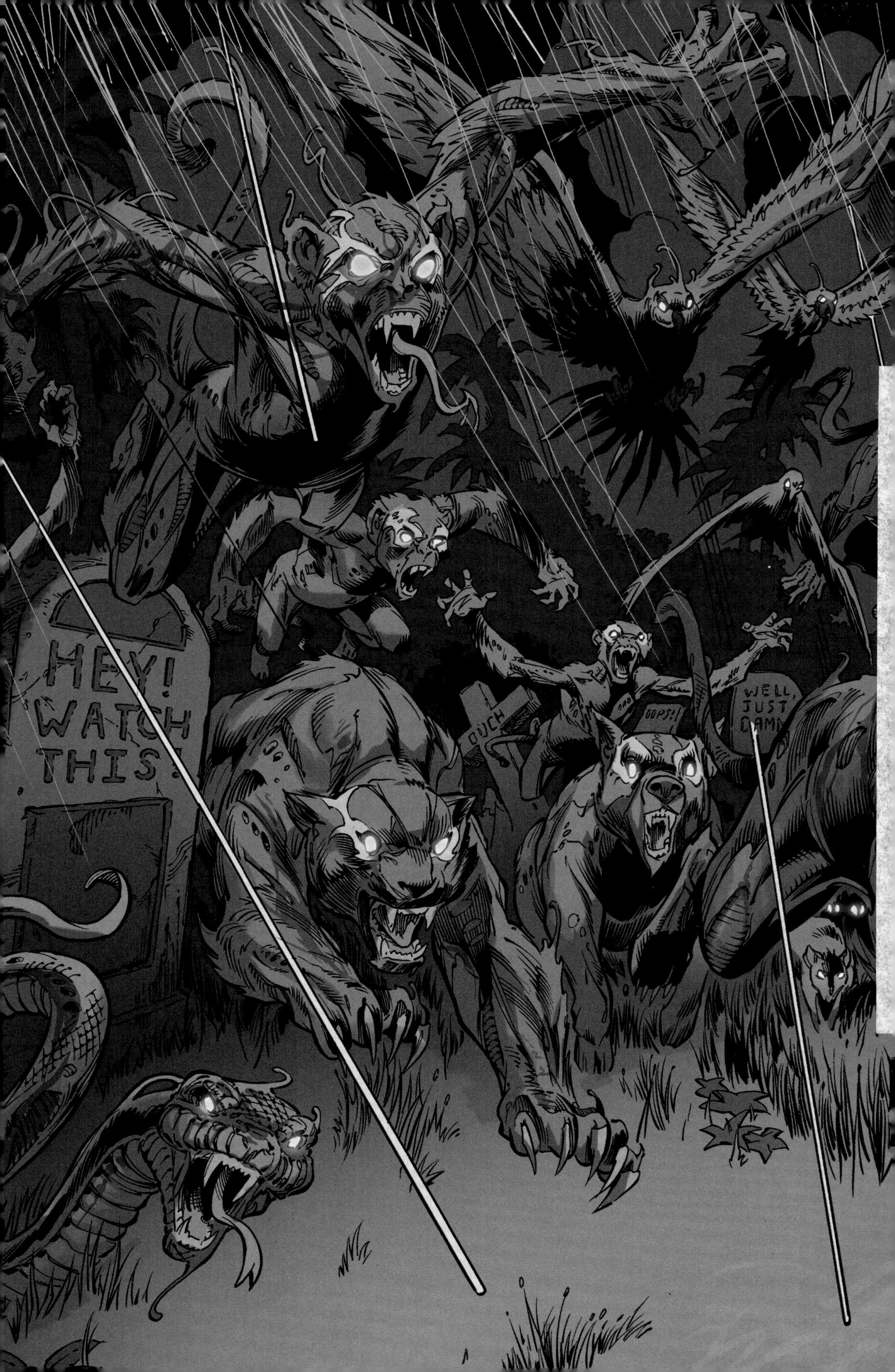
HEY! WATCH THIS
OUCH
OOPS!
WELL, JUST

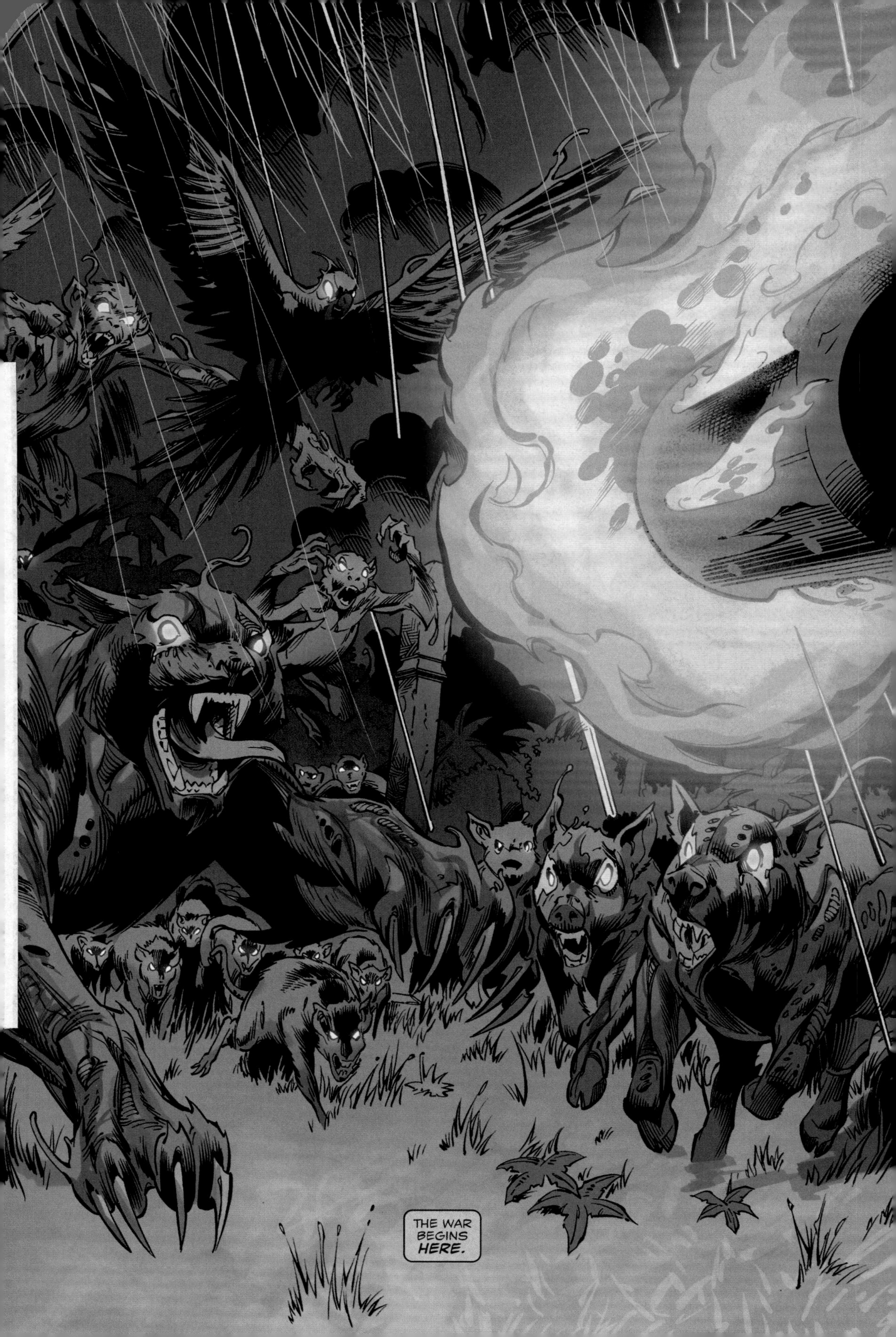
THE WAR BEGINS *HERE.*

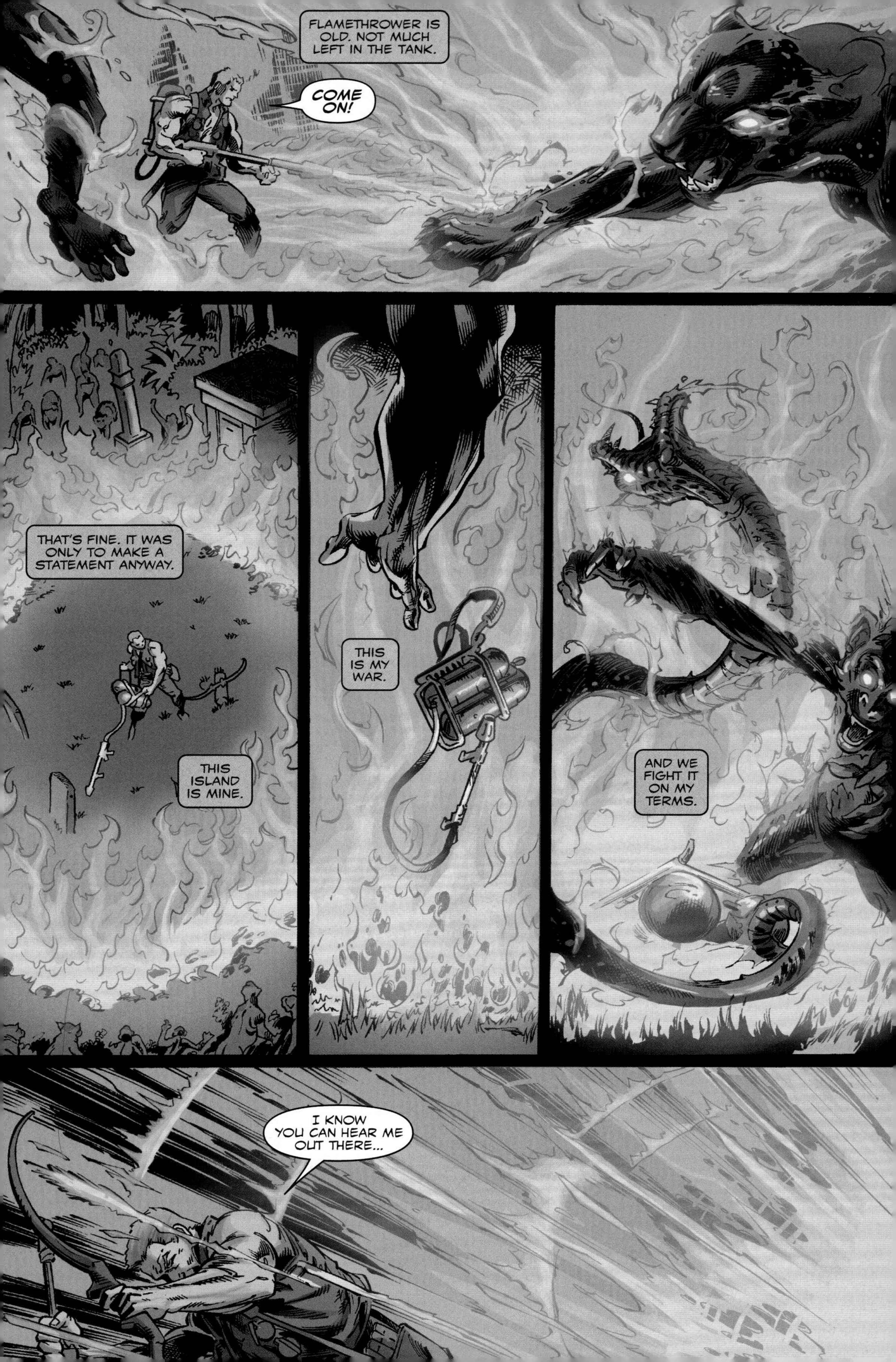
FLAMETHROWER IS OLD. NOT MUCH LEFT IN THE TANK.
COME ON!
THAT'S FINE. IT WAS ONLY TO MAKE A STATEMENT ANYWAY.
THIS ISLAND IS MINE.
THIS IS MY WAR.
AND WE FIGHT IT ON MY TERMS.
I KNOW YOU CAN HEAR ME OUT THERE...

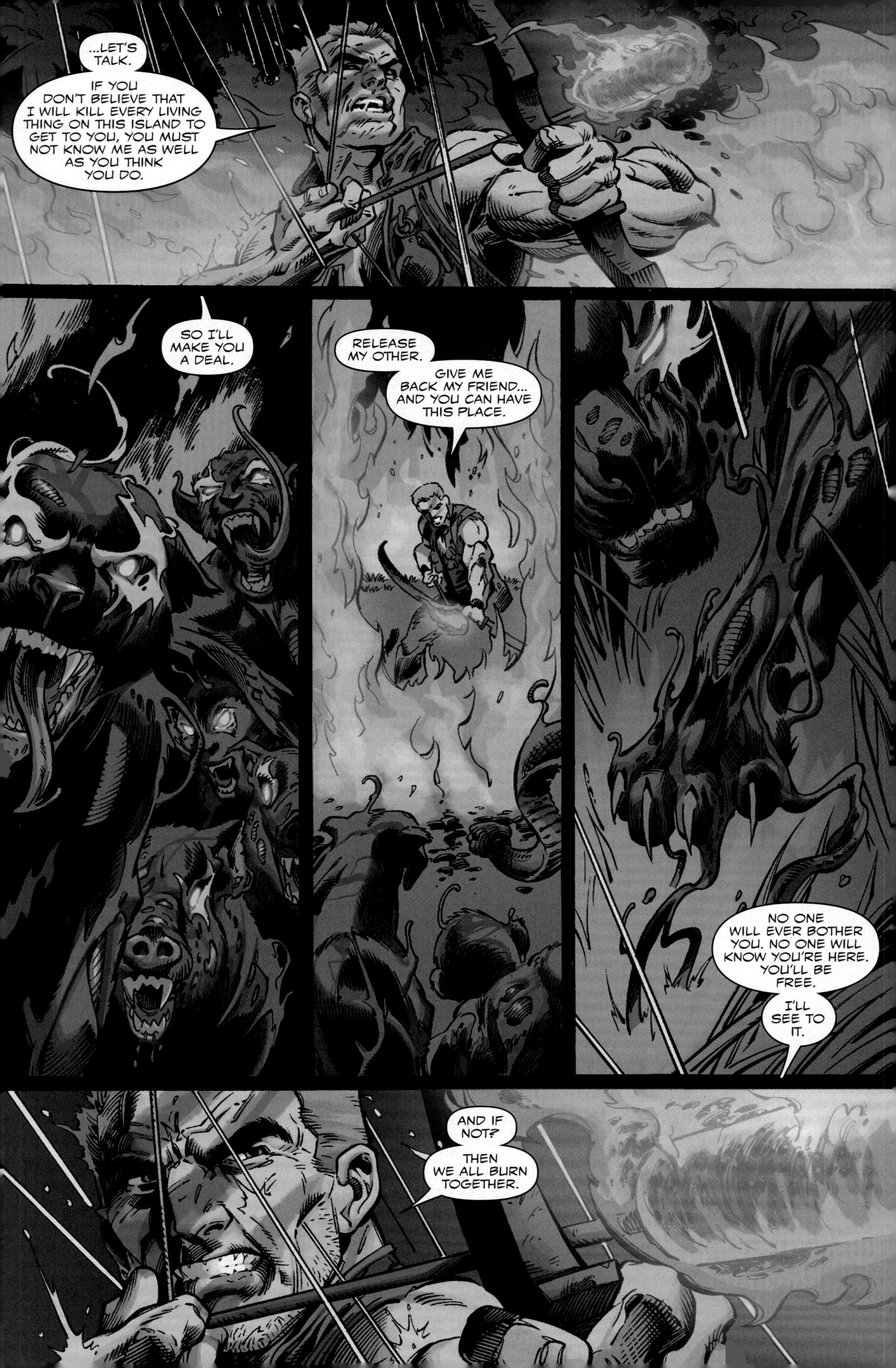
...LET'S TALK.
IF YOU DON'T BELIEVE THAT I WILL KILL EVERY LIVING THING ON THIS ISLAND TO GET TO YOU, YOU MUST NOT KNOW ME AS WELL AS YOU THINK YOU DO.
SO I'LL MAKE YOU A DEAL.
RELEASE MY OTHER.
GIVE ME BACK MY FRIEND... AND YOU CAN HAVE THIS PLACE.
NO ONE WILL EVER BOTHER YOU. NO ONE WILL KNOW YOU'RE HERE. YOU'LL BE FREE.
I'LL SEE TO IT.
AND IF NOT?
THEN WE ALL BURN TOGETHER.

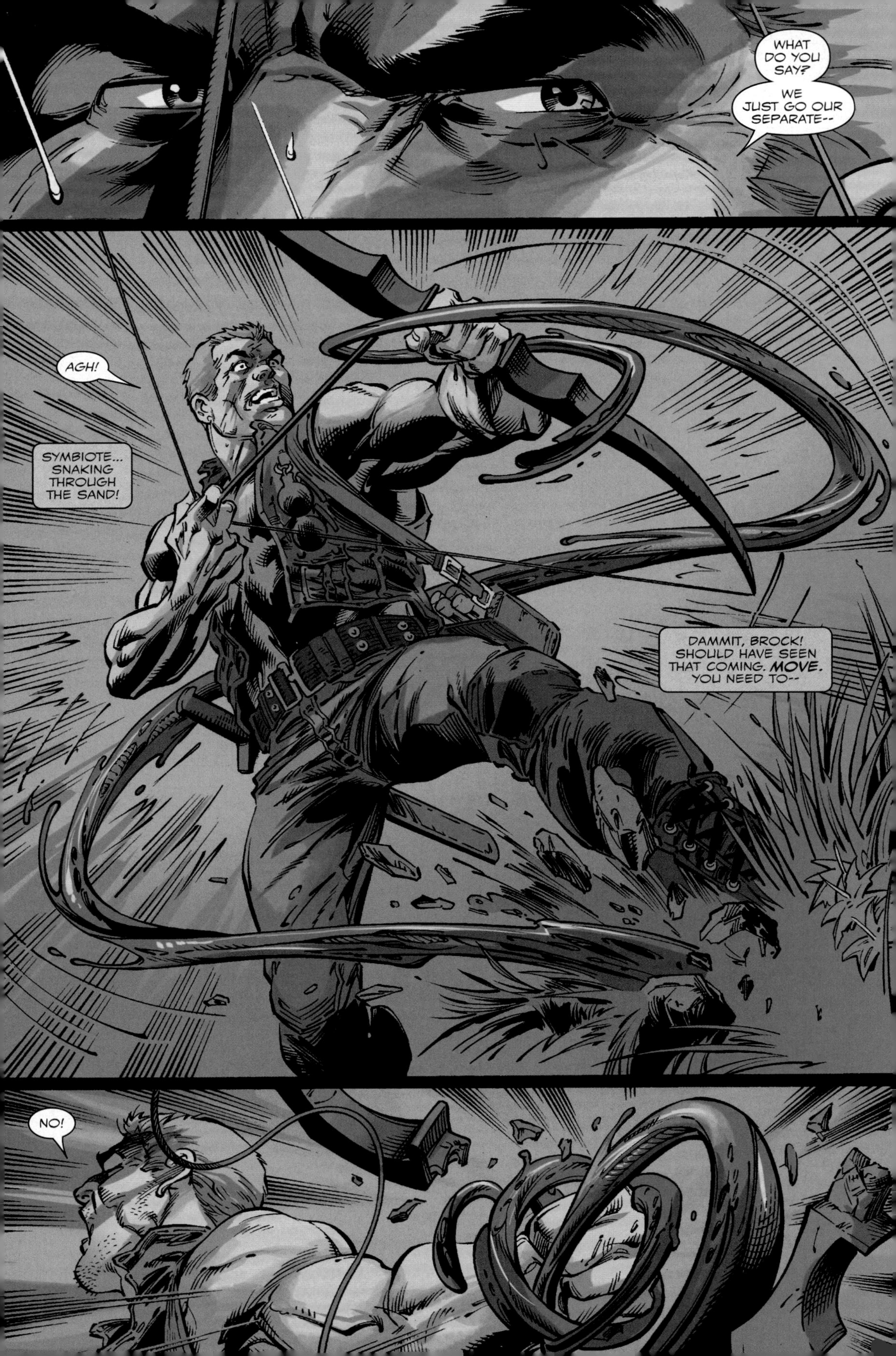
WHAT DO YOU SAY?
WE JUST GO OUR SEPARATE--
AGH!
SYMBIOTE... SNAKING THROUGH THE SAND!
DAMMIT, BROCK! SHOULD HAVE SEEN THAT COMING. MOVE. YOU NEED TO--
NO!

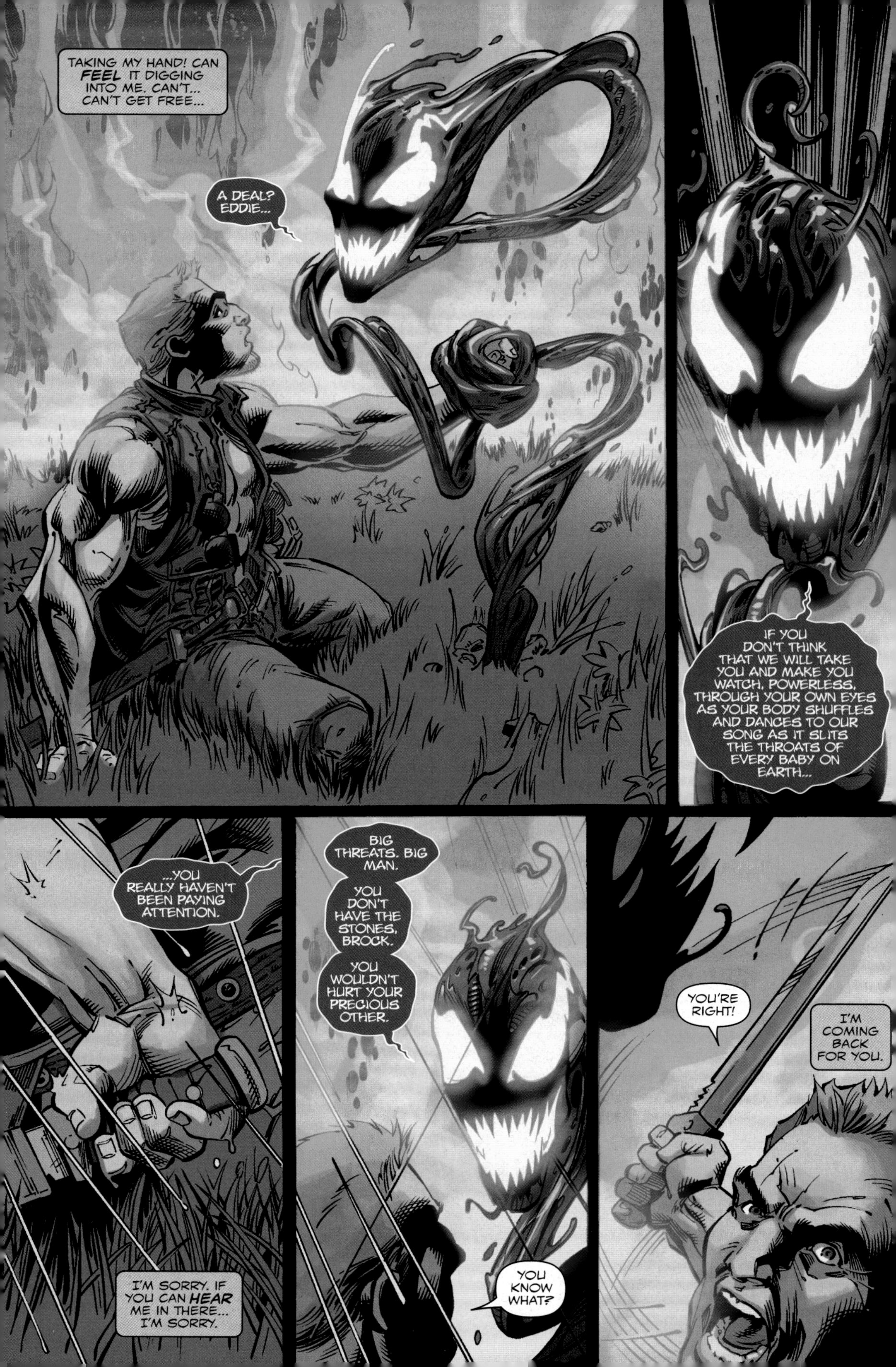
TAKING MY HAND! CAN FEEL IT DIGGING INTO ME. CAN'T... CAN'T GET FREE...
A DEAL? EDDIE...
IF YOU DON'T THINK THAT WE WILL TAKE YOU AND MAKE YOU WATCH, POWERLESS, THROUGH YOUR OWN EYES AS YOUR BODY SHUFFLES AND DANCES TO OUR SONG AS IT SLITS THE THROATS OF EVERY BABY ON EARTH...
...YOU REALLY HAVEN'T BEEN PAYING ATTENTION.
I'M SORRY. IF YOU CAN HEAR ME IN THERE... I'M SORRY.
BIG THREATS. BIG MAN.
YOU DON'T HAVE THE STONES, BROCK.
YOU WOULDN'T HURT YOUR PRECIOUS OTHER.
YOU KNOW WHAT?
YOU'RE RIGHT!
I'M COMING BACK FOR YOU.

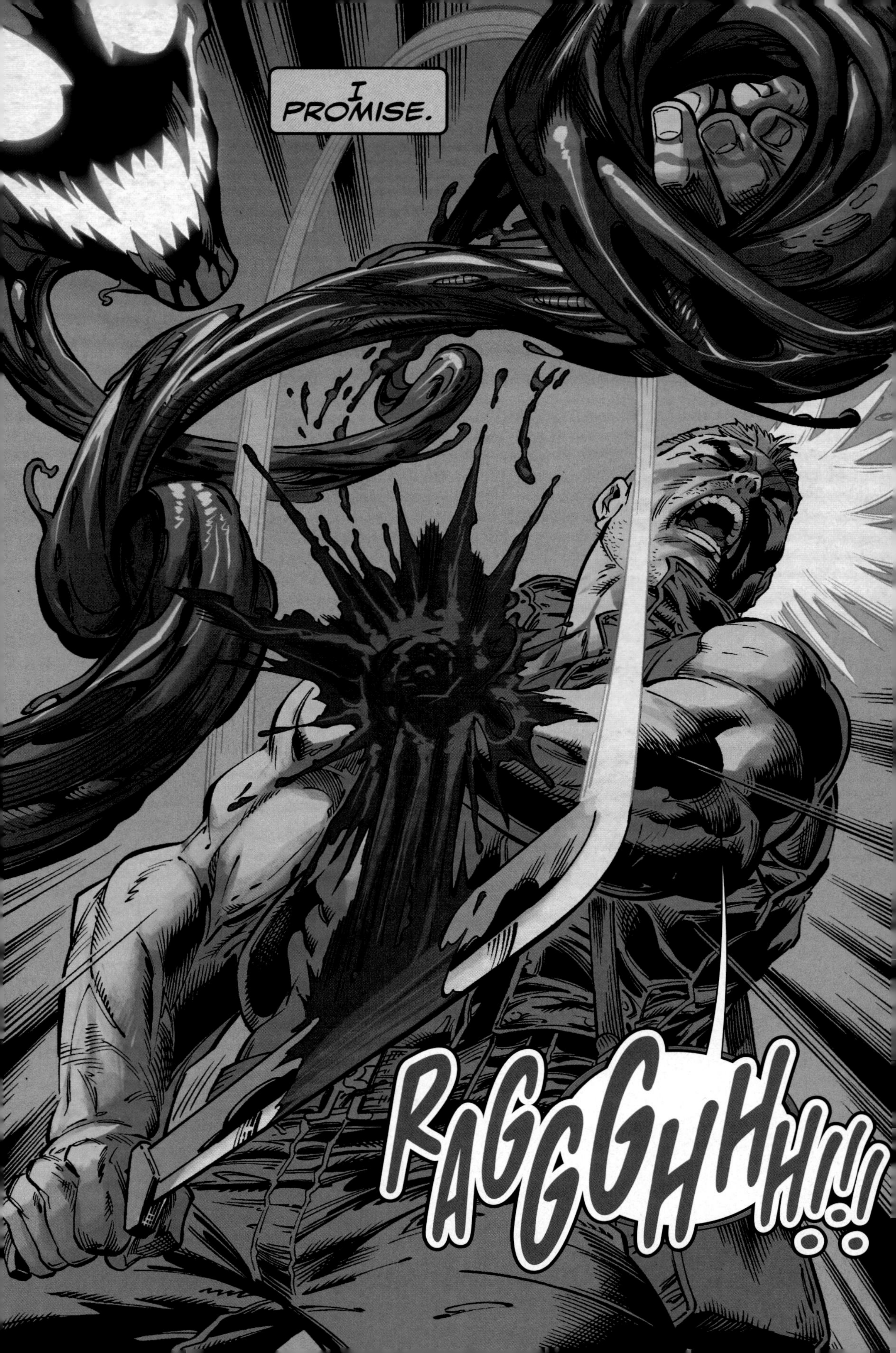
I PROMISE.
RAGGGHHHH!!!

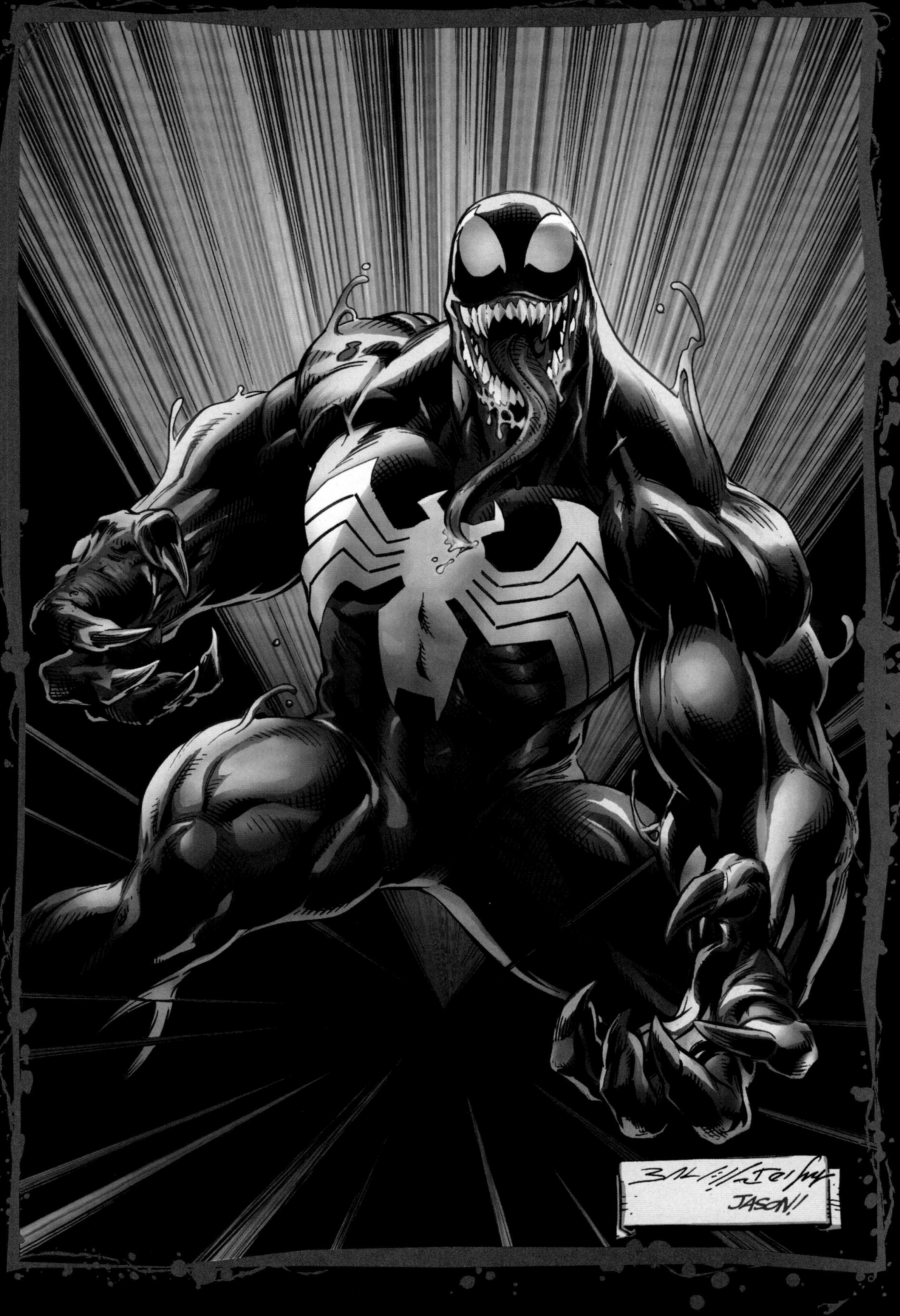
JASON!!

#21 VARIANT BY **MARK BAGLEY, JOHN DELL** & **JASON KEITH**

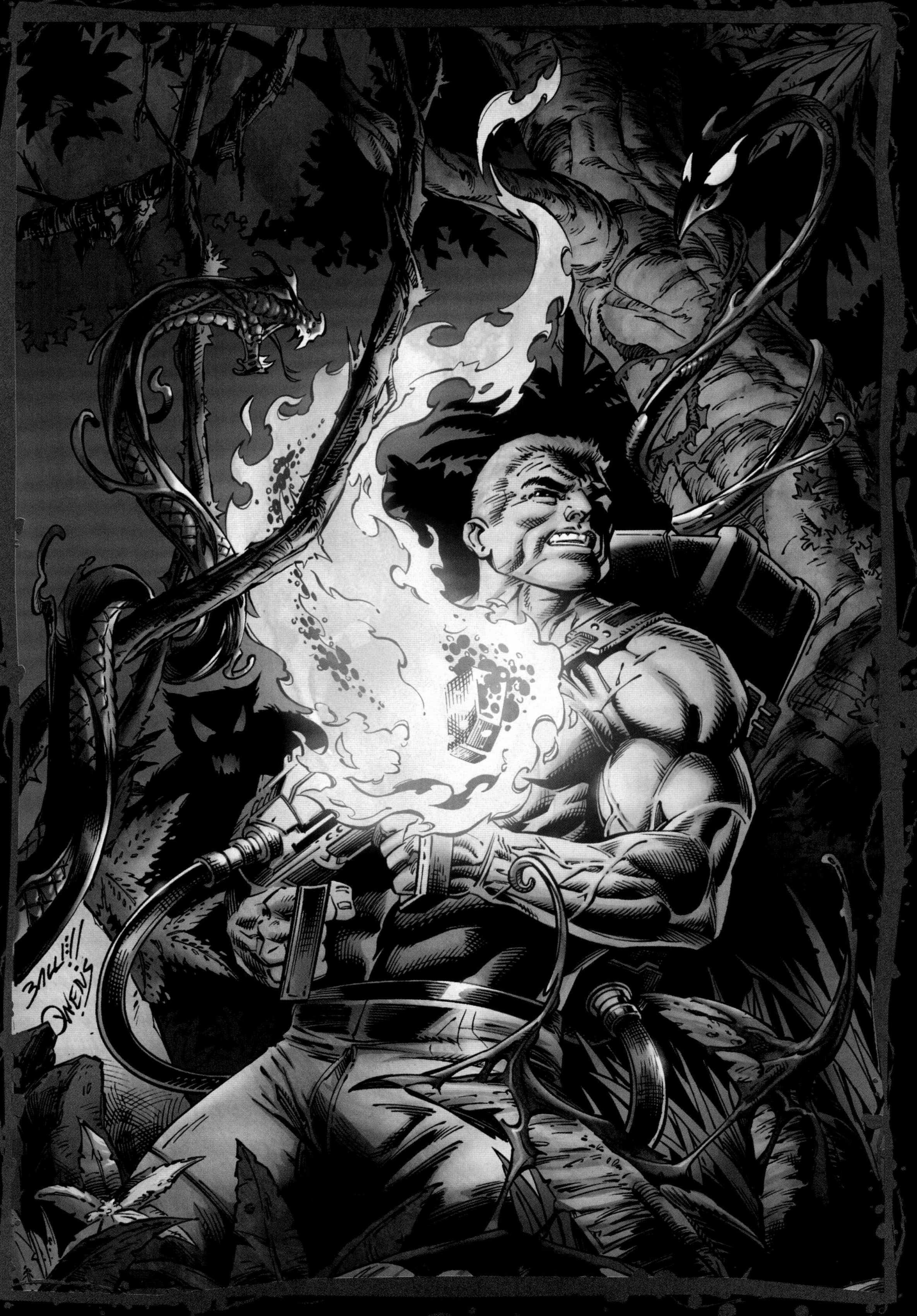
BALL!!!
OWENS

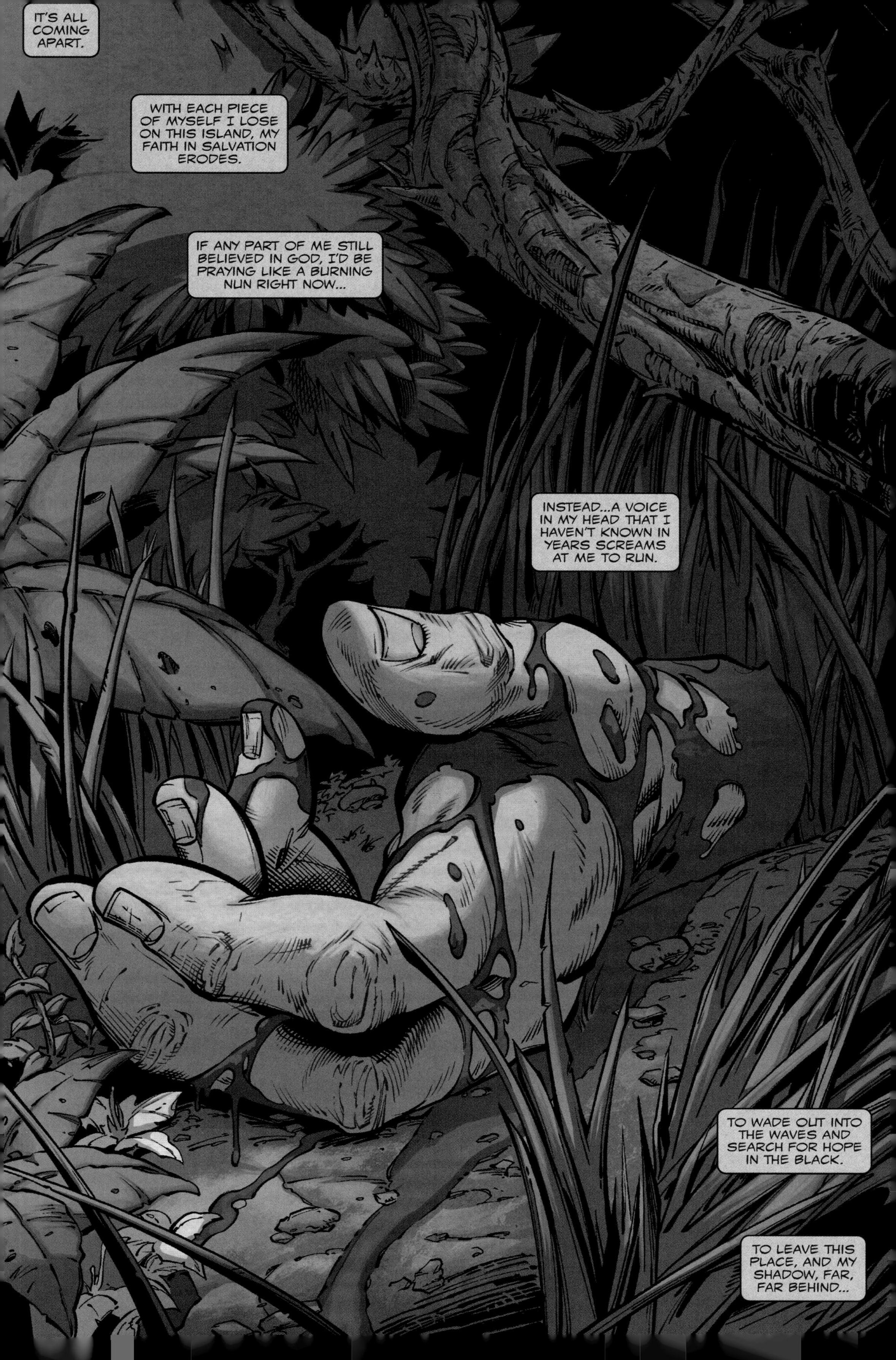
IT'S ALL COMING APART.
WITH EACH PIECE OF MYSELF I LOSE ON THIS ISLAND, MY FAITH IN SALVATION ERODES.
IF ANY PART OF ME STILL BELIEVED IN GOD, I'D BE PRAYING LIKE A BURNING NUN RIGHT NOW...
INSTEAD...A VOICE IN MY HEAD THAT I HAVEN'T KNOWN IN YEARS SCREAMS AT ME TO RUN.
TO WADE OUT INTO THE WAVES AND SEARCH FOR HOPE IN THE BLACK.
TO LEAVE THIS PLACE, AND MY SHADOW, FAR, FAR BEHIND...

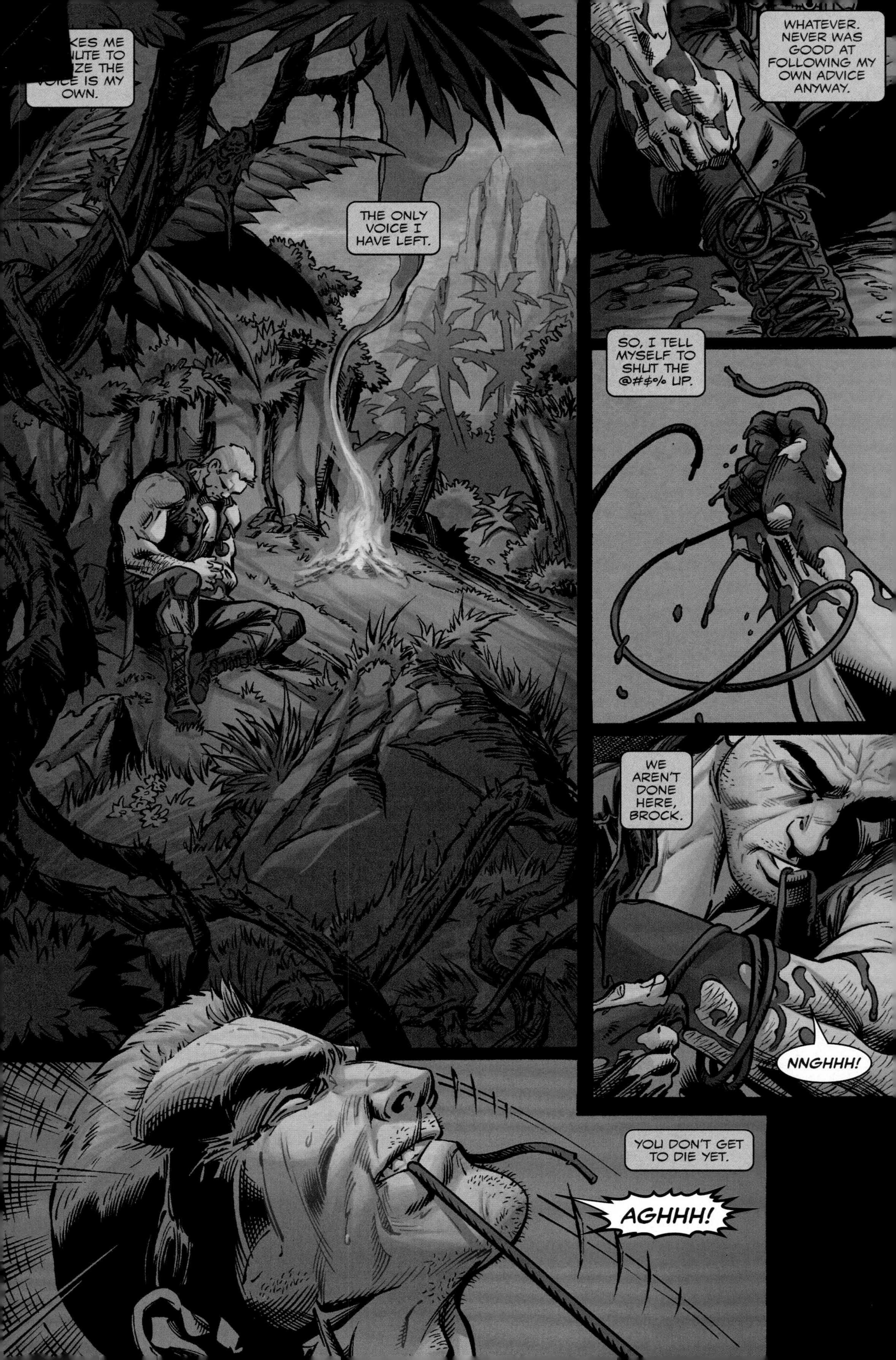
KES ME NUTE TO ZE THE VOICE IS MY OWN.
THE ONLY VOICE I HAVE LEFT.
WHATEVER. NEVER WAS GOOD AT FOLLOWING MY OWN ADVICE ANYWAY.
SO, I TELL MYSELF TO SHUT THE @#$% UP.
WE AREN'T DONE HERE, BROCK.
NNGHHH!
YOU DON'T GET TO DIE YET.
AGHHH!

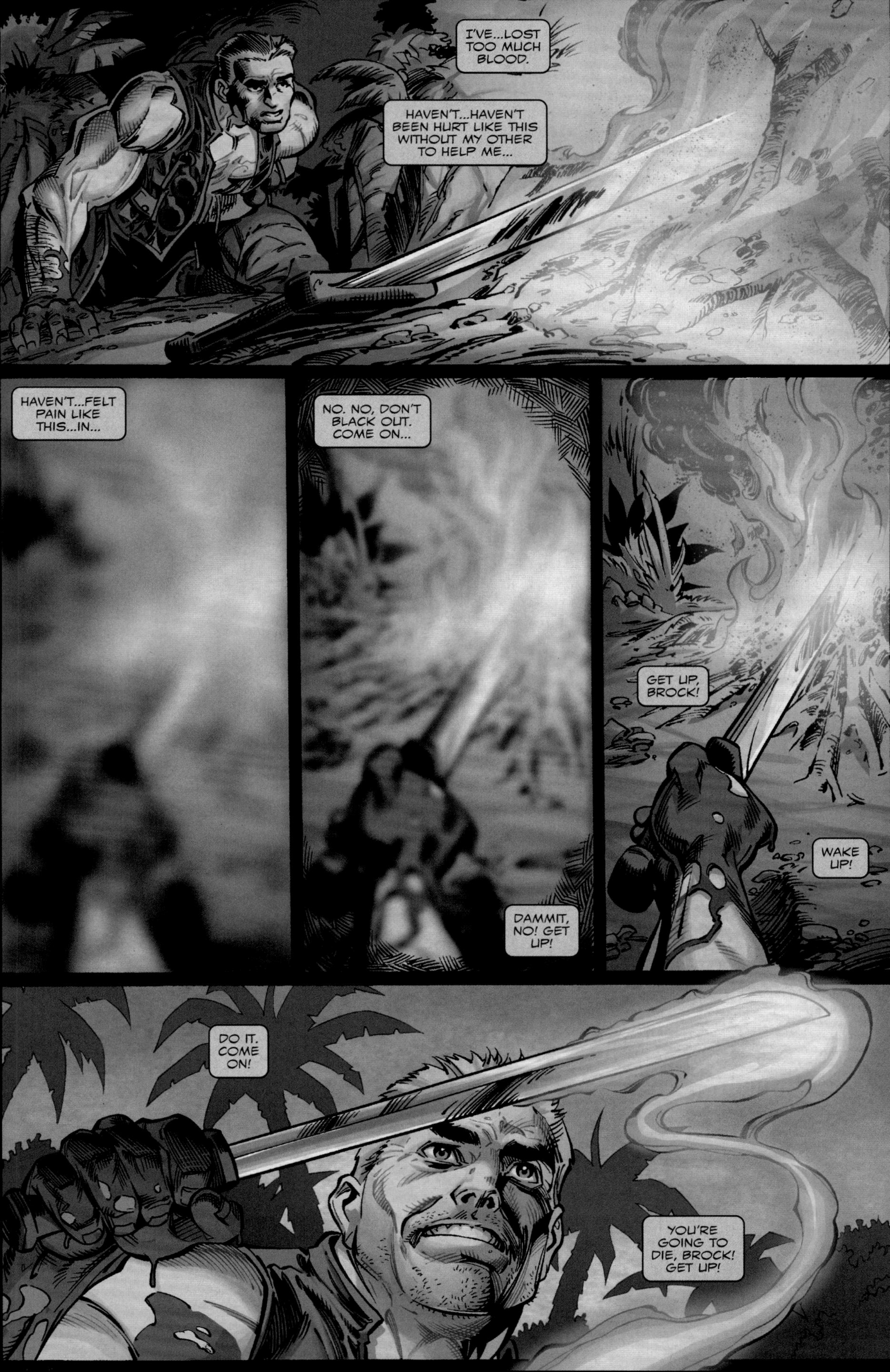
I'VE...LOST TOO MUCH BLOOD.
HAVEN'T...HAVEN'T BEEN HURT LIKE THIS WITHOUT MY OTHER TO HELP ME...
HAVEN'T...FELT PAIN LIKE THIS...IN...
NO. NO, DON'T BLACK OUT. COME ON...
DAMMIT, NO! GET UP!
GET UP, BROCK!
WAKE UP!
DO IT. COME ON!
YOU'RE GOING TO DIE, BROCK! GET UP!

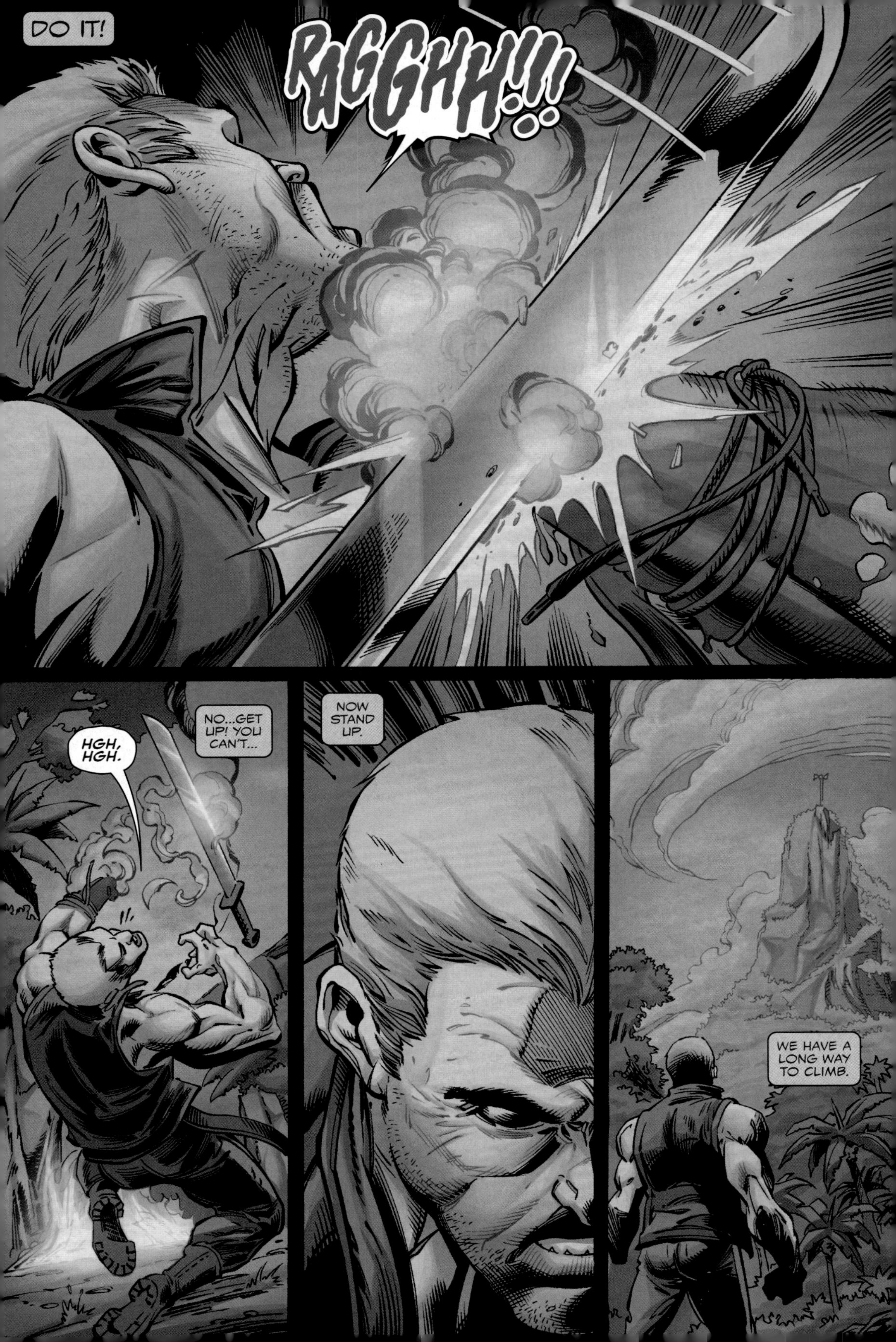
DO IT!
RAGGHH!!!
HGH, HGH.
NO...GET UP! YOU CAN'T...
NOW STAND UP.
WE HAVE A LONG WAY TO CLIMB.

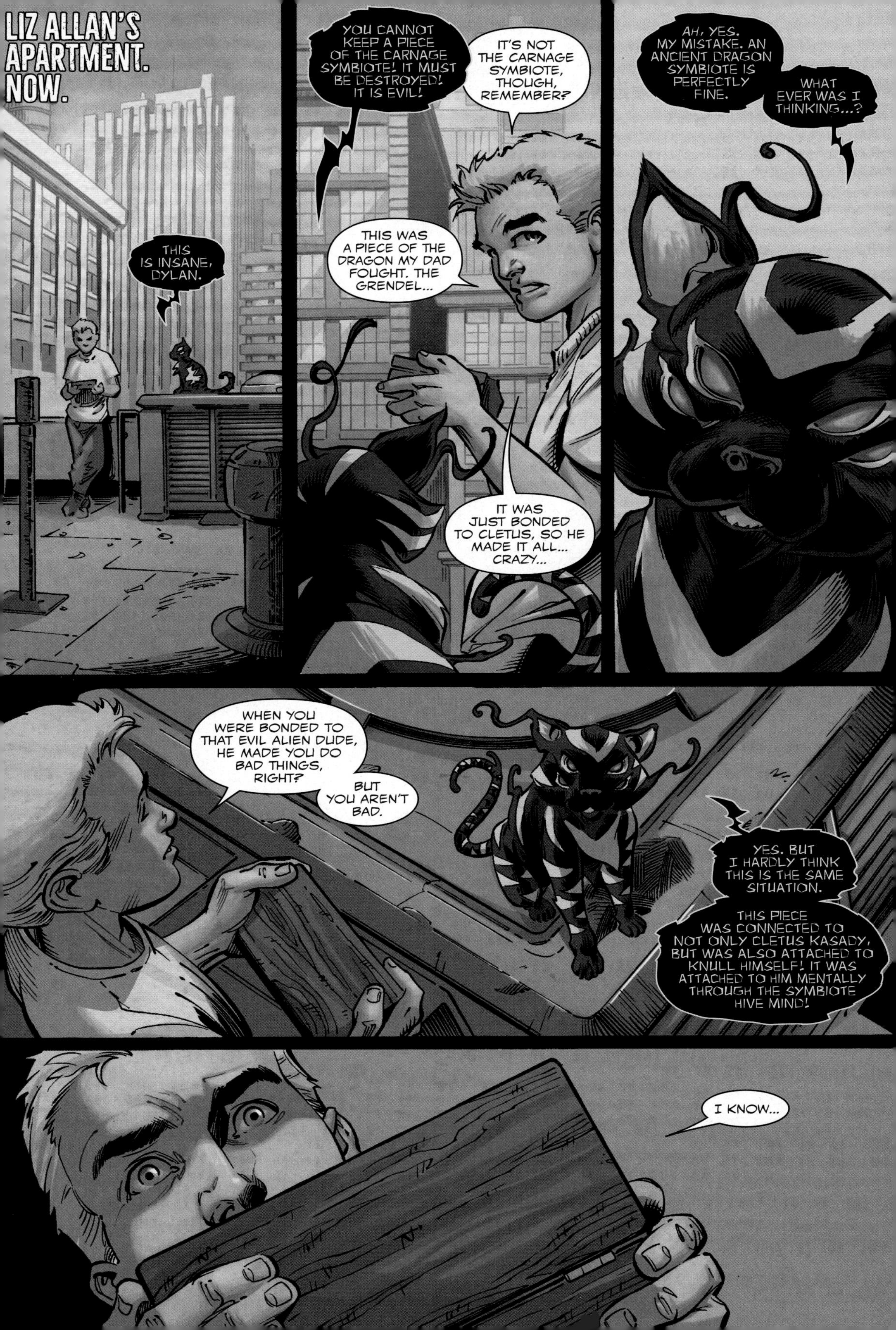
LIZ ALLAN'S APARTMENT. NOW.
THIS IS INSANE, DYLAN.
YOU CANNOT KEEP A PIECE OF THE CARNAGE SYMBIOTE! IT MUST BE DESTROYED! IT IS EVIL!
IT'S NOT THE CARNAGE SYMBIOTE, THOUGH, REMEMBER?
THIS WAS A PIECE OF THE DRAGON MY DAD FOUGHT. THE GRENDEL...
IT WAS JUST BONDED TO CLETUS, SO HE MADE IT ALL... CRAZY...
AH, YES. MY MISTAKE. AN ANCIENT DRAGON SYMBIOTE IS PERFECTLY FINE.
WHAT EVER WAS I THINKING...?
WHEN YOU WERE BONDED TO THAT EVIL ALIEN DUDE, HE MADE YOU DO BAD THINGS, RIGHT?
BUT YOU AREN'T BAD.
YES. BUT I HARDLY THINK THIS IS THE SAME SITUATION.
THIS PIECE WAS CONNECTED TO NOT ONLY CLETUS KASADY, BUT WAS ALSO ATTACHED TO KNULL HIMSELF! IT WAS ATTACHED TO HIM MENTALLY THROUGH THE SYMBIOTE HIVE MIND!
I KNOW...

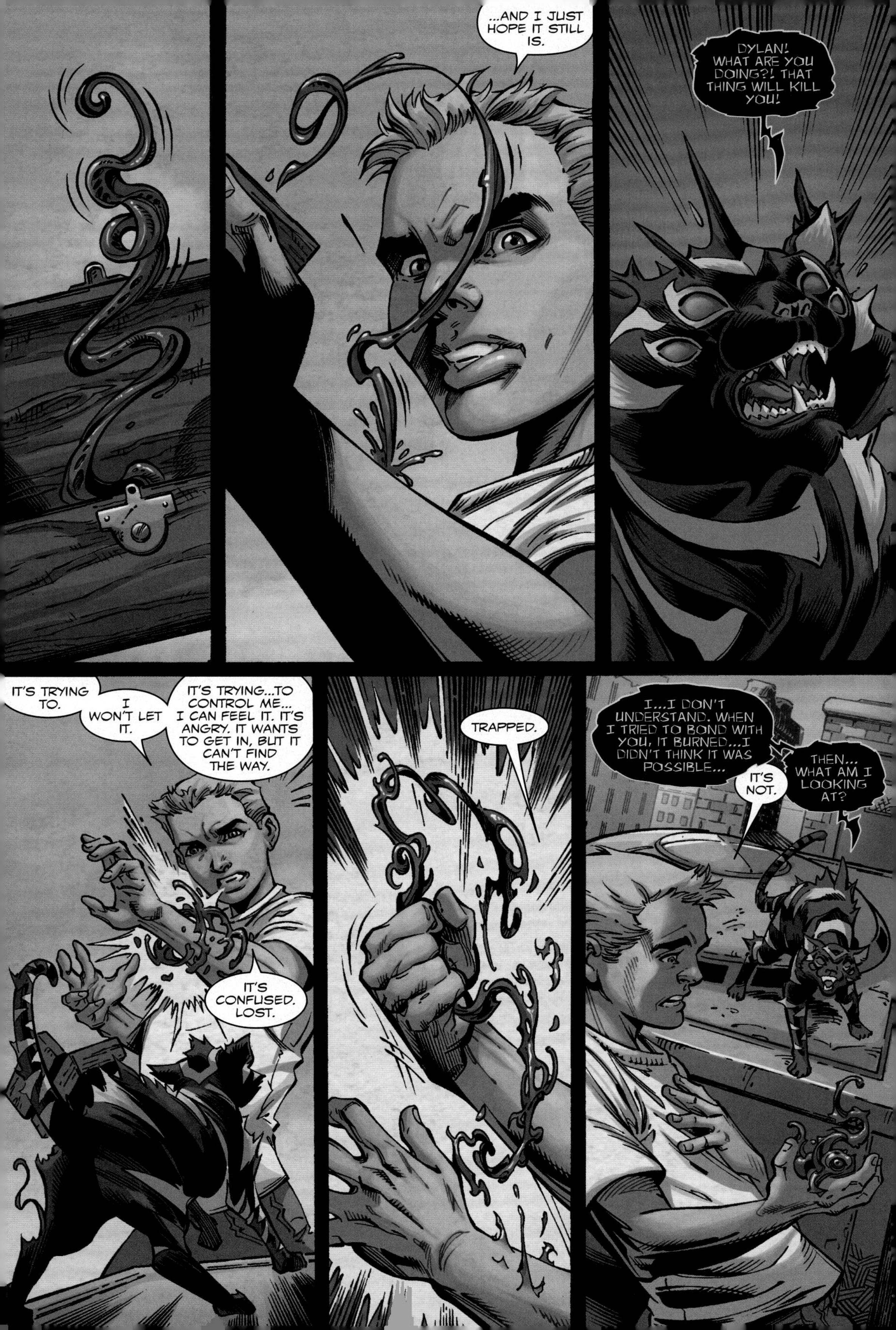
...AND I JUST HOPE IT STILL IS.
DYLAN! WHAT ARE YOU DOING?! THAT THING WILL KILL YOU!
IT'S TRYING TO.
I WON'T LET IT.
IT'S TRYING...TO CONTROL ME... I CAN FEEL IT. IT'S ANGRY. IT WANTS TO GET IN, BUT IT CAN'T FIND THE WAY.
IT'S CONFUSED. LOST.
TRAPPED.
I...I DON'T UNDERSTAND. WHEN I TRIED TO BOND WITH YOU, IT BURNED...I DIDN'T THINK IT WAS POSSIBLE...
IT'S NOT.
THEN... WHAT AM I LOOKING AT?

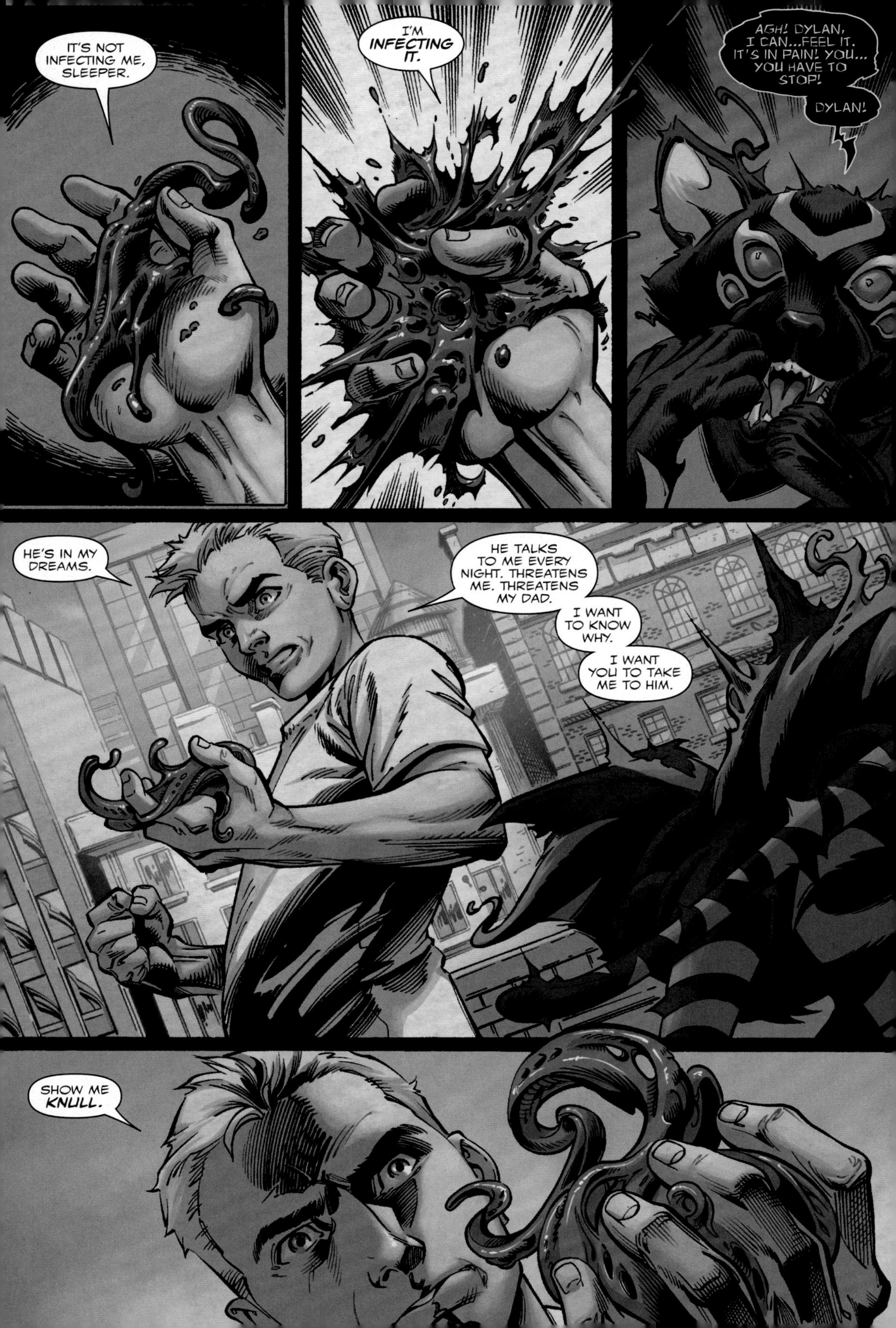

IT'S NOT INFECTING ME, SLEEPER.
I'M *INFECTING IT.*
AGH! DYLAN, I CAN...FEEL IT. IT'S IN PAIN! YOU... YOU HAVE TO STOP!
DYLAN!
HE'S IN MY DREAMS.
HE TALKS TO ME EVERY NIGHT. THREATENS ME. THREATENS MY DAD.
I WANT TO KNOW WHY.
I WANT YOU TO TAKE ME TO HIM.
SHOW ME *KNULL.*

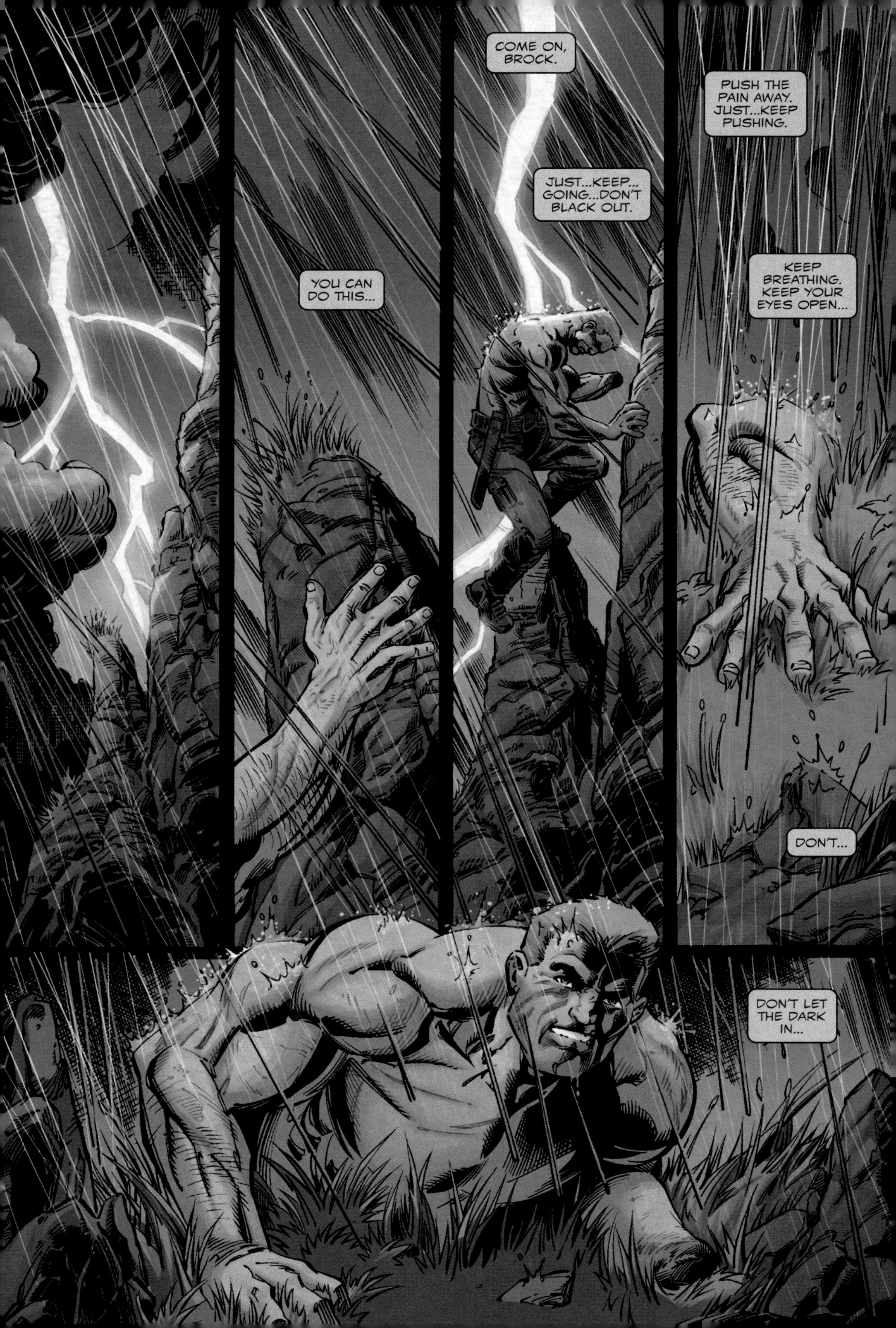
YOU CAN DO THIS...
COME ON, BROCK.
JUST...KEEP... GOING...DON'T BLACK OUT.
PUSH THE PAIN AWAY. JUST...KEEP PUSHING.
KEEP BREATHING. KEEP YOUR EYES OPEN...
DON'T...
DON'T LET THE DARK IN...

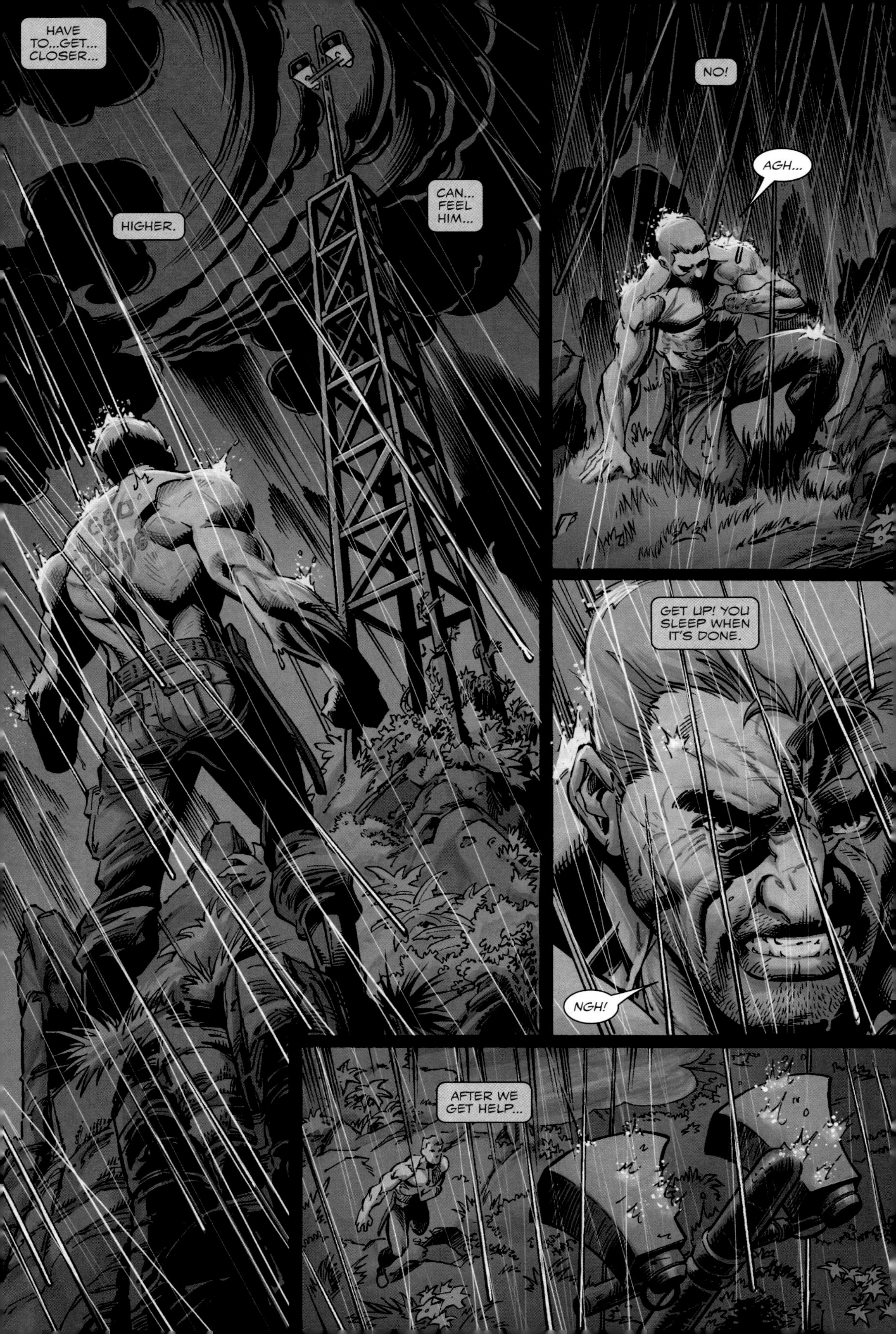
HAVE TO...GET... CLOSER...
HIGHER.
CAN... FEEL HIM...
NO!
AGH...
GET UP! YOU SLEEP WHEN IT'S DONE.
NGH!
AFTER WE GET HELP...

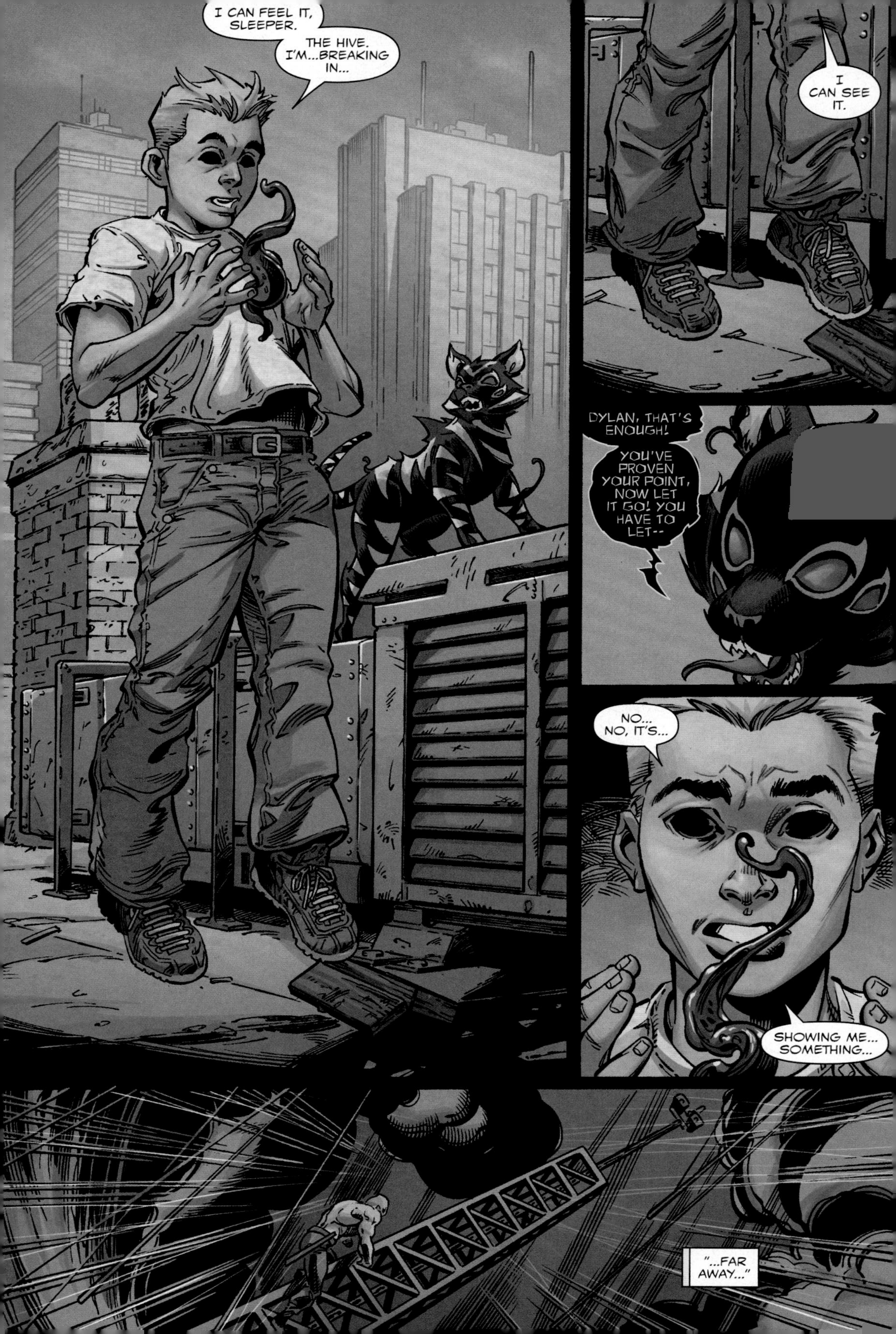
I CAN FEEL IT, SLEEPER.
THE HIVE. I'M...BREAKING IN...
I CAN SEE IT.
DYLAN, THAT'S ENOUGH!
YOU'VE PROVEN YOUR POINT, NOW LET IT GO! YOU HAVE TO LET--
NO... NO, IT'S...
SHOWING ME... SOMETHING...
"...FAR AWAY..."

I...I DON'T UNDERSTAND. WHAT...
"...WHAT AM I SEEING?
"WHY ARE YOU SHOWING ME THIS?"
D-DYLAN?
YES! I... I CAN HEAR YOU!
T-TRAPPED, DYLAN. HE NEEDS YOU. H-HELP...
WHAT? WHO?
EDDIE! HELP EDDIE!
DAD?!

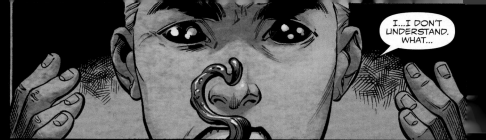

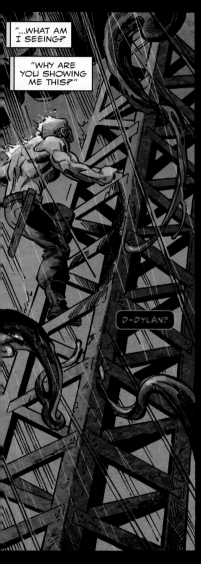

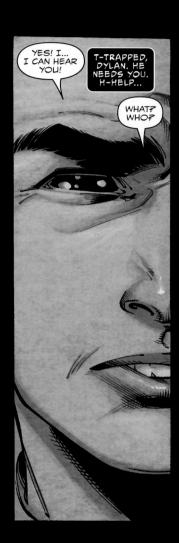

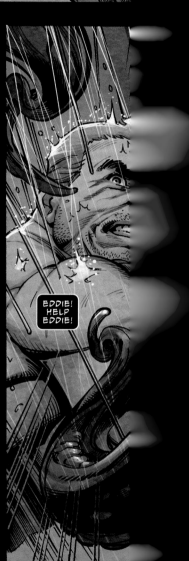

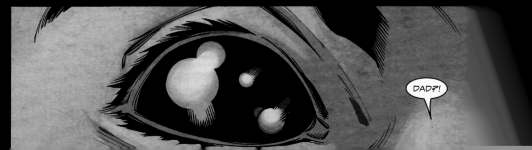

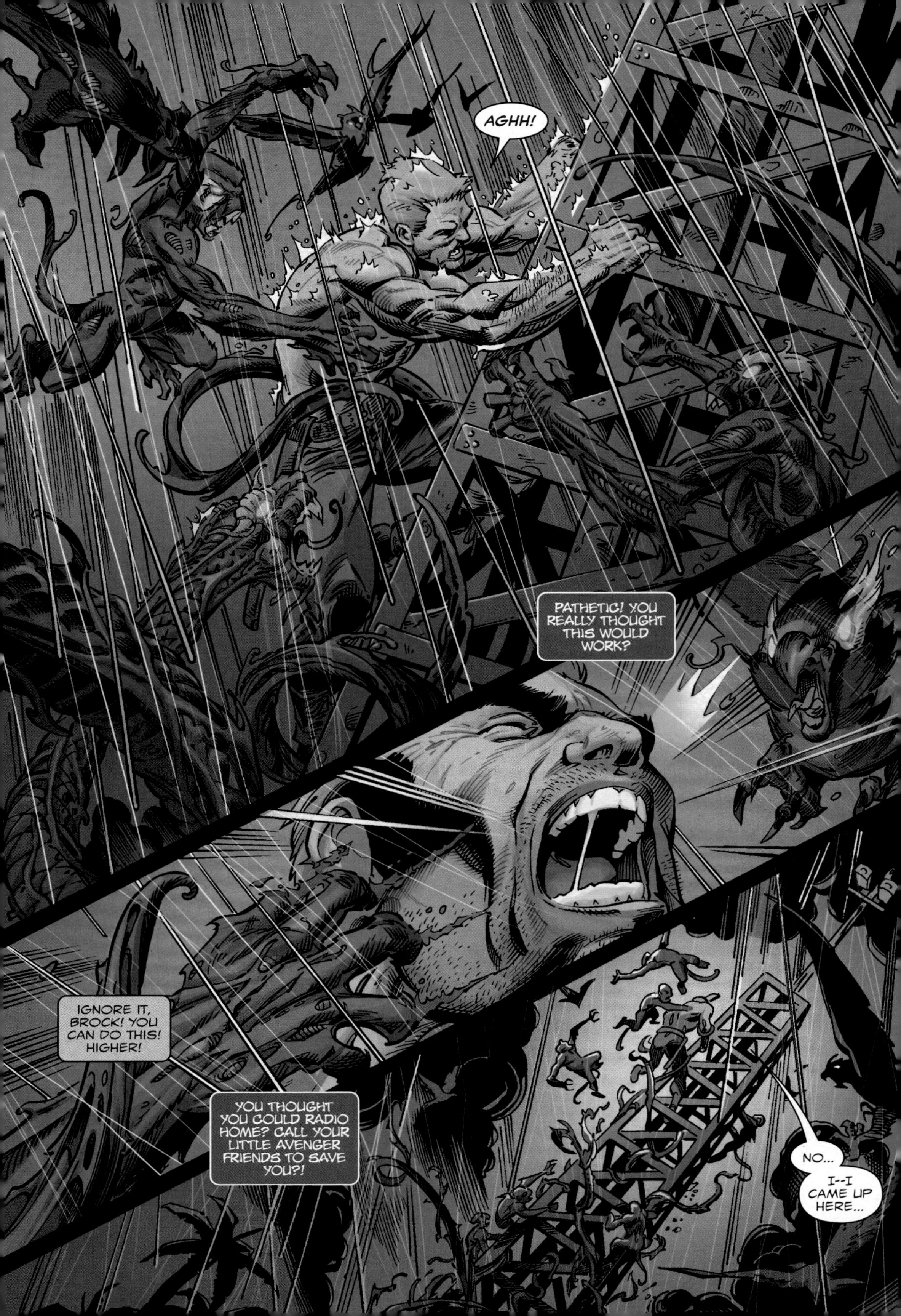
AGHH!
PATHETIC! YOU REALLY THOUGHT THIS WOULD WORK?
IGNORE IT, BROCK! YOU CAN DO THIS! HIGHER!
YOU THOUGHT YOU COULD RADIO HOME? CALL YOUR LITTLE AVENGER FRIENDS TO SAVE YOU?!
NO...
I--I CAME UP HERE...

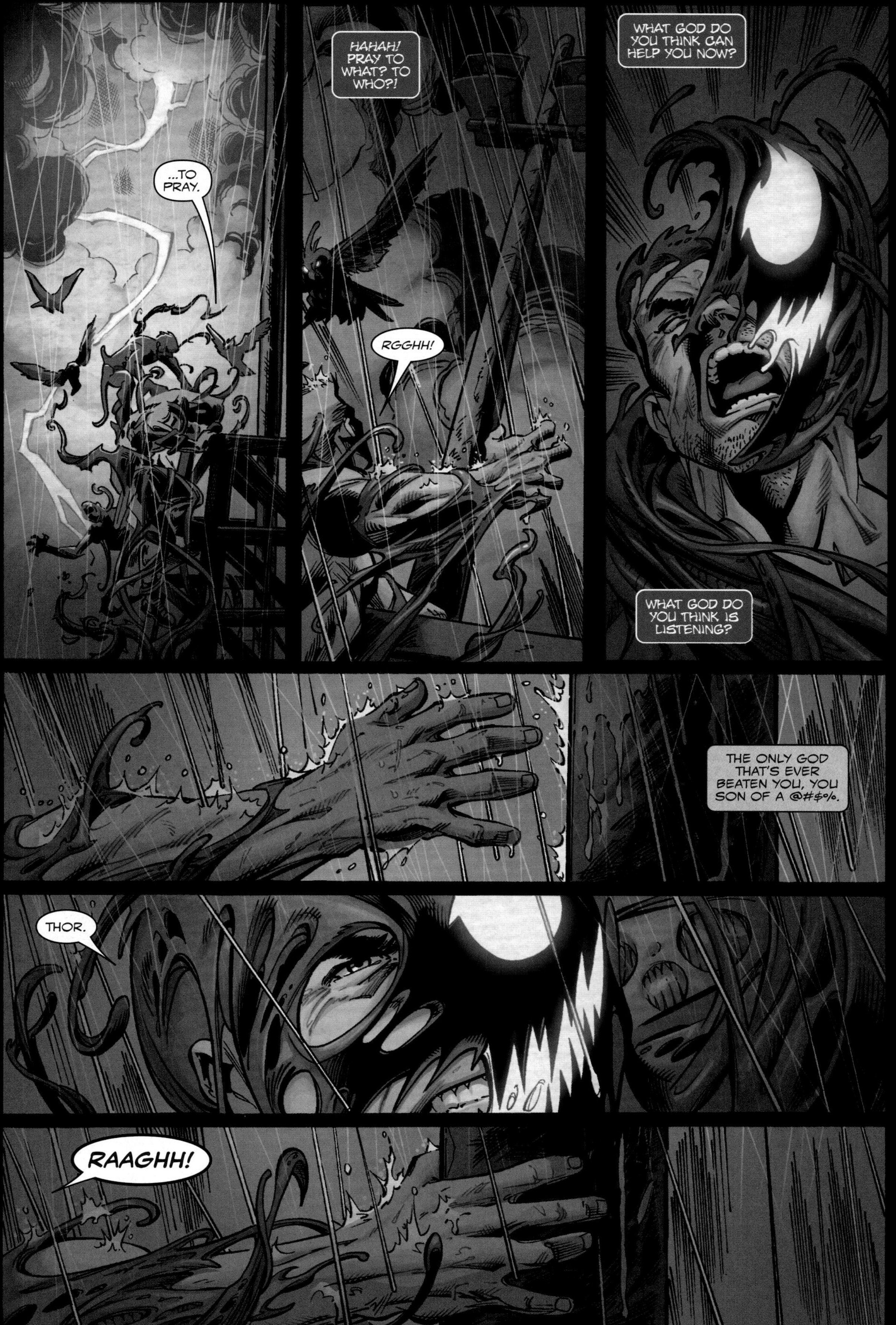
...TO PRAY.
HAHAH! PRAY TO WHAT? TO WHO?!
RGGHH!
WHAT GOD DO YOU THINK CAN HELP YOU NOW?
WHAT GOD DO YOU THINK IS LISTENING?
THE ONLY GOD THAT'S EVER BEATEN YOU, YOU SON OF A @#$%.
THOR.
RAAGHH!

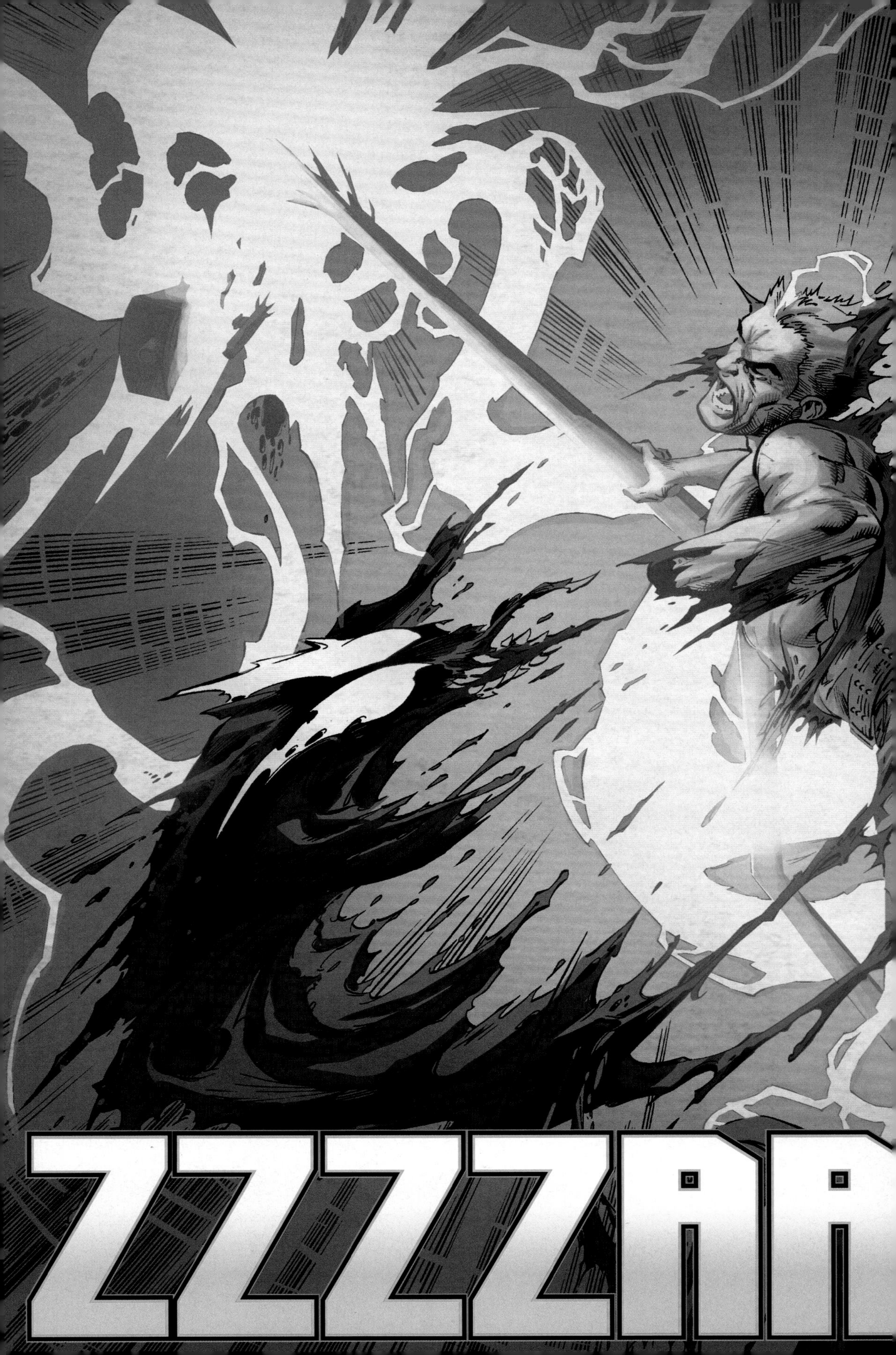
ZZZZAR

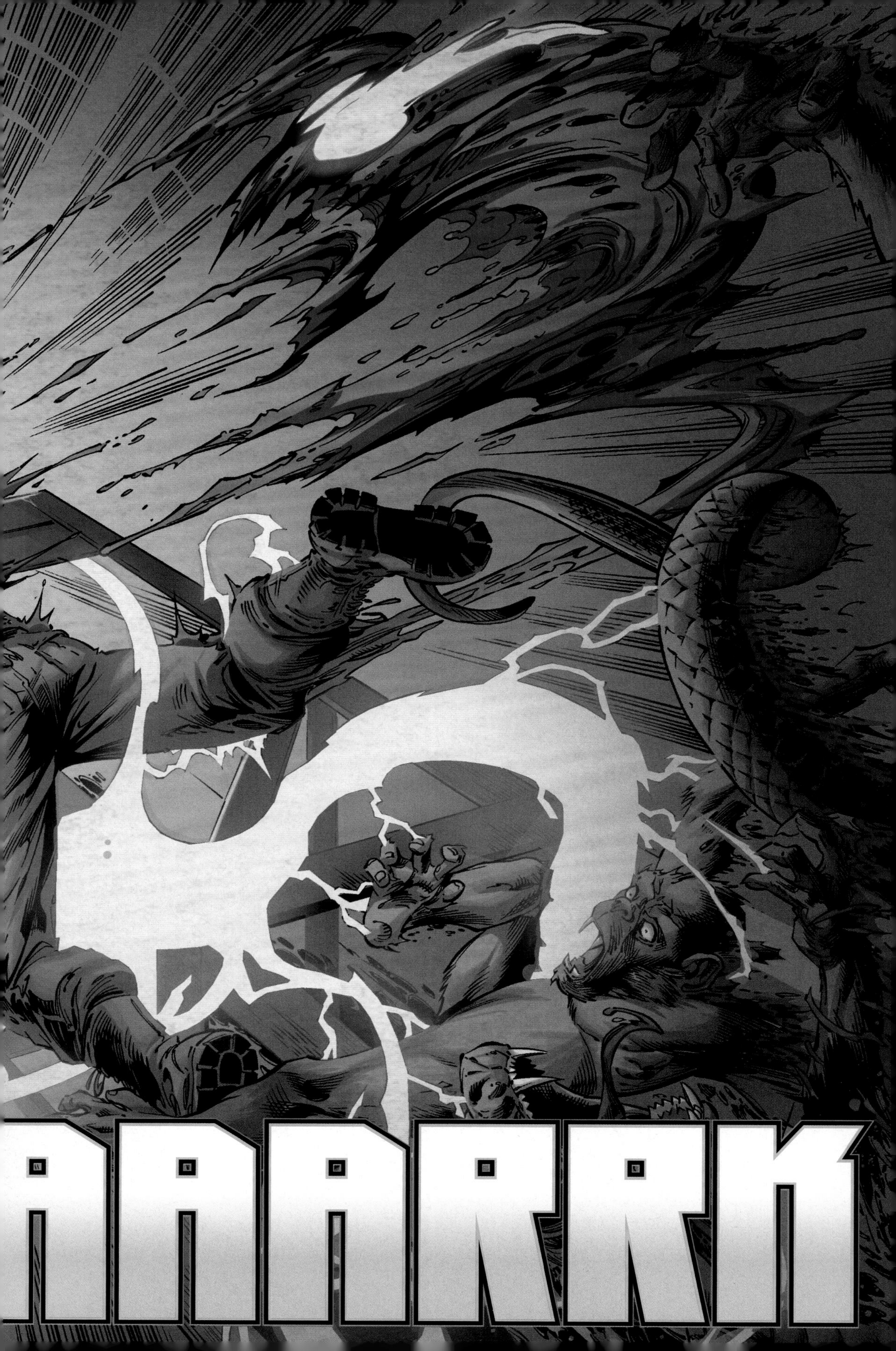
AARRRK

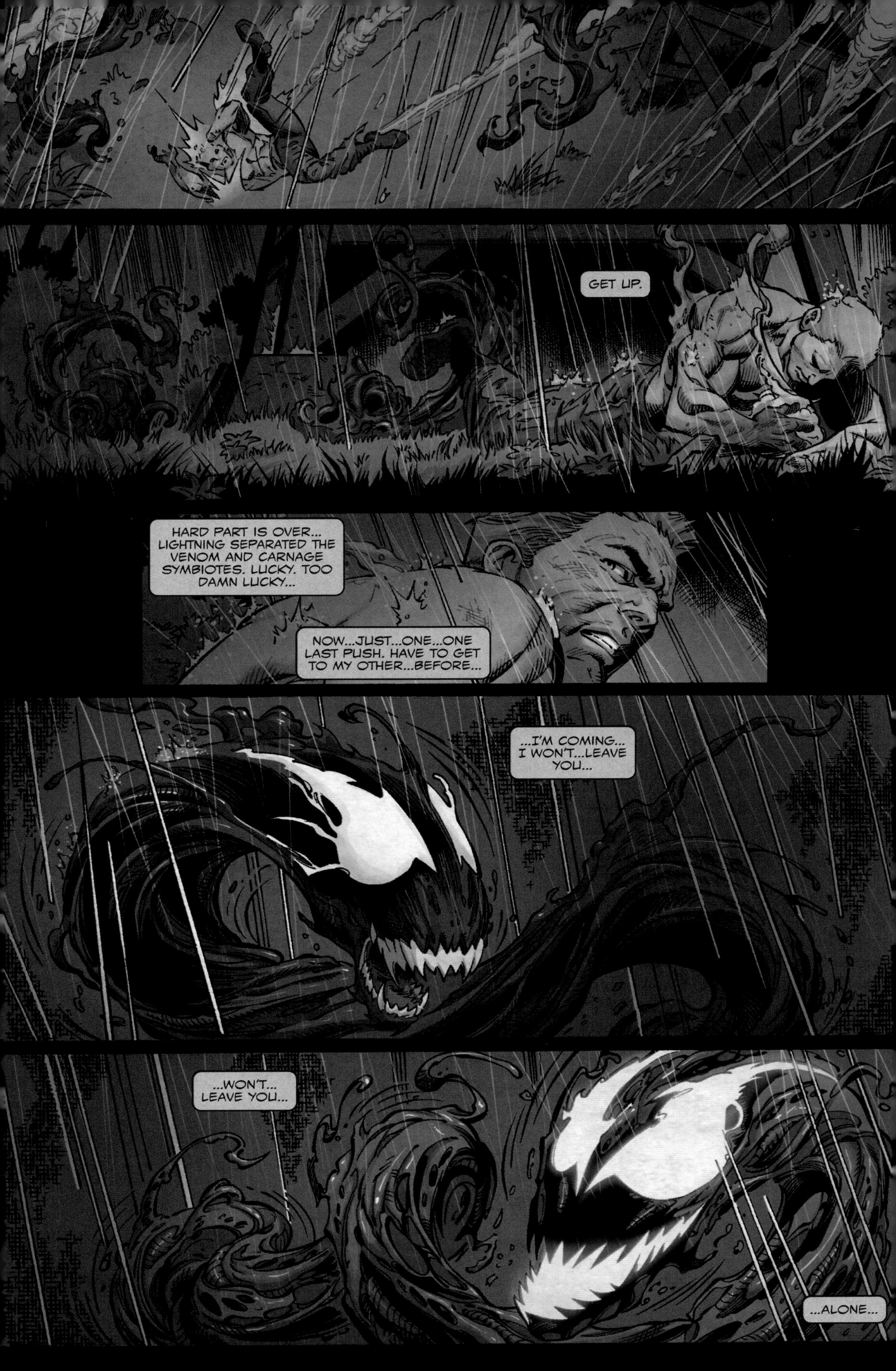
GET UP.
HARD PART IS OVER... LIGHTNING SEPARATED THE VENOM AND CARNAGE SYMBIOTES. LUCKY. TOO DAMN LUCKY...
NOW...JUST...ONE...ONE LAST PUSH. HAVE TO GET TO MY OTHER...BEFORE...
...I'M COMING... I WON'T...LEAVE YOU...
...WON'T... LEAVE YOU...
...ALONE...

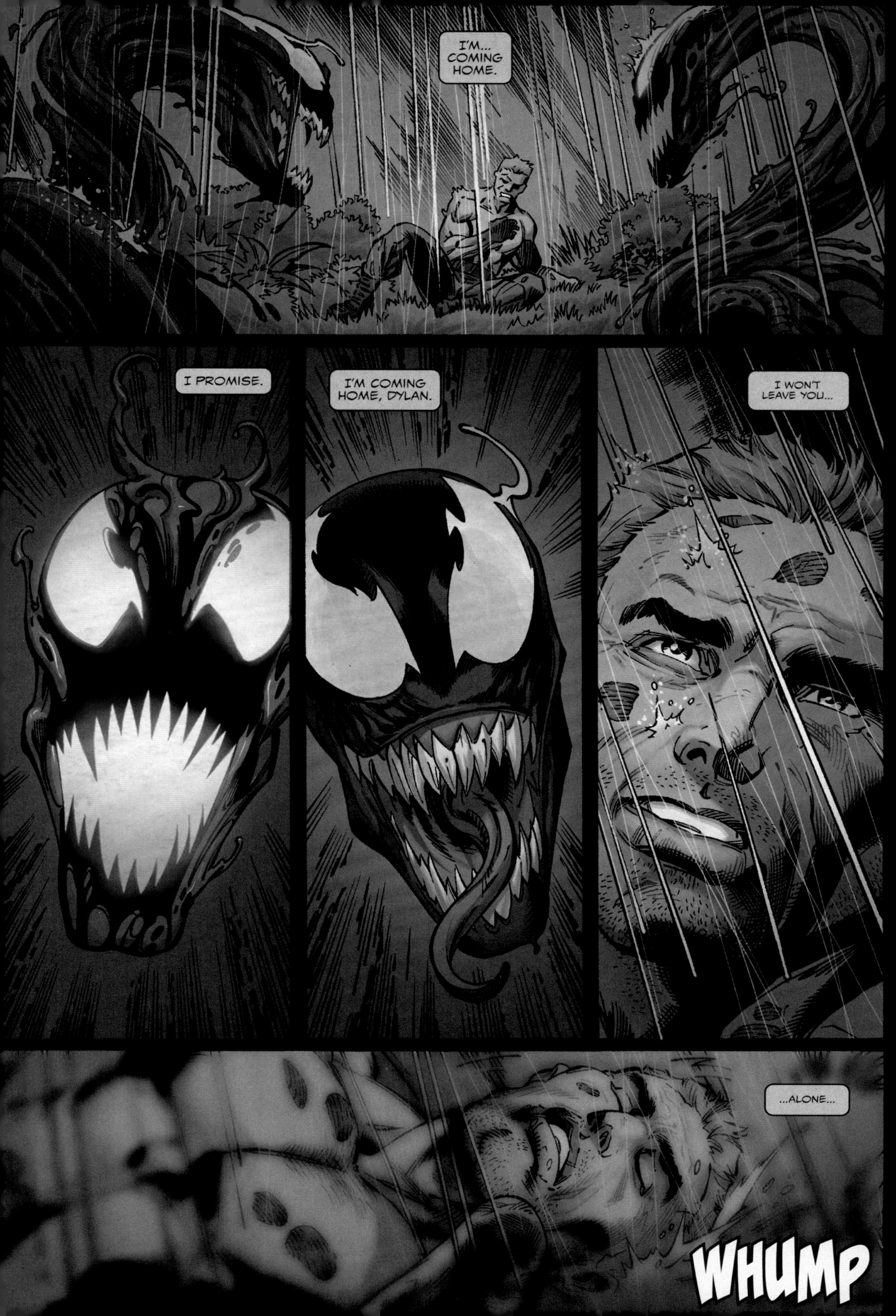
I'M... COMING HOME.
I PROMISE.
I'M COMING HOME, DYLAN.
I WON'T LEAVE YOU...
...ALONE...
WHUMP

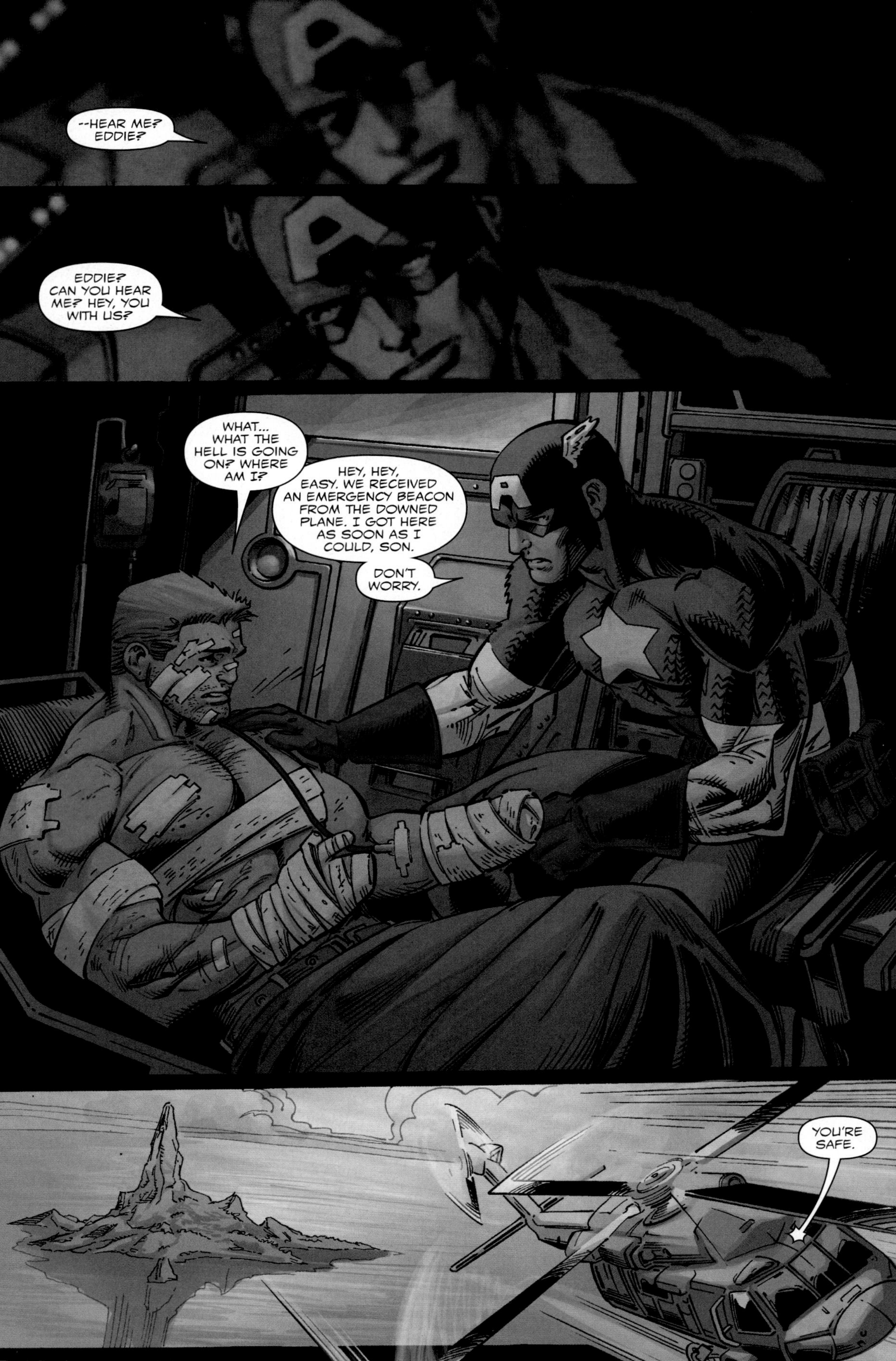
--HEAR ME? EDDIE?
EDDIE? CAN YOU HEAR ME? HEY, YOU WITH US?
WHAT... WHAT THE HELL IS GOING ON? WHERE AM I?
HEY, HEY, EASY. WE RECEIVED AN EMERGENCY BEACON FROM THE DOWNED PLANE. I GOT HERE AS SOON AS I COULD, SON.
DON'T WORRY.
YOU'RE SAFE.

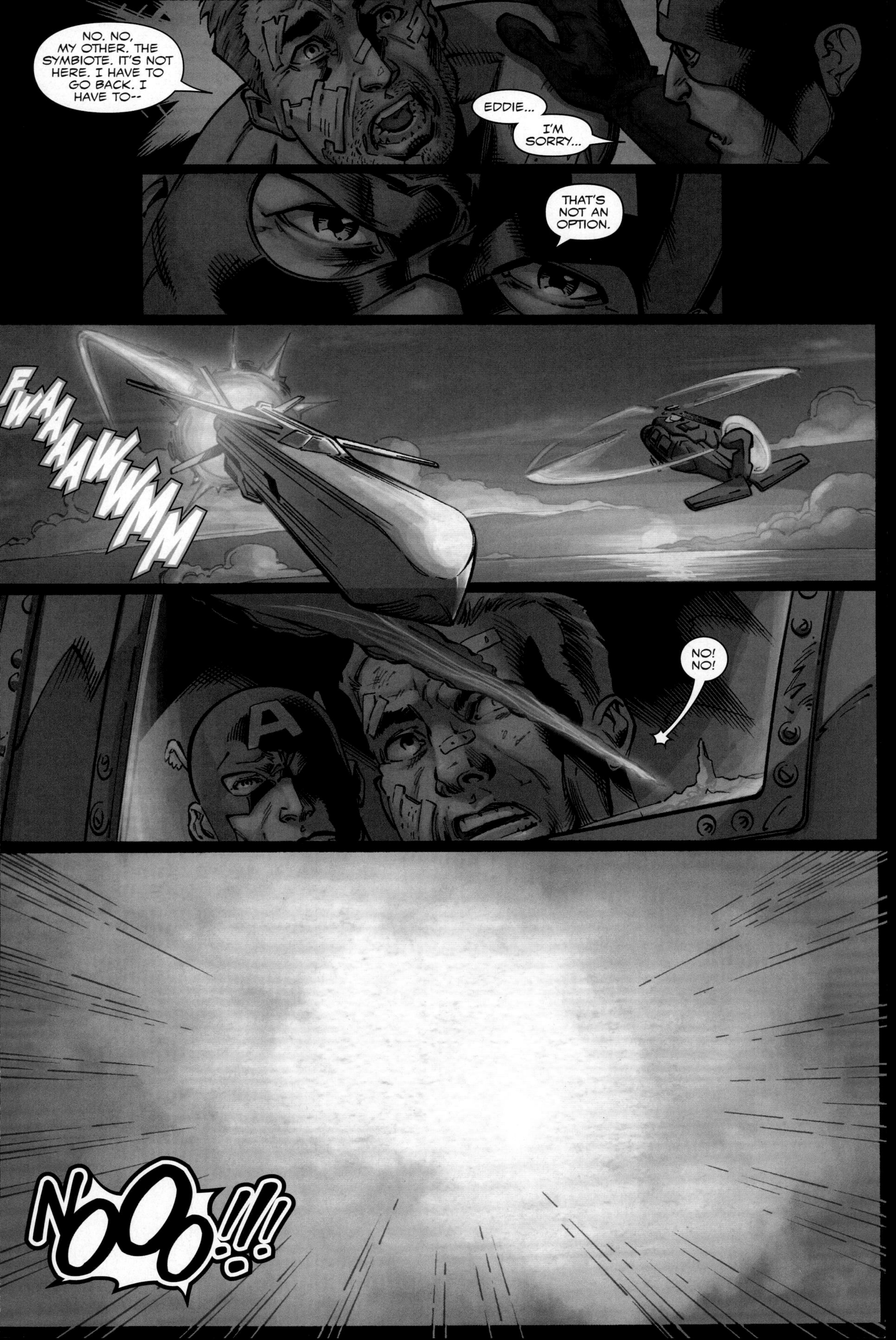
NO. NO, MY OTHER. THE SYMBIOTE. IT'S NOT HERE. I HAVE TO GO BACK. I HAVE TO--
EDDIE...
I'M SORRY...
THAT'S NOT AN OPTION.
FWAAAAWWMM
NO! NO!
NOOO!!!

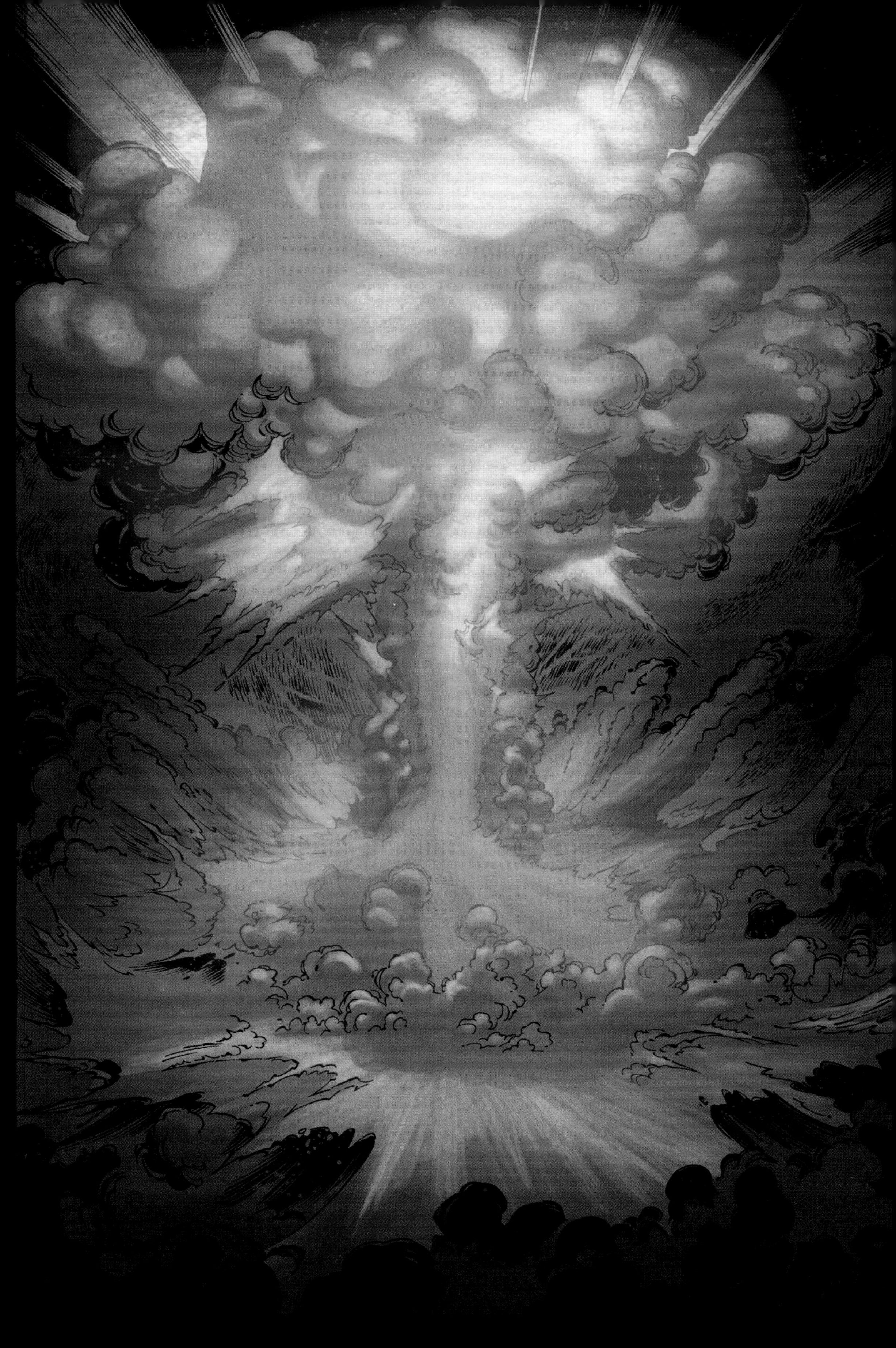

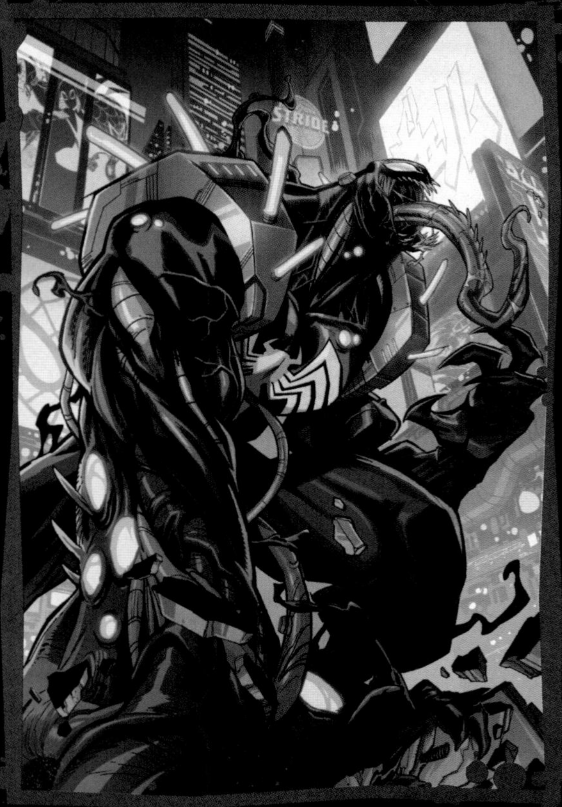
STRIDE

#21 2020 VARIANT
BY **KHARY RANDOLPH** & **EMILIO LOPEZ**

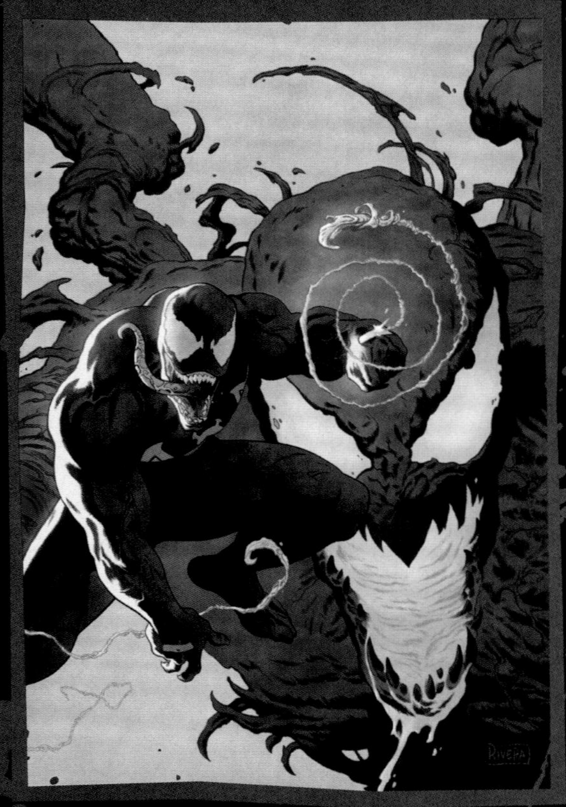
RIVERA

#21 VARIANT
BY **PAOLO RIVERA**

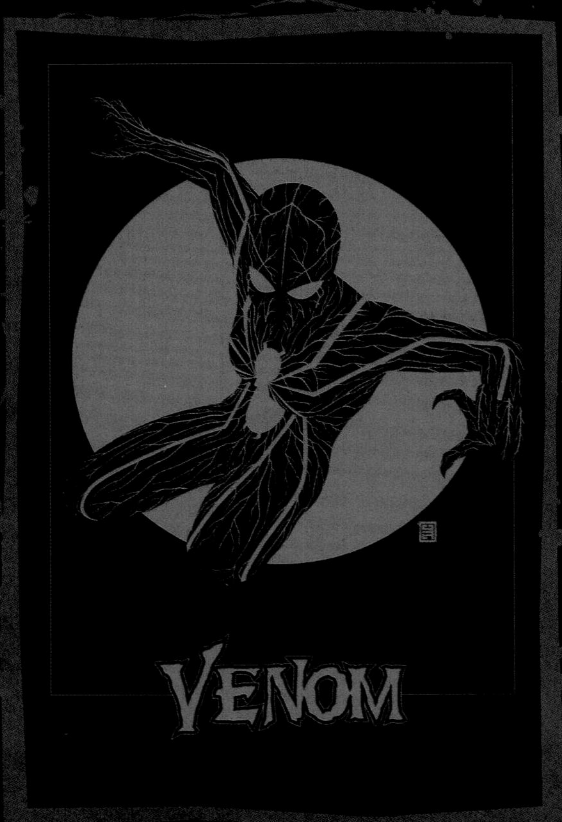
VENOM

#22 *MARVELS X* VARIANT
BY **JOHN TYLER CHRISTOPHER**

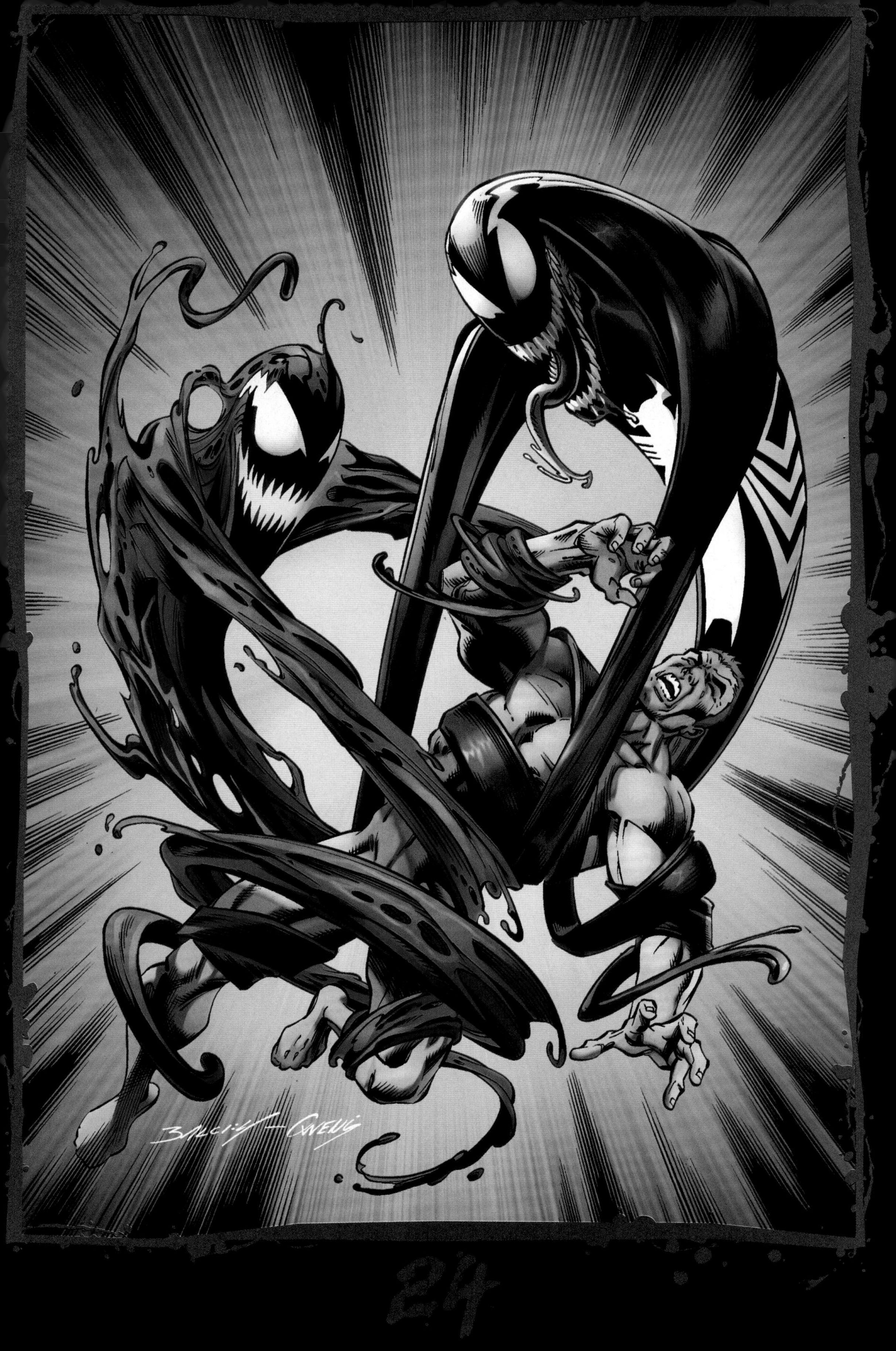
24

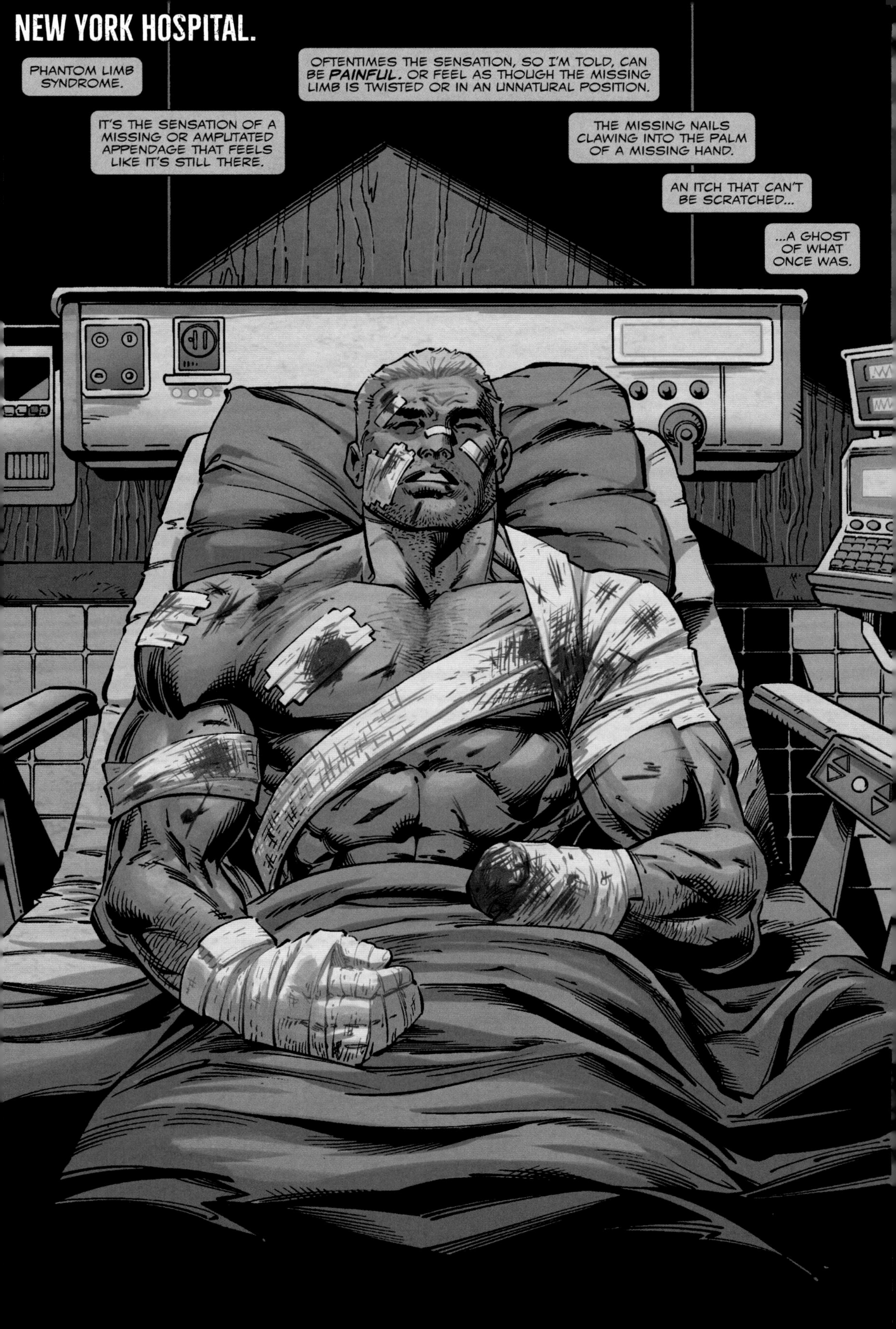
NEW YORK HOSPITAL.
PHANTOM LIMB SYNDROME.
IT'S THE SENSATION OF A MISSING OR AMPUTATED APPENDAGE THAT FEELS LIKE IT'S STILL THERE.
OFTENTIMES THE SENSATION, SO I'M TOLD, CAN BE PAINFUL. OR FEEL AS THOUGH THE MISSING LIMB IS TWISTED OR IN AN UNNATURAL POSITION.
THE MISSING NAILS CLAWING INTO THE PALM OF A MISSING HAND.
AN ITCH THAT CAN'T BE SCRATCHED...
...A GHOST OF WHAT ONCE WAS.

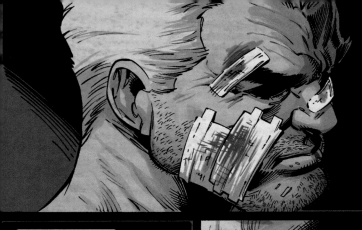

I'VE BEEN IN THIS BED FOR *THREE WEEKS* NOW.

THREE WEEKS SINCE I WAS AIRLIFTED OFF OF A DESERTED ISLAND.

THREE WEEKS SINCE...

...SINCE...

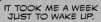

IT TOOK ME A WEEK JUST TO WAKE UP.

AND WHEN I DID, THE DOCTOR ASKED ME IF I WAS HAVING ANY SIGNS OF PHANTOM LIMB...

ANY FEELINGS, ANY SENSATIONS THAT BELONGED TO SOMETHING THAT WASN'T THERE ANYMORE.

I TOLD HIM I DID.

TOLD HIM ABOUT THE *SCREAMING PAIN* I FELT IN THE PART OF ME THAT WAS GONE...

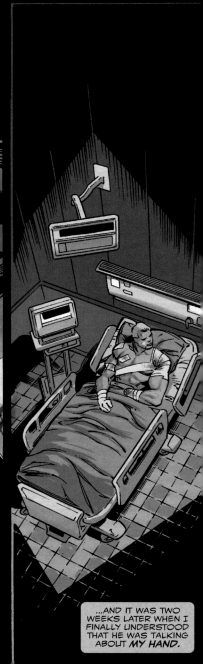

...AND IT WAS TWO WEEKS LATER WHEN I FINALLY UNDERSTOOD THAT HE WAS TALKING ABOUT *MY HAND.*

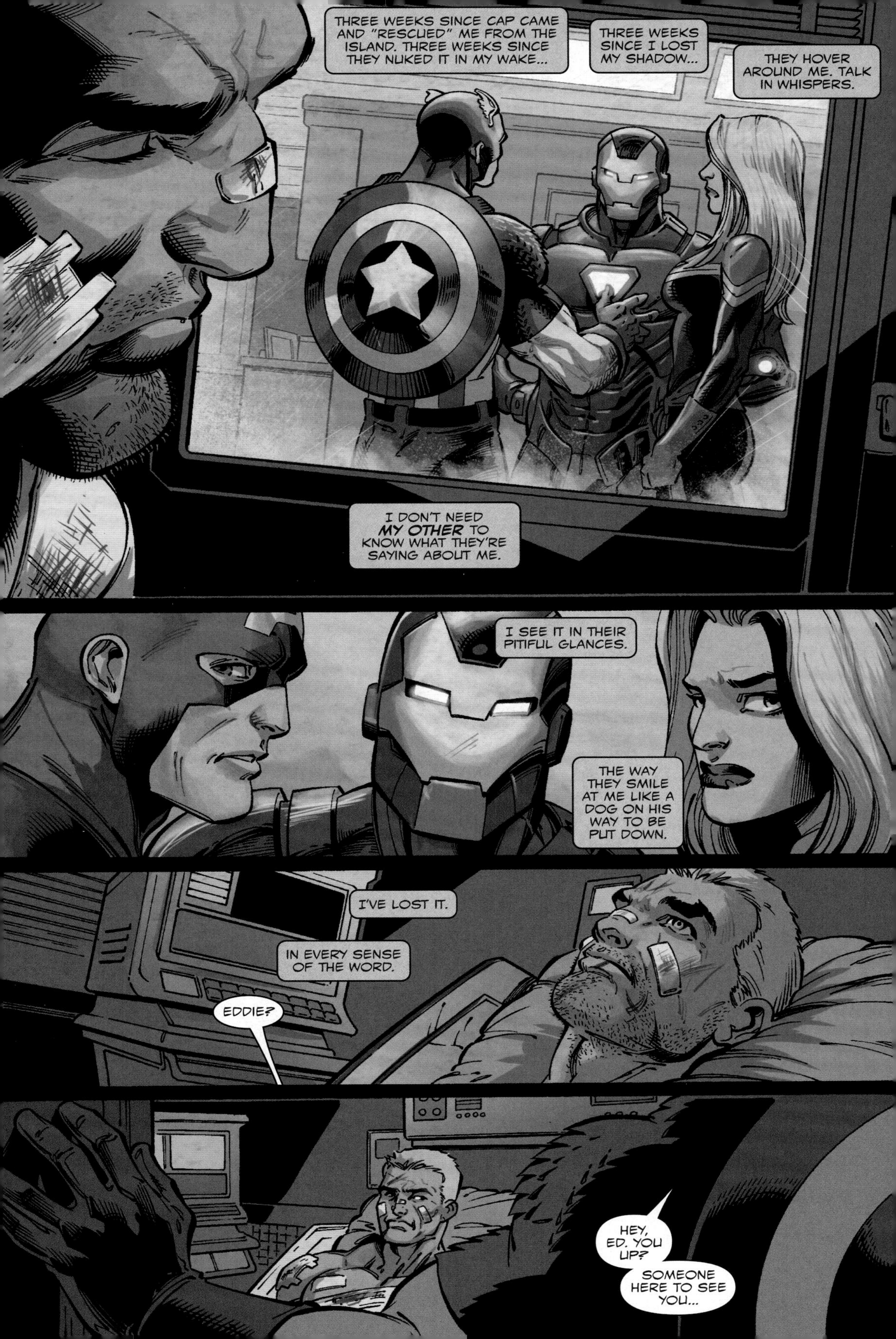
THREE WEEKS SINCE CAP CAME AND "RESCUED" ME FROM THE ISLAND. THREE WEEKS SINCE THEY NUKED IT IN MY WAKE...
THREE WEEKS SINCE I LOST MY SHADOW...
THEY HOVER AROUND ME. TALK IN WHISPERS.
I DON'T NEED MY OTHER TO KNOW WHAT THEY'RE SAYING ABOUT ME.
I SEE IT IN THEIR PITIFUL GLANCES.
THE WAY THEY SMILE AT ME LIKE A DOG ON HIS WAY TO BE PUT DOWN.
I'VE LOST IT.
IN EVERY SENSE OF THE WORD.
EDDIE?
HEY, ED. YOU UP?
SOMEONE HERE TO SEE YOU...

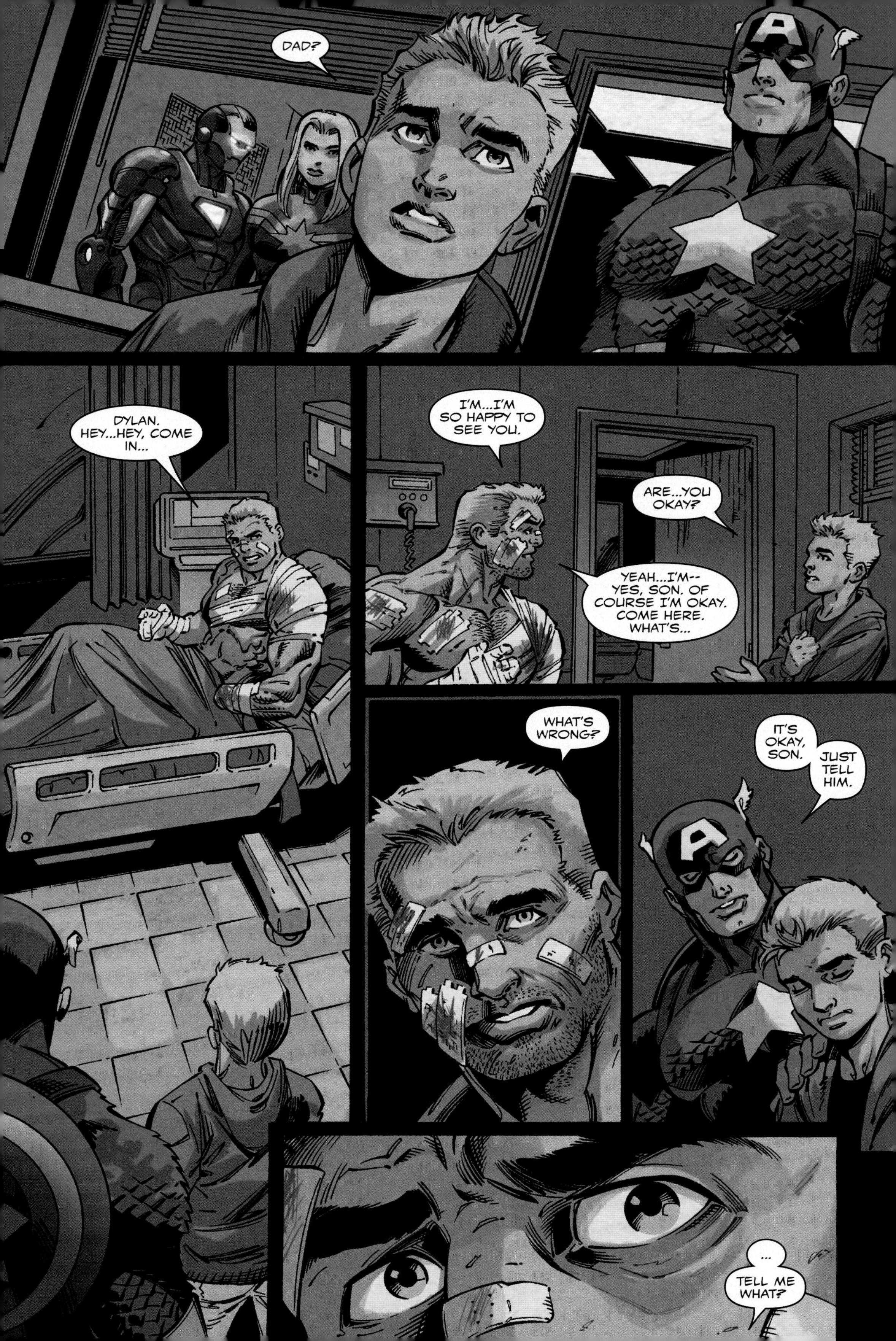
DAD?
DYLAN. HEY...HEY, COME IN...
I'M...I'M SO HAPPY TO SEE YOU.
ARE...YOU OKAY?
YEAH...I'M-- YES, SON. OF COURSE I'M OKAY. COME HERE. WHAT'S...
WHAT'S WRONG?
IT'S OKAY, SON.
JUST TELL HIM.
...
TELL ME WHAT?

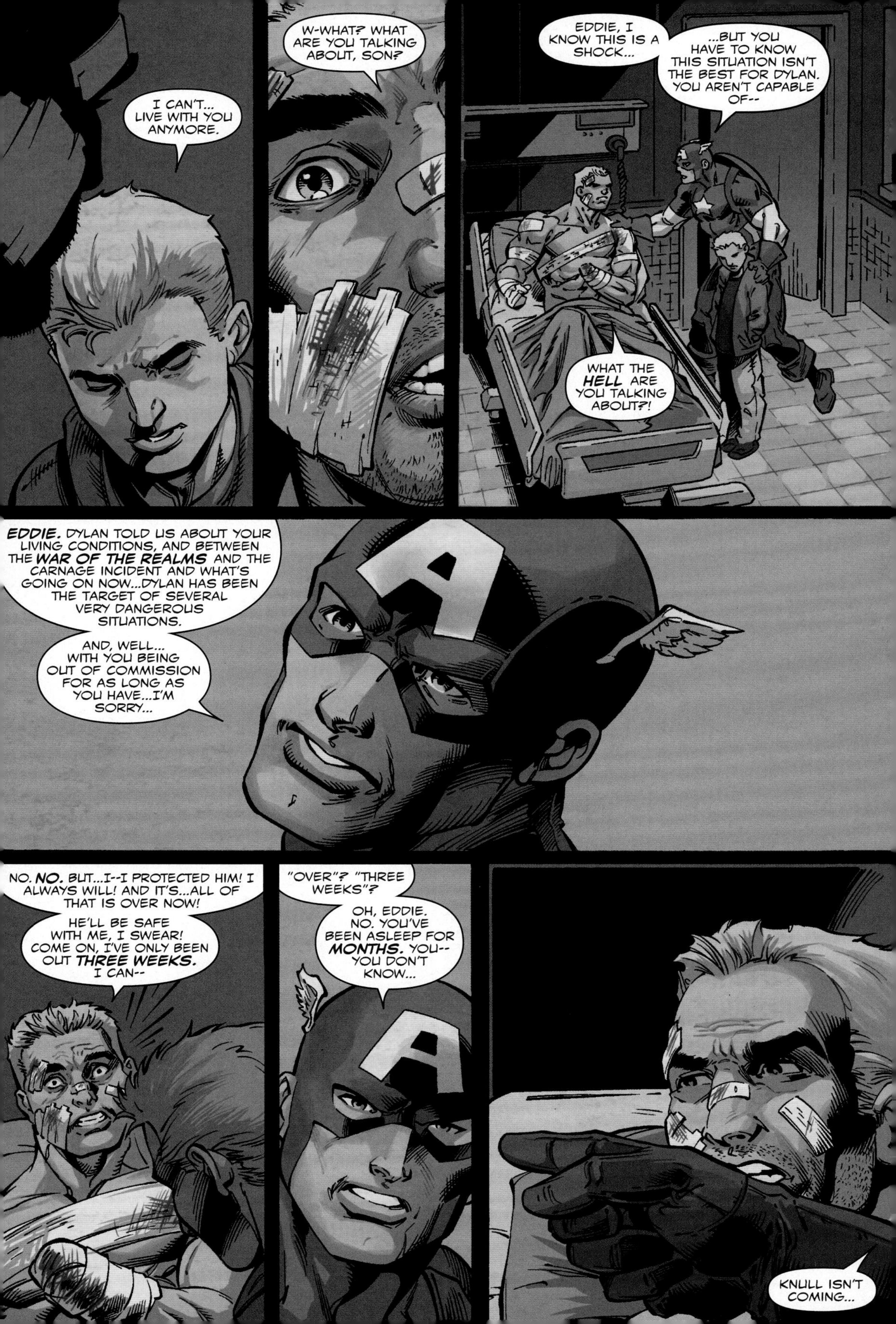
I CAN'T... LIVE WITH YOU ANYMORE.
W-WHAT? WHAT ARE YOU TALKING ABOUT, SON?
EDDIE, I KNOW THIS IS A SHOCK...
...BUT YOU HAVE TO KNOW THIS SITUATION ISN'T THE BEST FOR DYLAN. YOU AREN'T CAPABLE OF--
WHAT THE HELL ARE YOU TALKING ABOUT?!
EDDIE. DYLAN TOLD US ABOUT YOUR LIVING CONDITIONS, AND BETWEEN THE WAR OF THE REALMS AND THE CARNAGE INCIDENT AND WHAT'S GOING ON NOW...DYLAN HAS BEEN THE TARGET OF SEVERAL VERY DANGEROUS SITUATIONS.
AND, WELL... WITH YOU BEING OUT OF COMMISSION FOR AS LONG AS YOU HAVE...I'M SORRY...
NO. NO. BUT...I--I PROTECTED HIM! I ALWAYS WILL! AND IT'S...ALL OF THAT IS OVER NOW!
HE'LL BE SAFE WITH ME, I SWEAR! COME ON, I'VE ONLY BEEN OUT THREE WEEKS. I CAN--
"OVER"? "THREE WEEKS"?
OH, EDDIE. NO. YOU'VE BEEN ASLEEP FOR MONTHS. YOU-- YOU DON'T KNOW...
KNULL ISN'T COMING...

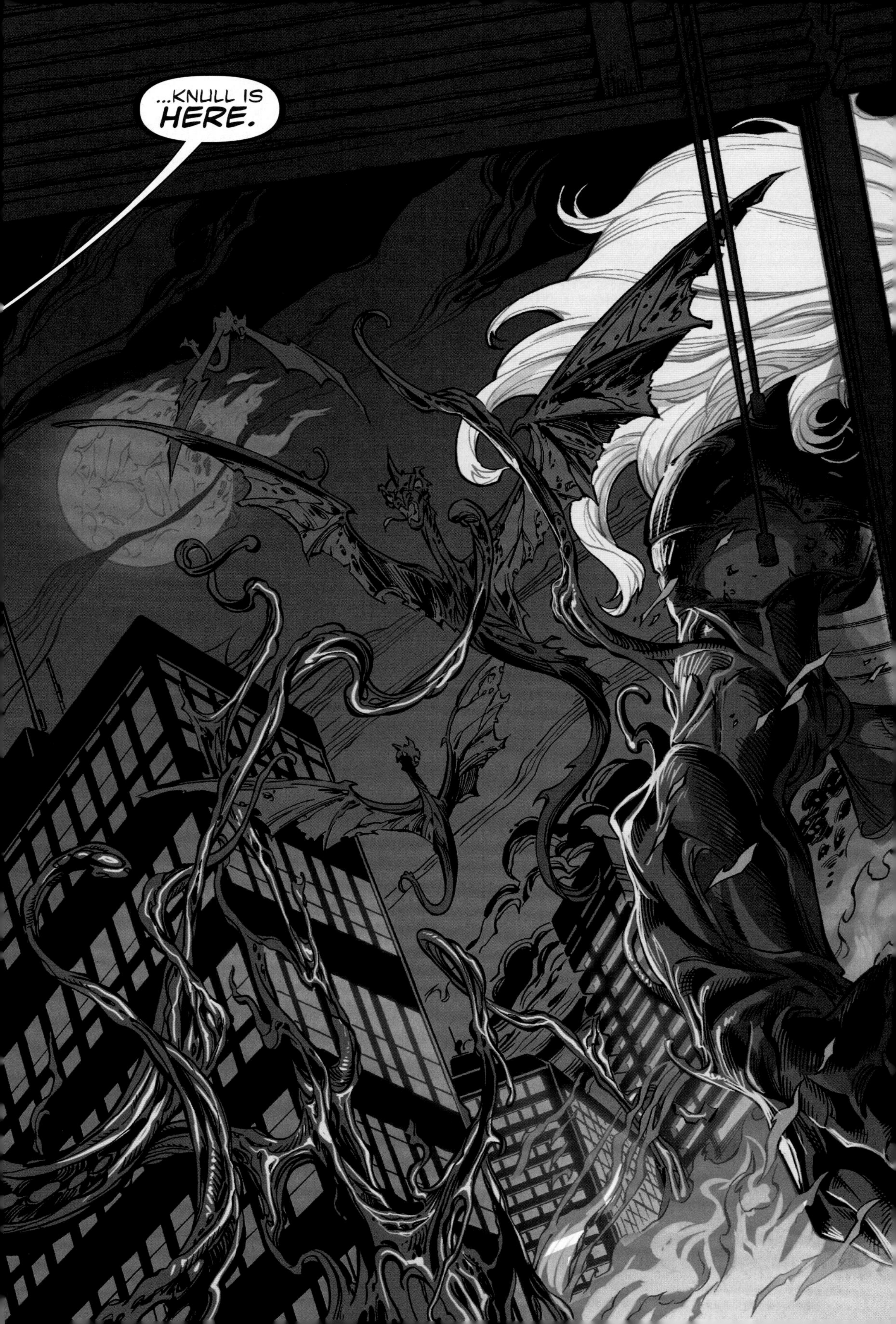
...KNULL IS HERE.

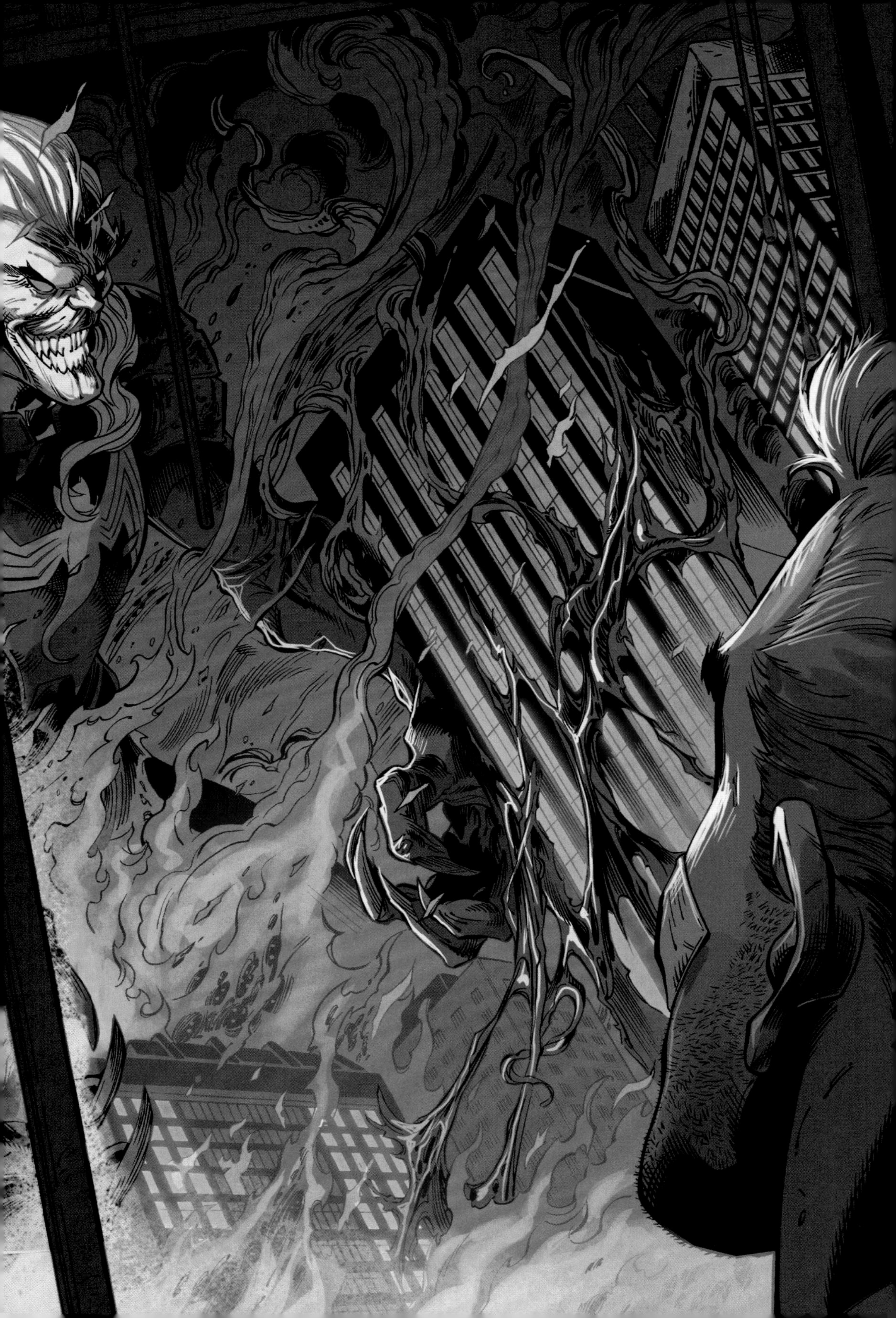

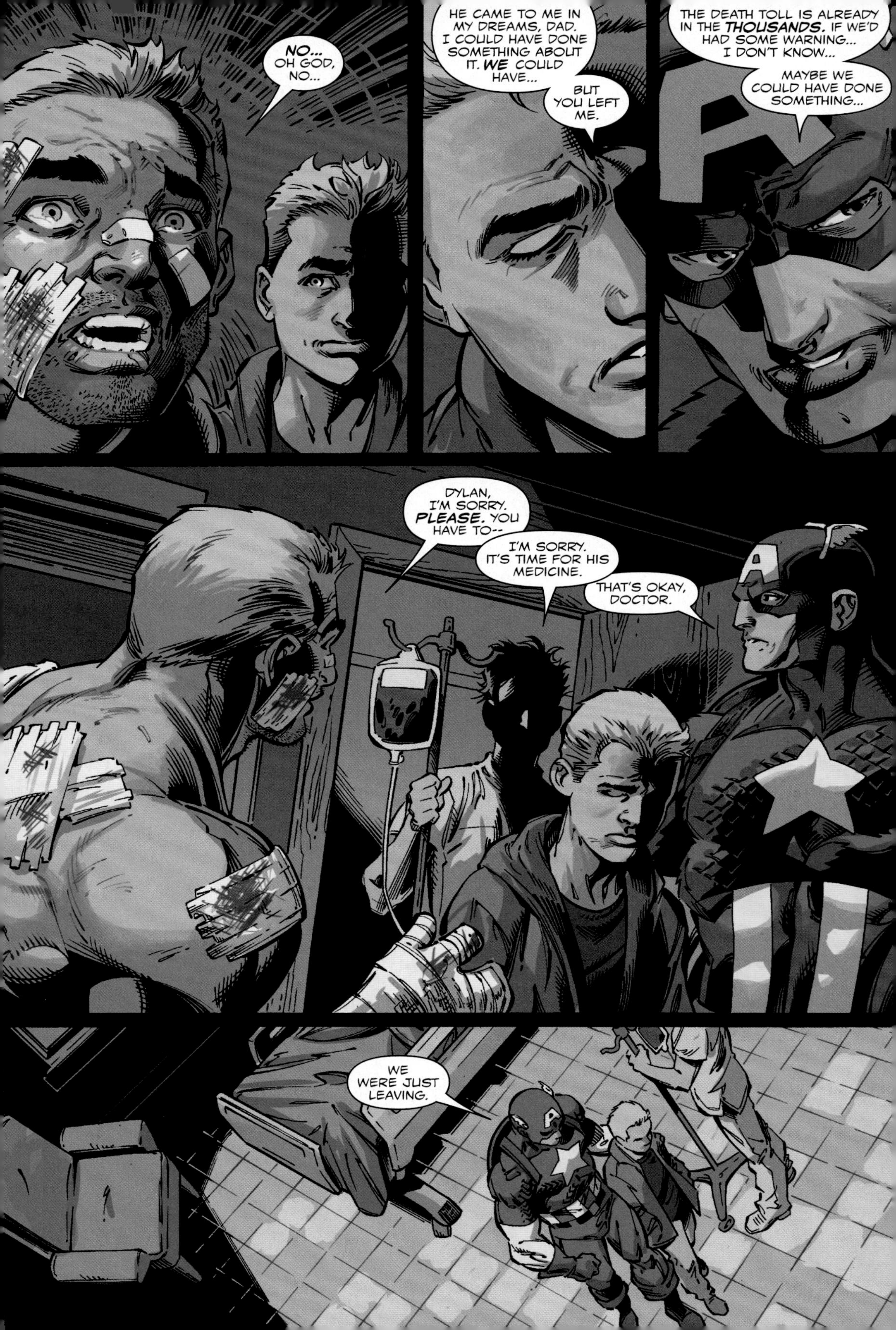
NO... OH GOD, NO...
HE CAME TO ME IN MY DREAMS, DAD. I COULD HAVE DONE SOMETHING ABOUT IT. WE COULD HAVE...
BUT YOU LEFT ME.
THE DEATH TOLL IS ALREADY IN THE THOUSANDS. IF WE'D HAD SOME WARNING... I DON'T KNOW...
MAYBE WE COULD HAVE DONE SOMETHING...
DYLAN, I'M SORRY. PLEASE. YOU HAVE TO--
I'M SORRY. IT'S TIME FOR HIS MEDICINE.
THAT'S OKAY, DOCTOR.
WE WERE JUST LEAVING.

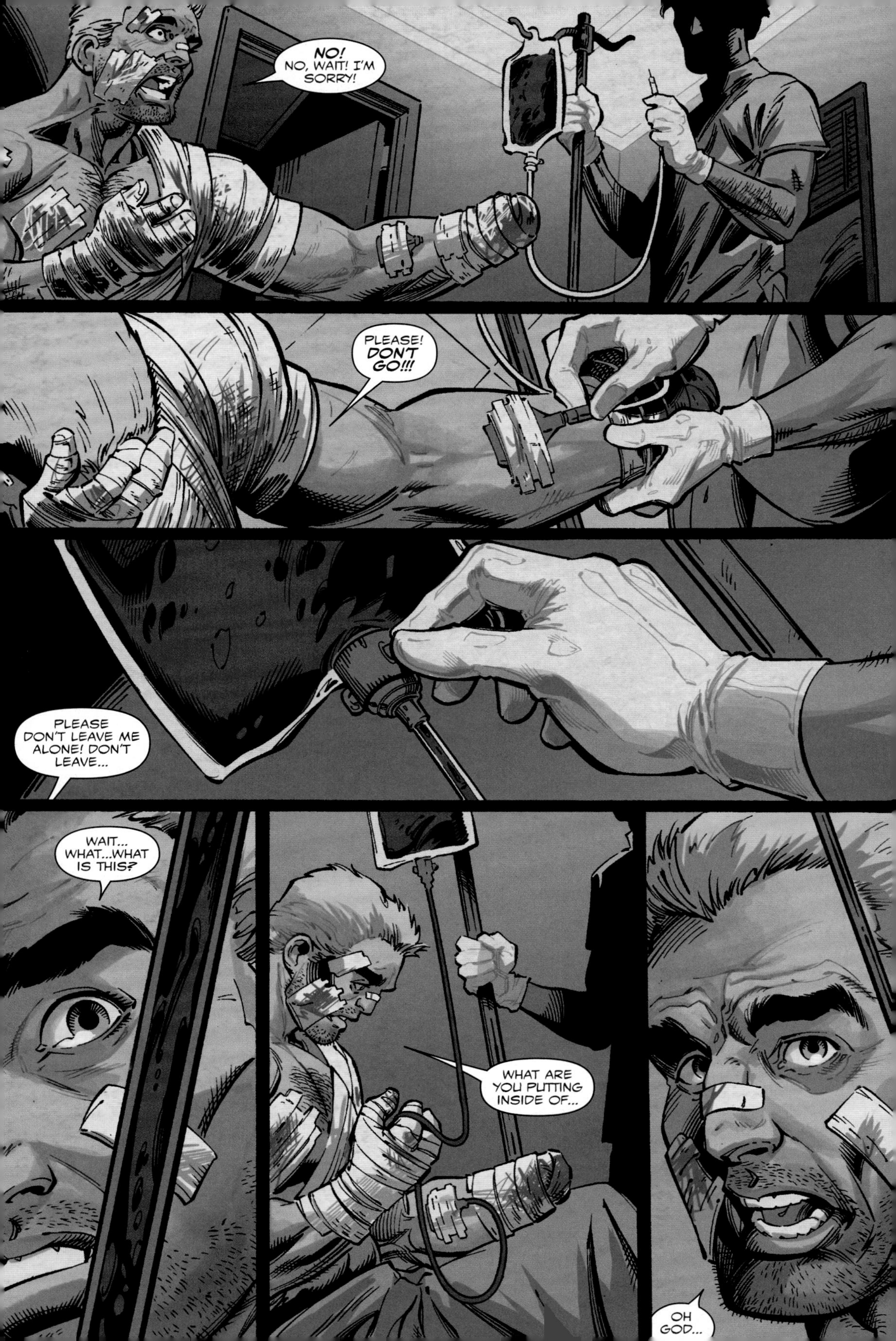

NO! NO, WAIT! I'M SORRY!
PLEASE! DON'T GO!!!
PLEASE DON'T LEAVE ME ALONE! DON'T LEAVE...
WAIT... WHAT...WHAT IS THIS?
WHAT ARE YOU PUTTING INSIDE OF...
OH GOD...

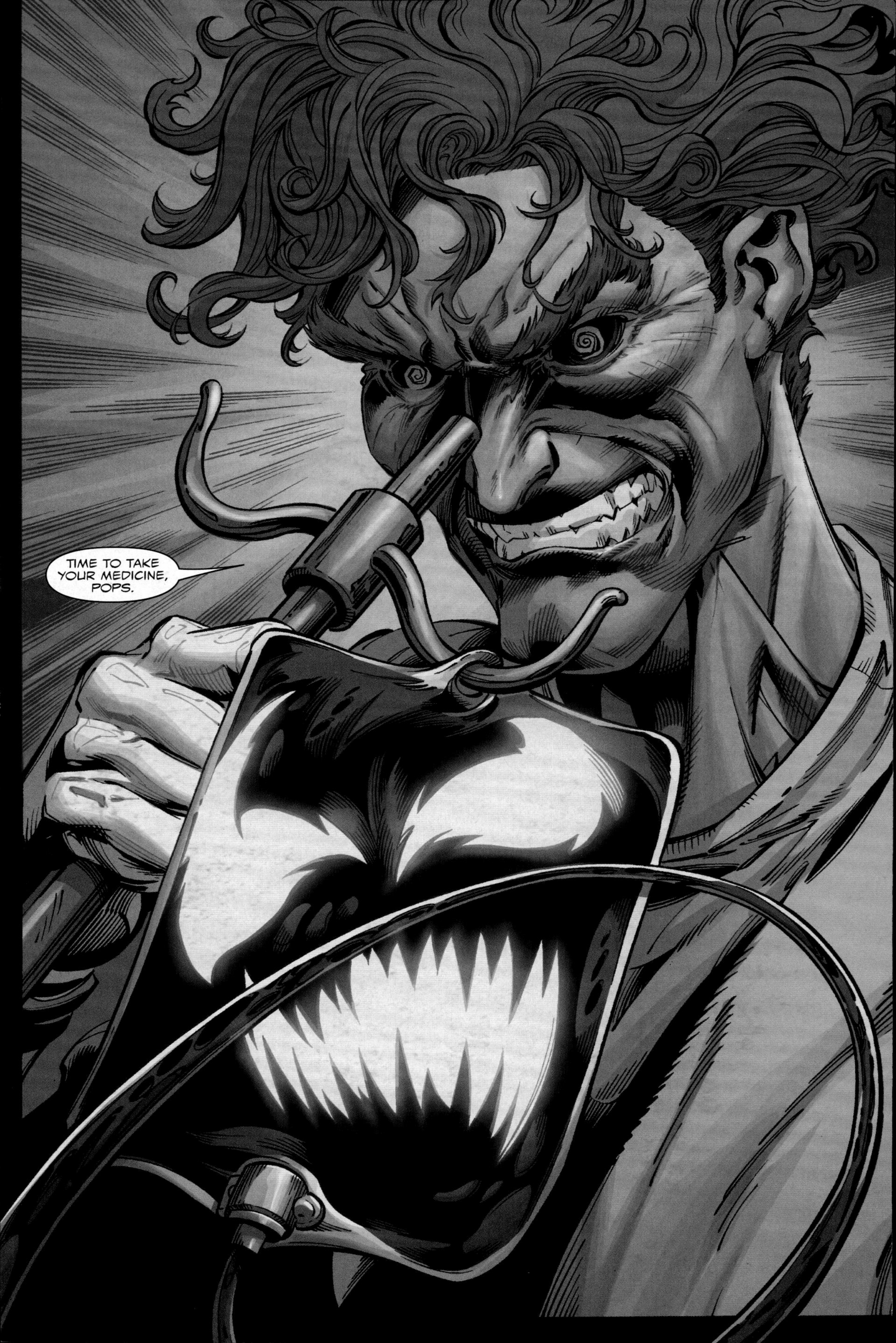
TIME TO TAKE YOUR MEDICINE, POPS.

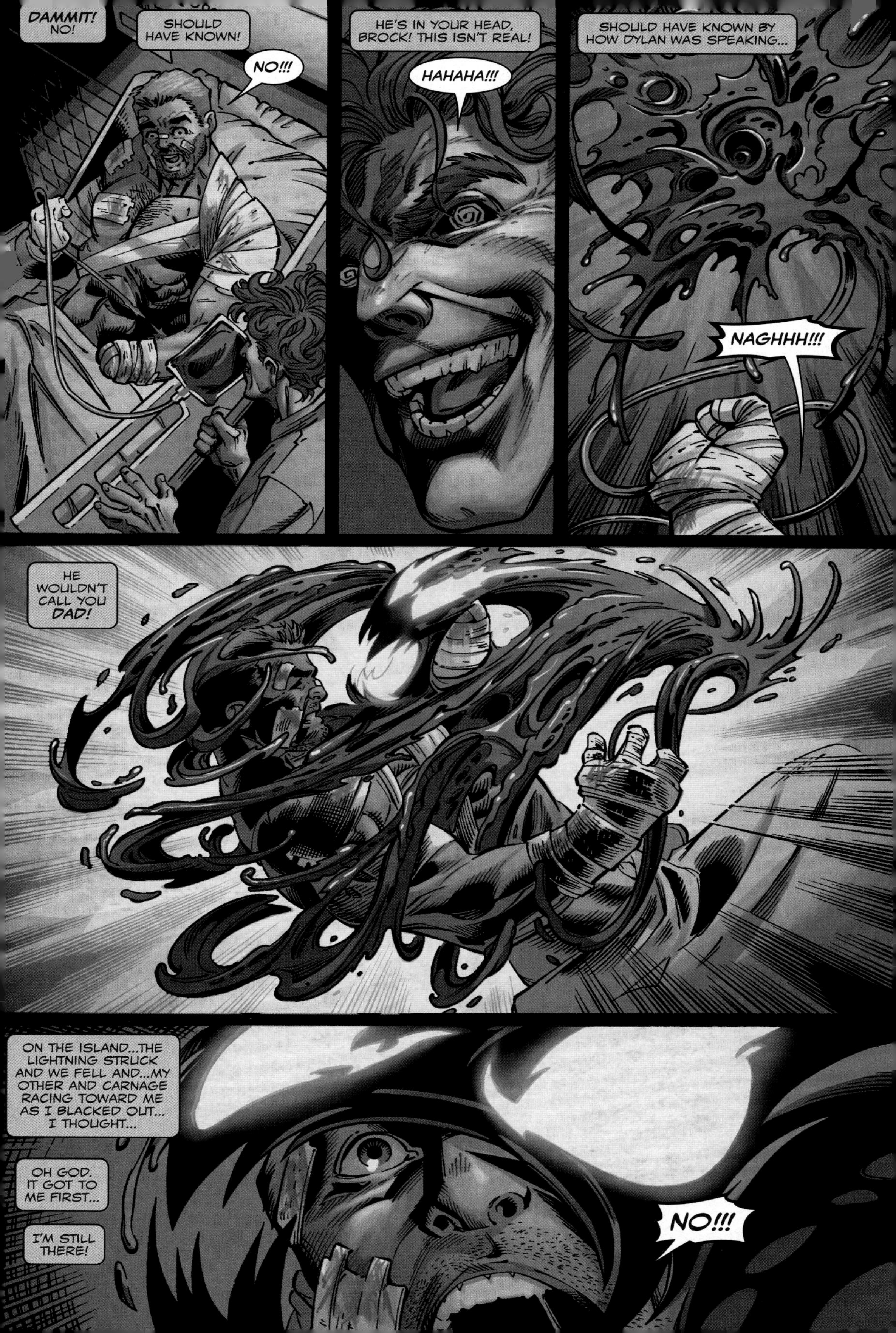
DAMMIT! NO!
SHOULD HAVE KNOWN!
NO!!!
HE'S IN YOUR HEAD, BROCK! THIS ISN'T REAL!
HAHAHA!!!
SHOULD HAVE KNOWN BY HOW DYLAN WAS SPEAKING...
NAGHHH!!!
HE WOULDN'T CALL YOU DAD!
ON THE ISLAND...THE LIGHTNING STRUCK AND WE FELL AND...MY OTHER AND CARNAGE RACING TOWARD ME AS I BLACKED OUT... I THOUGHT...
OH GOD. IT GOT TO ME FIRST...
I'M STILL THERE!
NO!!!

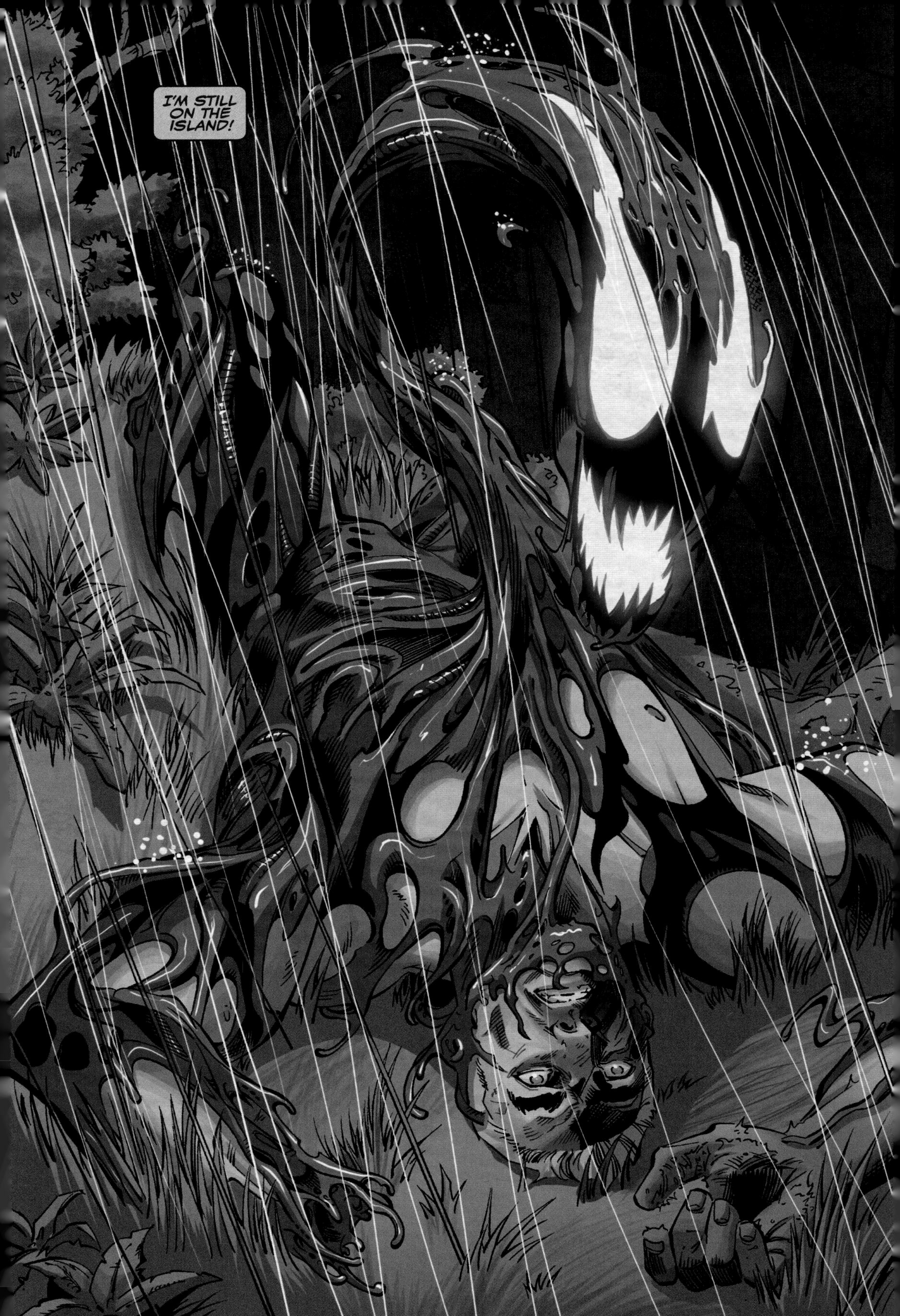
I'M STILL ON THE ISLAND!

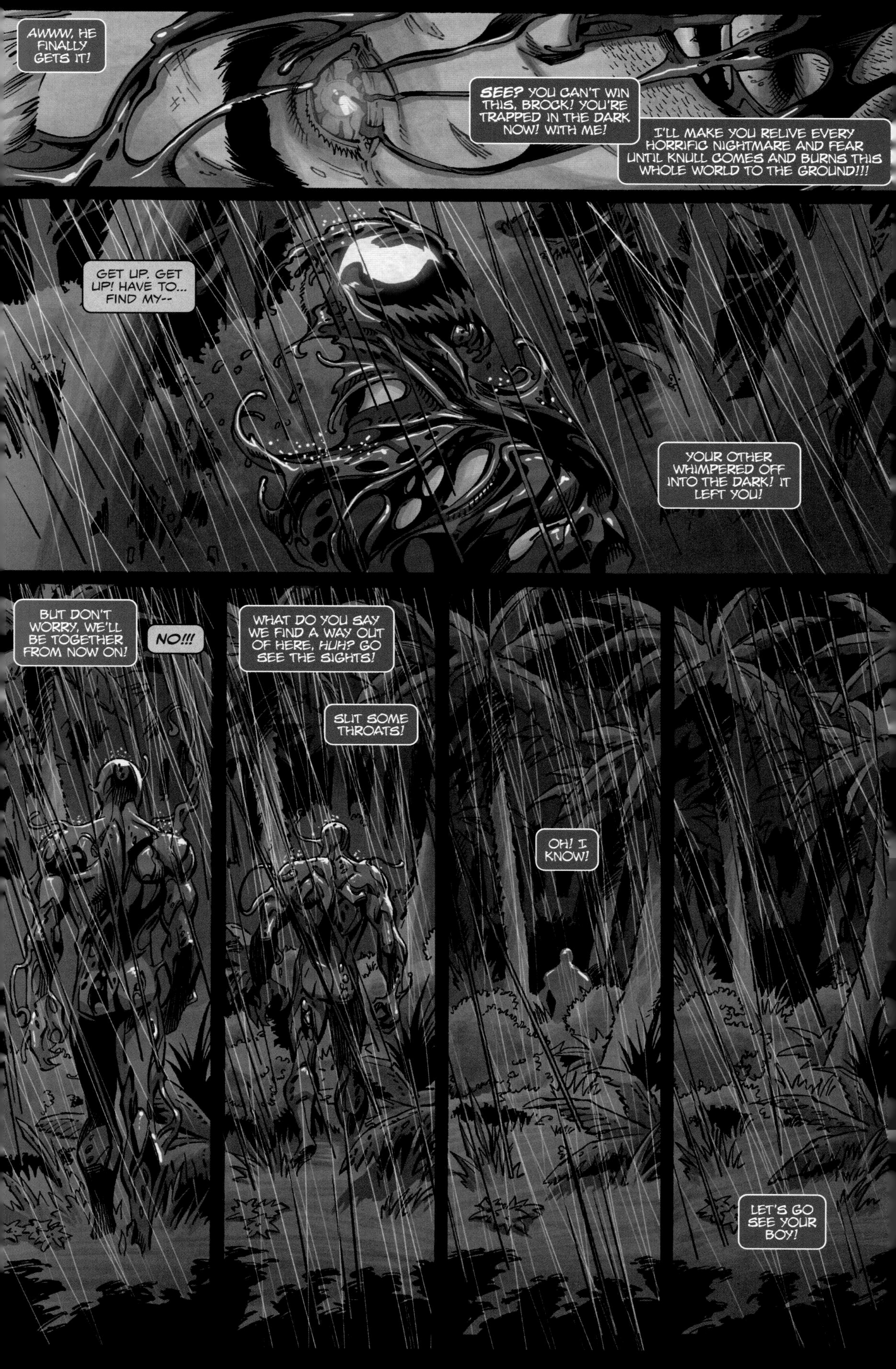
AWWW, HE FINALLY GETS IT!
SEE? YOU CAN'T WIN THIS, BROCK! YOU'RE TRAPPED IN THE DARK NOW! WITH ME!
I'LL MAKE YOU RELIVE EVERY HORRIFIC NIGHTMARE AND FEAR UNTIL KNULL COMES AND BURNS THIS WHOLE WORLD TO THE GROUND!!!
GET UP. GET UP! HAVE TO... FIND MY--
YOUR OTHER WHIMPERED OFF INTO THE DARK! IT LEFT YOU!
BUT DON'T WORRY, WE'LL BE TOGETHER FROM NOW ON!
NO!!!
WHAT DO YOU SAY WE FIND A WAY OUT OF HERE, HUH? GO SEE THE SIGHTS!
SLIT SOME THROATS!
OH! I KNOW!
LET'S GO SEE YOUR BOY!

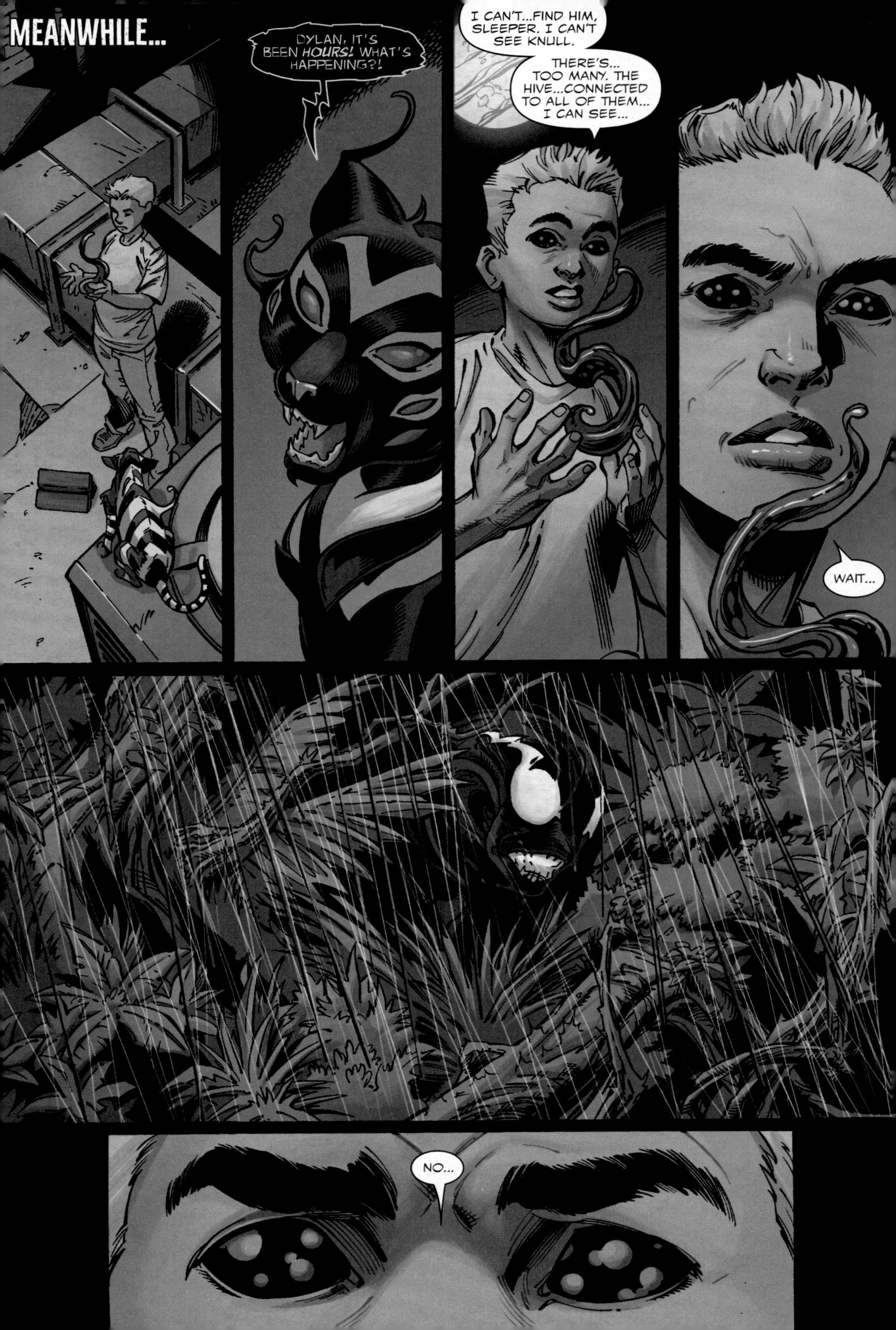
MEANWHILE...
DYLAN, IT'S BEEN HOURS! WHAT'S HAPPENING?!
I CAN'T...FIND HIM, SLEEPER. I CAN'T SEE KNULL.
THERE'S... TOO MANY. THE HIVE...CONNECTED TO ALL OF THEM... I CAN SEE...
WAIT...
NO...

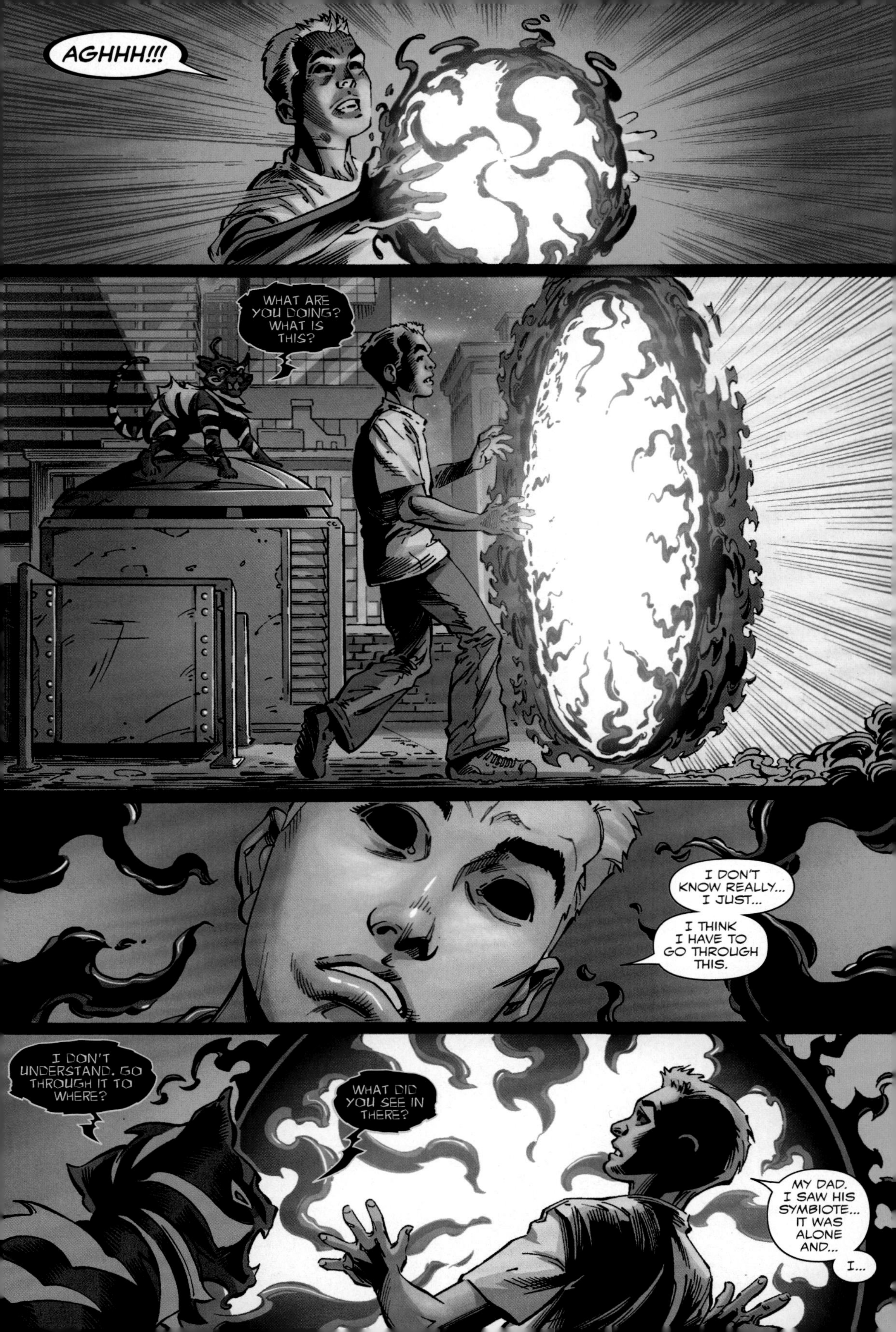
AGHHH!!!
WHAT ARE YOU DOING? WHAT IS THIS?
I DON'T KNOW REALLY... I JUST...
I THINK I HAVE TO GO THROUGH THIS.
I DON'T UNDERSTAND. GO THROUGH IT TO WHERE?
WHAT DID YOU SEE IN THERE?
MY DAD. I SAW HIS SYMBIOTE... IT WAS ALONE AND...
I...

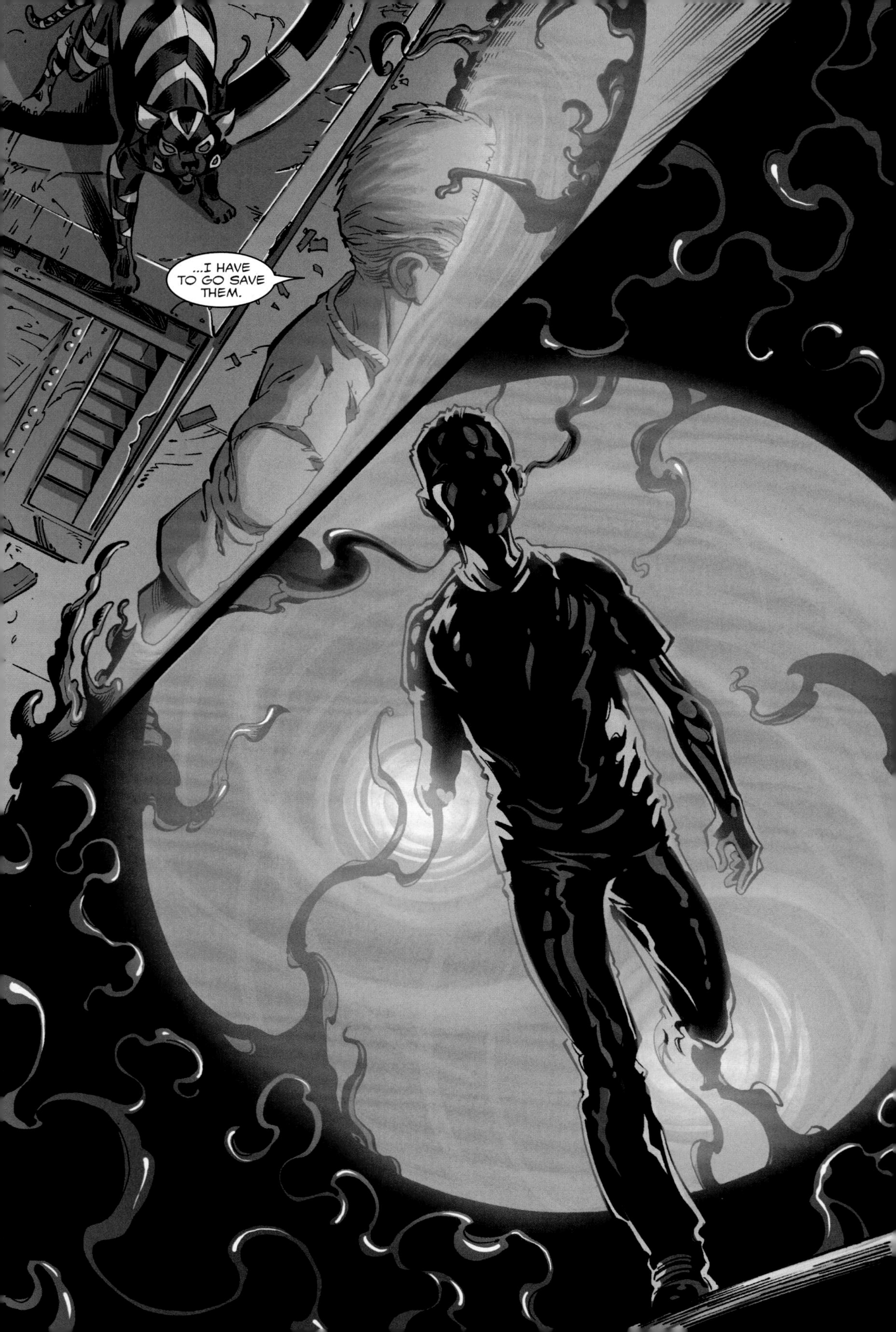
...I HAVE TO GO SAVE THEM.

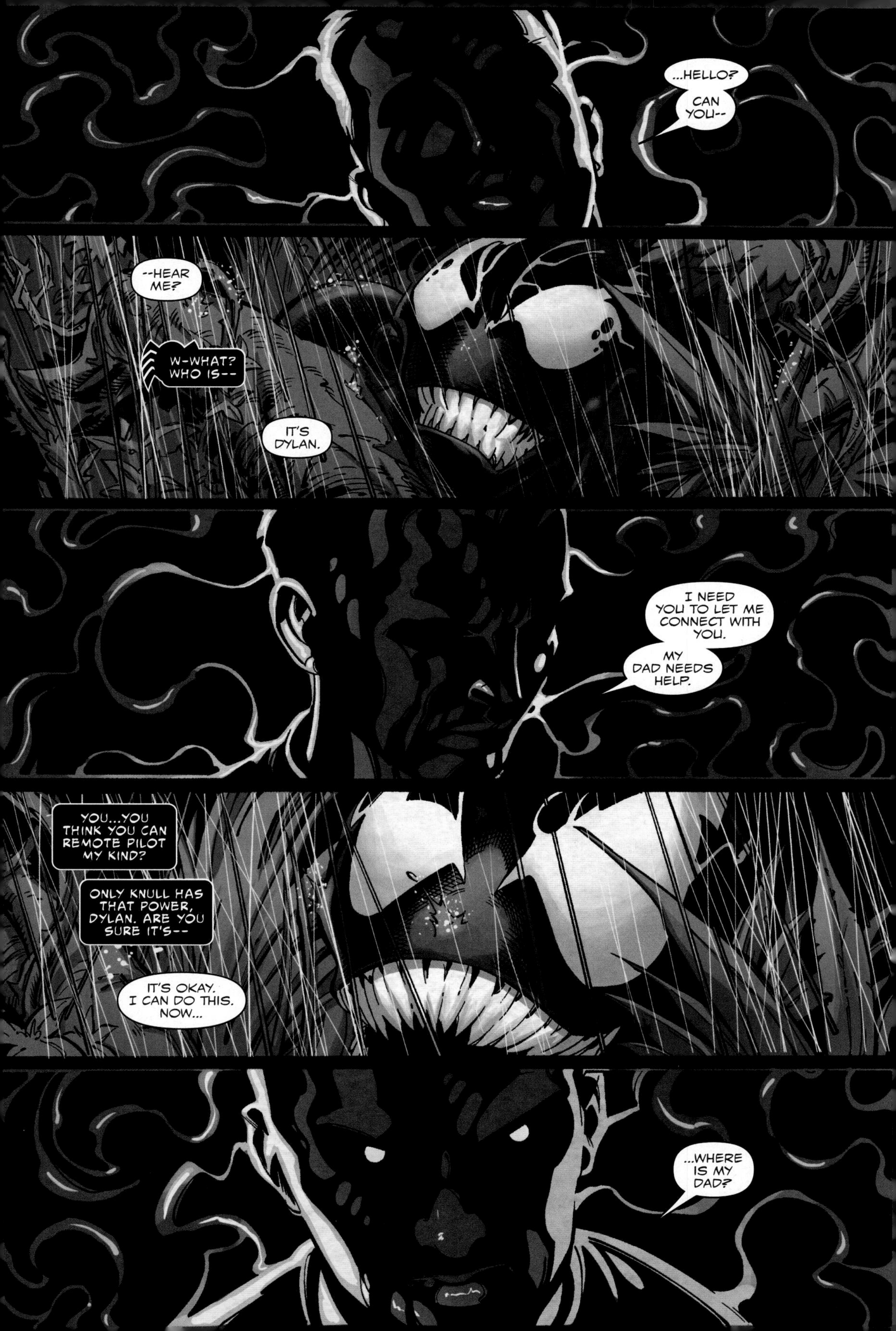

...HELLO?
CAN YOU--
--HEAR ME?
W-WHAT? WHO IS--
IT'S DYLAN.
I NEED YOU TO LET ME CONNECT WITH YOU.
MY DAD NEEDS HELP.
YOU...YOU THINK YOU CAN REMOTE PILOT MY KIND?
ONLY KNULL HAS THAT POWER, DYLAN. ARE YOU SURE IT'S--
IT'S OKAY. I CAN DO THIS. NOW...
...WHERE IS MY DAD?

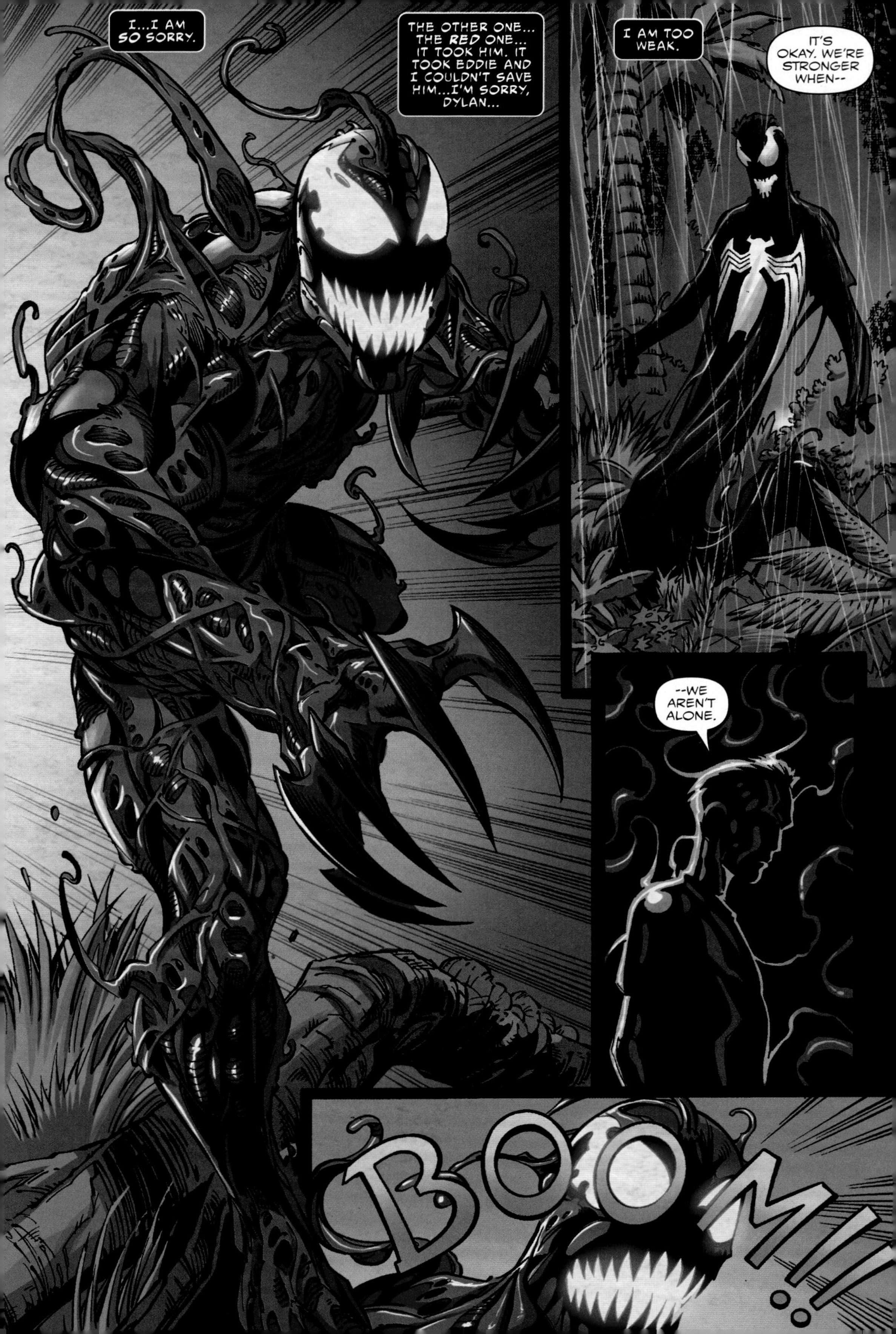
I...I AM SO SORRY.
THE OTHER ONE... THE RED ONE... IT TOOK HIM. IT TOOK EDDIE AND I COULDN'T SAVE HIM...I'M SORRY, DYLAN...
I AM TOO WEAK.
IT'S OKAY. WE'RE STRONGER WHEN--
--WE AREN'T ALONE.
BOOM!!

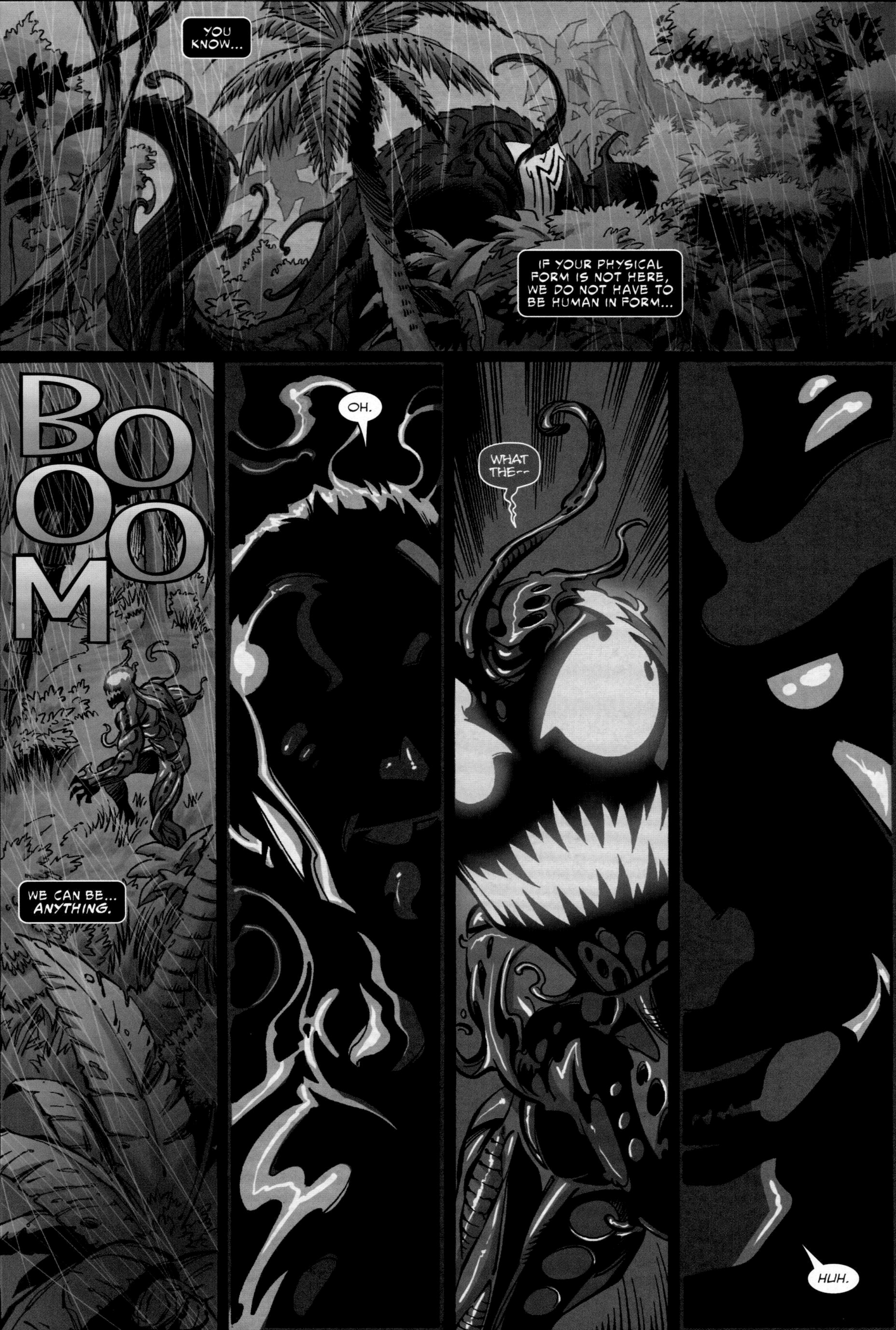
YOU KNOW...
IF YOUR PHYSICAL FORM IS NOT HERE, WE DO NOT HAVE TO BE HUMAN IN FORM...
BOOOOM
WE CAN BE... ANYTHING.
OH.
WHAT THE--
HUH.

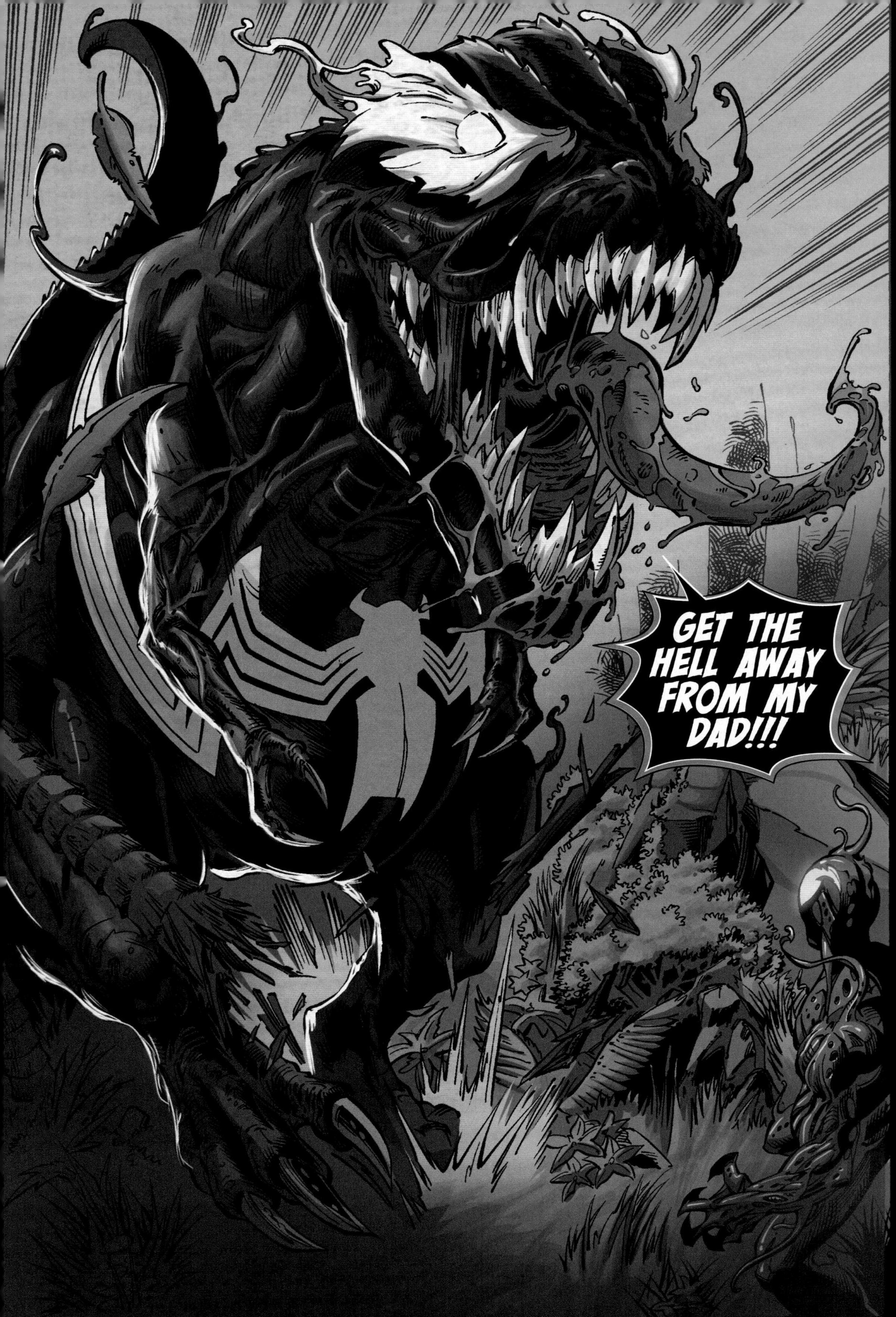
GET THE HELL AWAY FROM MY DAD!!!

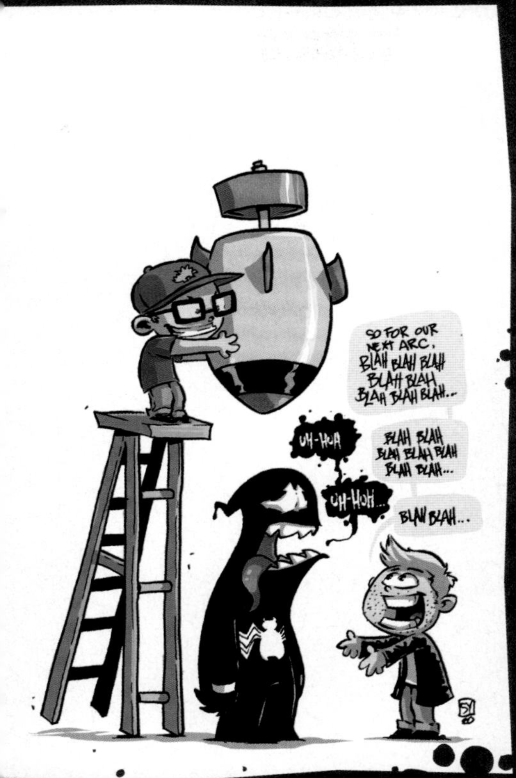
SO FOR OUR NEXT ARC, BLAH BLAH BLAH BLAH BLAH BLAH BLAH BLAH...
UH-HUH
BLAH BLAH BLAH BLAH BLAH BLAH BLAH...
UH-HUH...
BLAH BLAH...

#23 VARIANT
BY **SKOTTIE YOUNG**

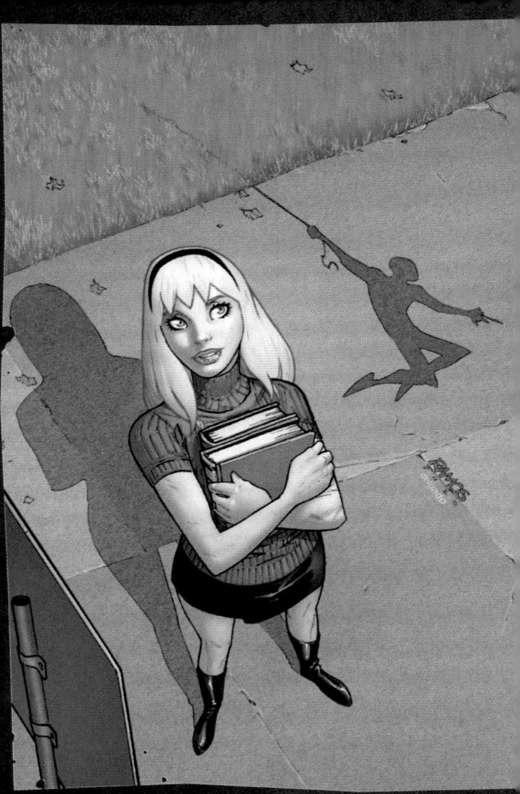

#23 GWEN STACY VARIANT
BY **HUMBERTO RAMOS** & **EDGAR DELGADO**

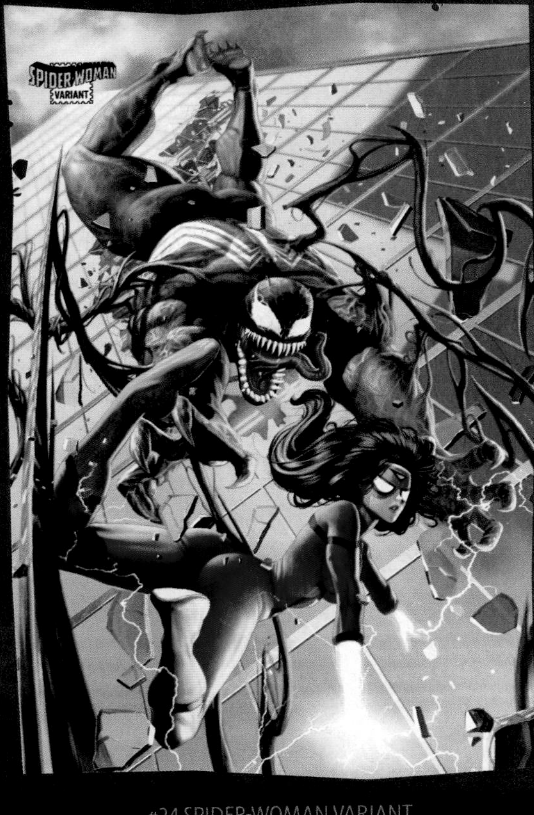
SPIDER-WOMAN
VARIANT

#24 SPIDER-WOMAN VARIANT
BY **ROCK-HE KIM**

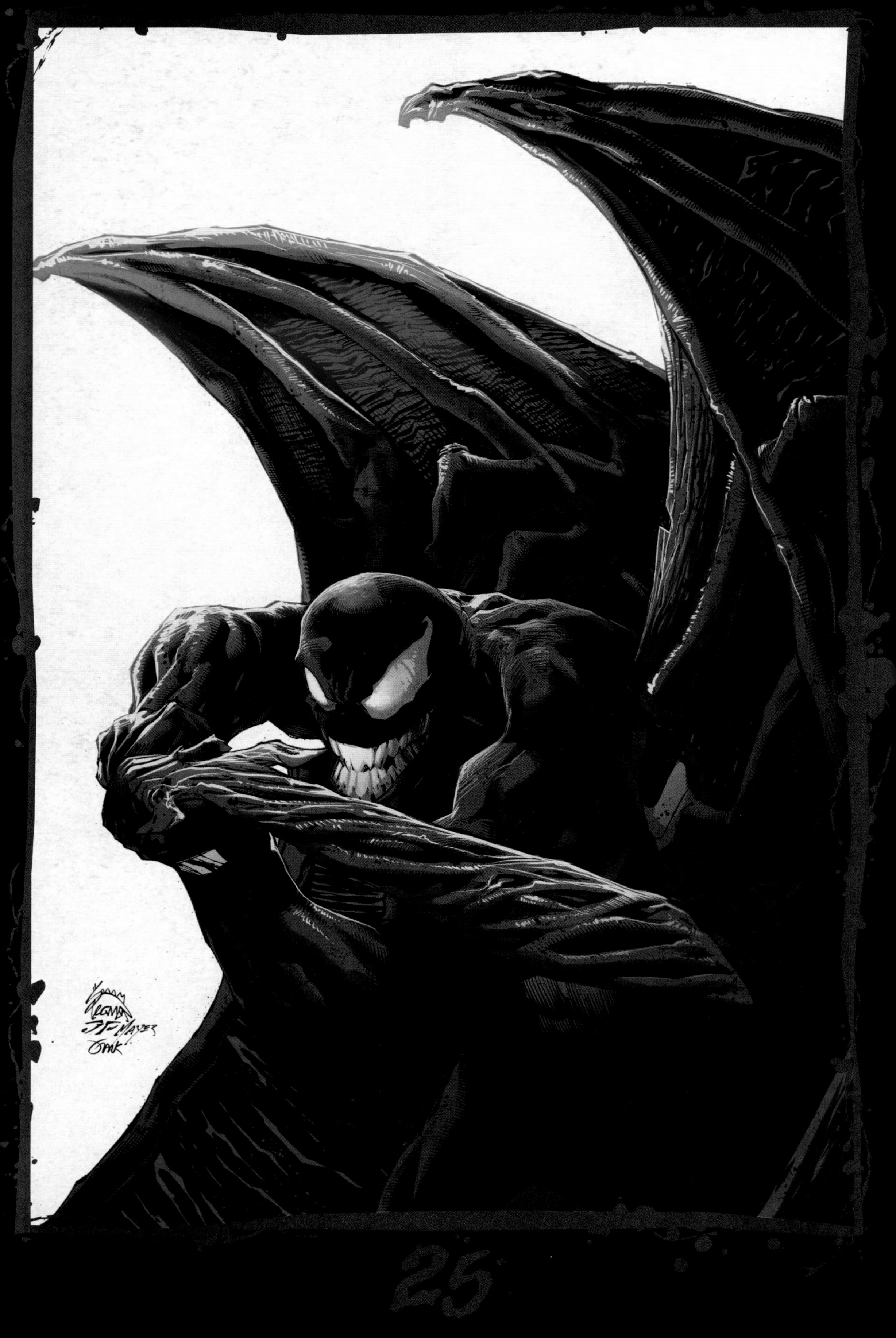
25

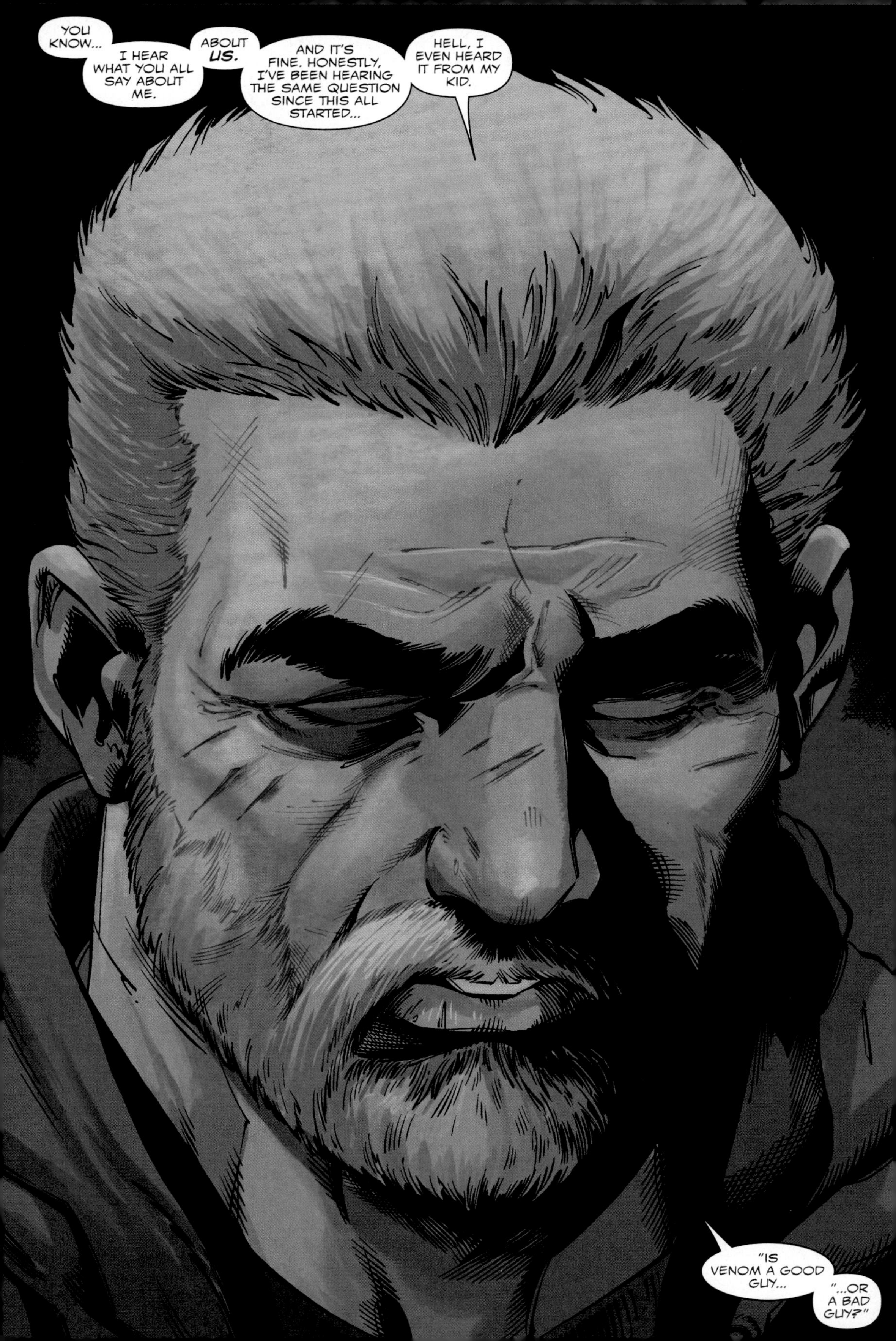
YOU KNOW...
I HEAR WHAT YOU ALL SAY ABOUT ME.
ABOUT US.
AND IT'S FINE. HONESTLY, I'VE BEEN HEARING THE SAME QUESTION SINCE THIS ALL STARTED...
HELL, I EVEN HEARD IT FROM MY KID.
"IS VENOM A GOOD GUY...
"...OR A BAD GUY?"

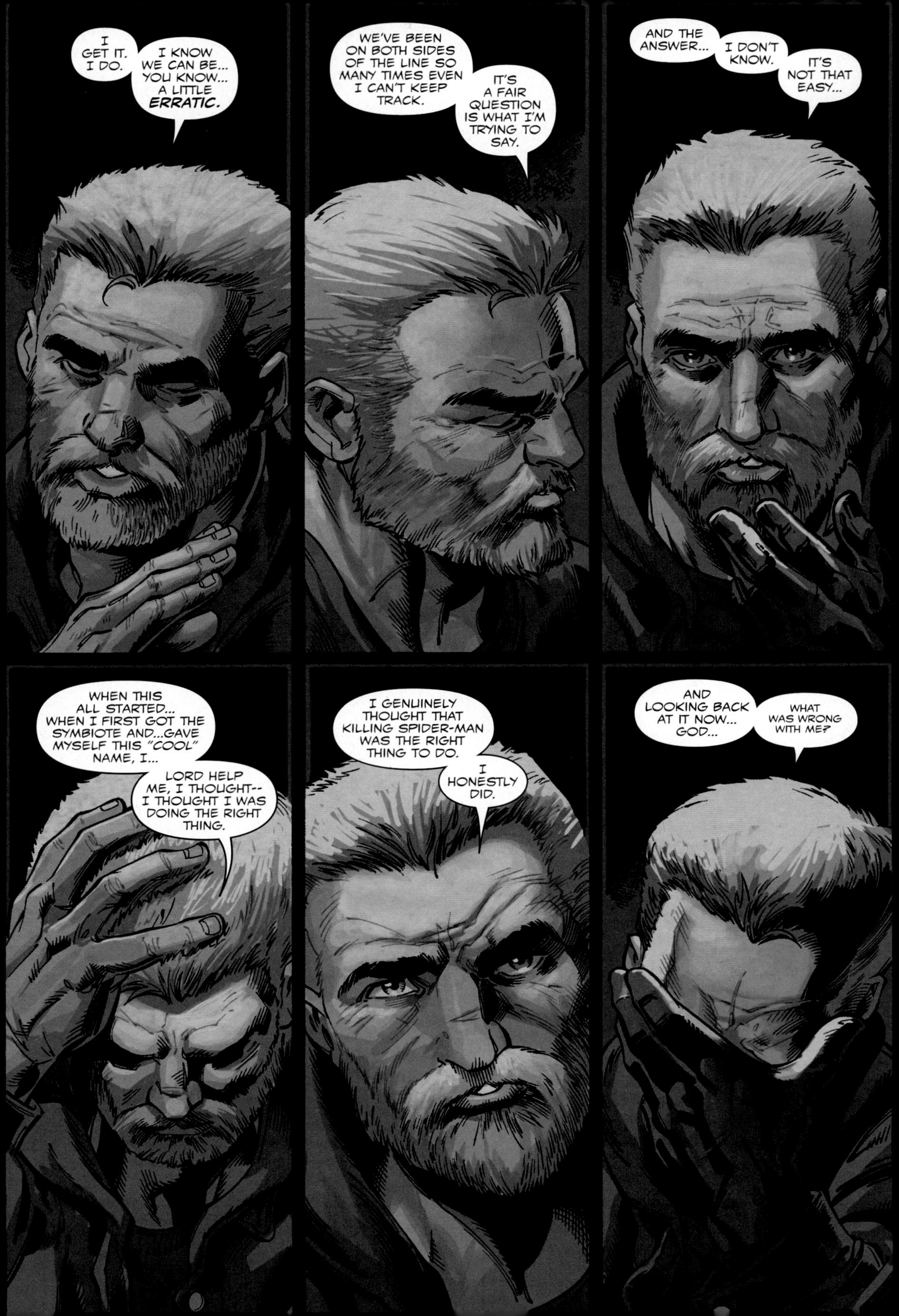
I GET IT. I DO.
I KNOW WE CAN BE... YOU KNOW... A LITTLE **ERRATIC.**
WE'VE BEEN ON BOTH SIDES OF THE LINE SO MANY TIMES EVEN I CAN'T KEEP TRACK.
IT'S A FAIR QUESTION IS WHAT I'M TRYING TO SAY.
AND THE ANSWER...
I DON'T KNOW.
IT'S NOT THAT EASY...
WHEN THIS ALL STARTED... WHEN I FIRST GOT THE SYMBIOTE AND...GAVE MYSELF THIS "COOL" NAME, I...
LORD HELP ME, I THOUGHT-- I THOUGHT I WAS DOING THE RIGHT THING.
I GENUINELY THOUGHT THAT KILLING SPIDER-MAN WAS THE RIGHT THING TO DO.
I HONESTLY DID.
AND LOOKING BACK AT IT NOW... GOD...
WHAT WAS WRONG WITH ME?

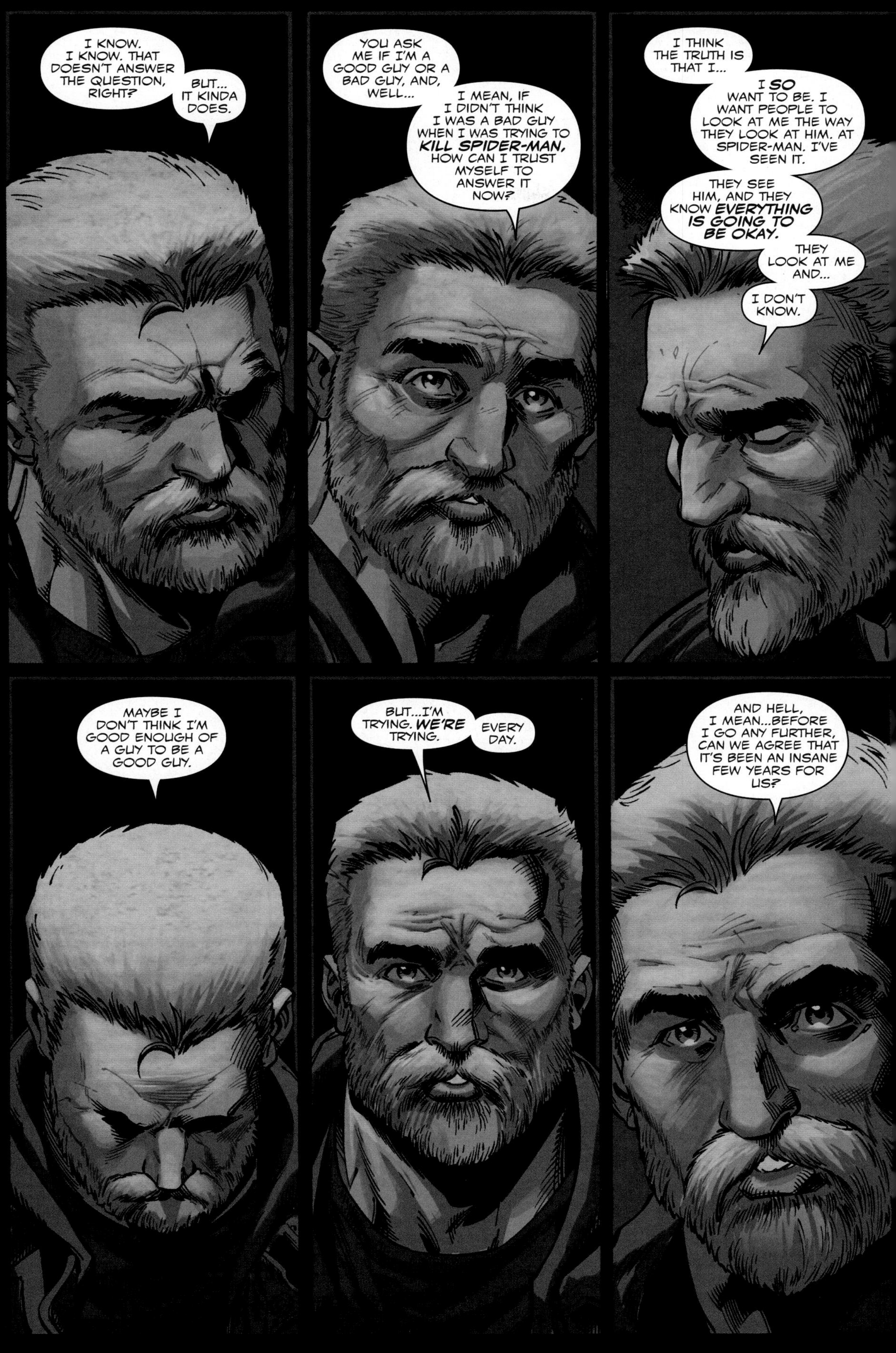
I KNOW. I KNOW. THAT DOESN'T ANSWER THE QUESTION, RIGHT?
BUT... IT KINDA DOES.
YOU ASK ME IF I'M A GOOD GUY OR A BAD GUY, AND, WELL...
I MEAN, IF I DIDN'T THINK I WAS A BAD GUY WHEN I WAS TRYING TO KILL SPIDER-MAN, HOW CAN I TRUST MYSELF TO ANSWER IT NOW?
I THINK THE TRUTH IS THAT I...
I SO WANT TO BE. I WANT PEOPLE TO LOOK AT ME THE WAY THEY LOOK AT HIM. AT SPIDER-MAN. I'VE SEEN IT.
THEY SEE HIM, AND THEY KNOW EVERYTHING IS GOING TO BE OKAY.
THEY LOOK AT ME AND...
I DON'T KNOW.
MAYBE I DON'T THINK I'M GOOD ENOUGH OF A GUY TO BE A GOOD GUY.
BUT...I'M TRYING. WE'RE TRYING.
EVERY DAY.
AND HELL, I MEAN...BEFORE I GO ANY FURTHER, CAN WE AGREE THAT IT'S BEEN AN INSANE FEW YEARS FOR US?

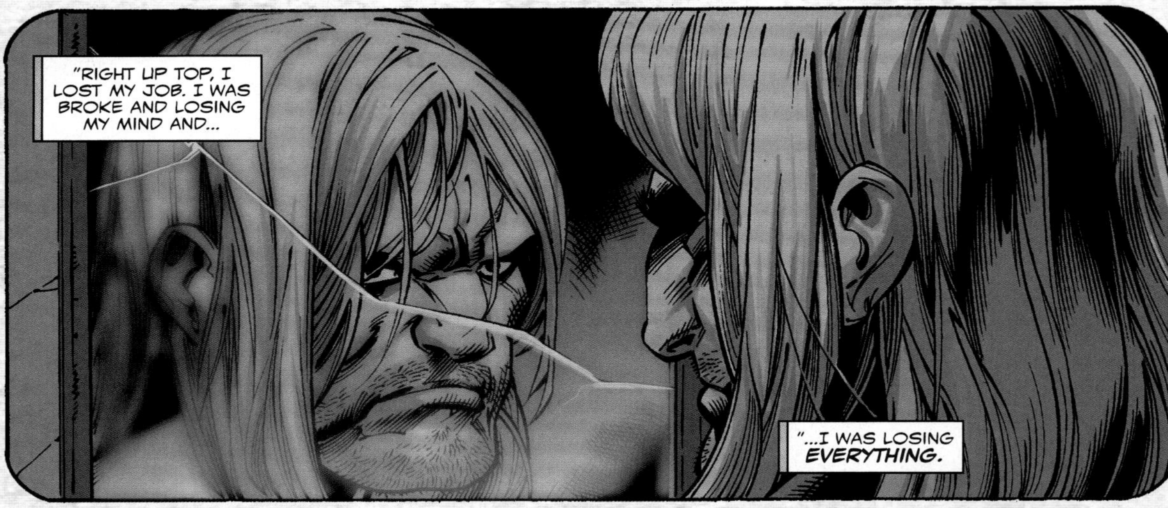
"RIGHT UP TOP, I LOST MY JOB. I WAS BROKE AND LOSING MY MIND AND...
"...I WAS LOSING *EVERYTHING.*

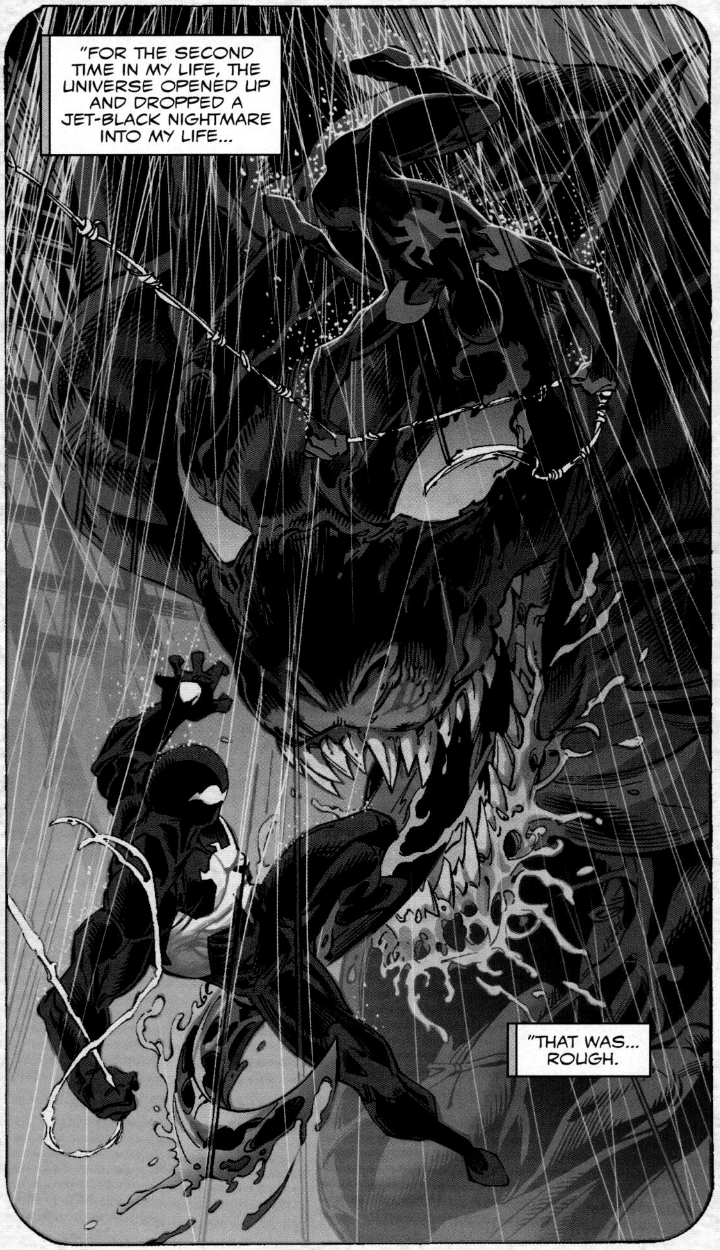
"FOR THE SECOND TIME IN MY LIFE, THE UNIVERSE OPENED UP AND DROPPED A JET-BLACK NIGHTMARE INTO MY LIFE...
"THAT WAS... ROUGH.

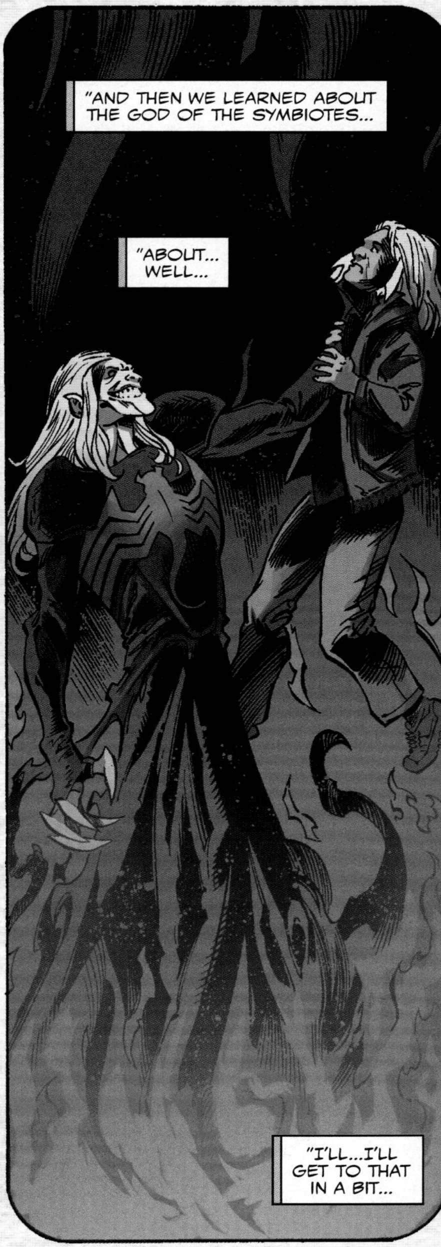
"AND THEN WE LEARNED ABOUT THE GOD OF THE SYMBIOTES...
"ABOUT... WELL...
"I'LL...I'LL GET TO THAT IN A BIT...

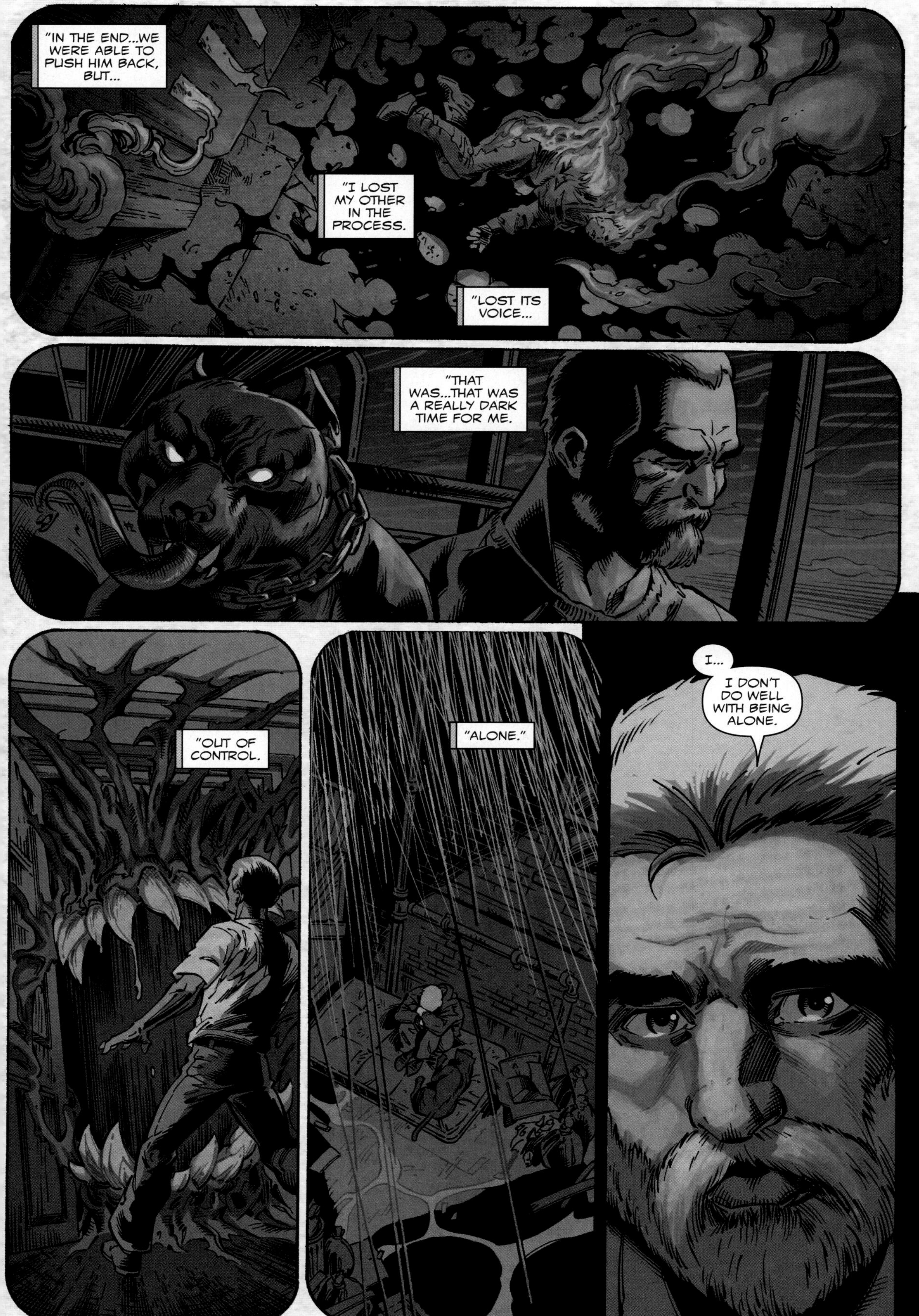
"IN THE END...WE WERE ABLE TO PUSH HIM BACK, BUT...
"I LOST MY OTHER IN THE PROCESS.
"LOST ITS VOICE...
"THAT WAS...THAT WAS A REALLY DARK TIME FOR ME.
"OUT OF CONTROL.
"ALONE."
I...
I DON'T DO WELL WITH BEING ALONE.

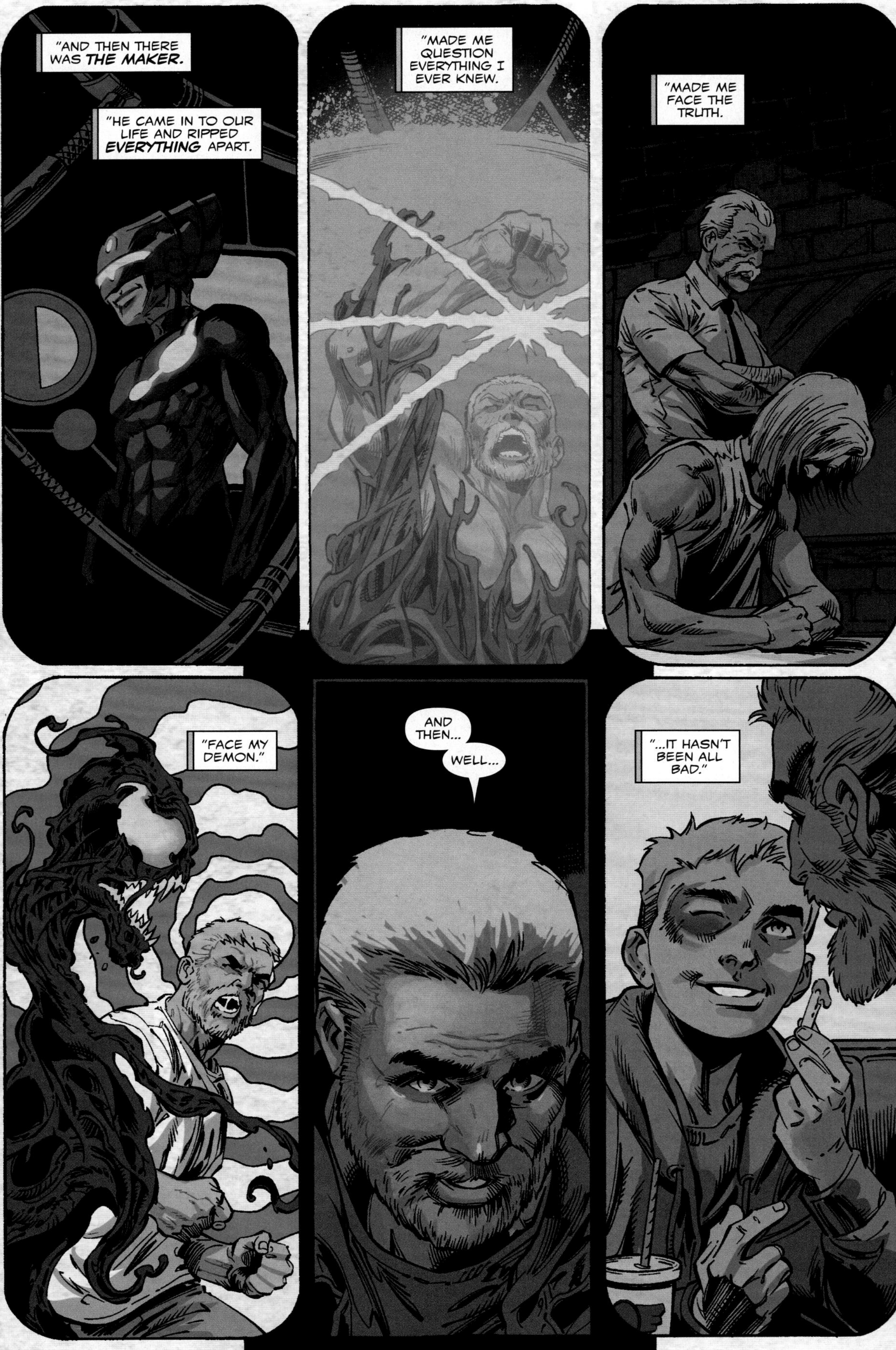
"AND THEN THERE WAS THE MAKER.
"HE CAME IN TO OUR LIFE AND RIPPED EVERYTHING APART.
"MADE ME QUESTION EVERYTHING I EVER KNEW.
"MADE ME FACE THE TRUTH.
"FACE MY DEMON."
AND THEN...
WELL...
"...IT HASN'T BEEN ALL BAD."

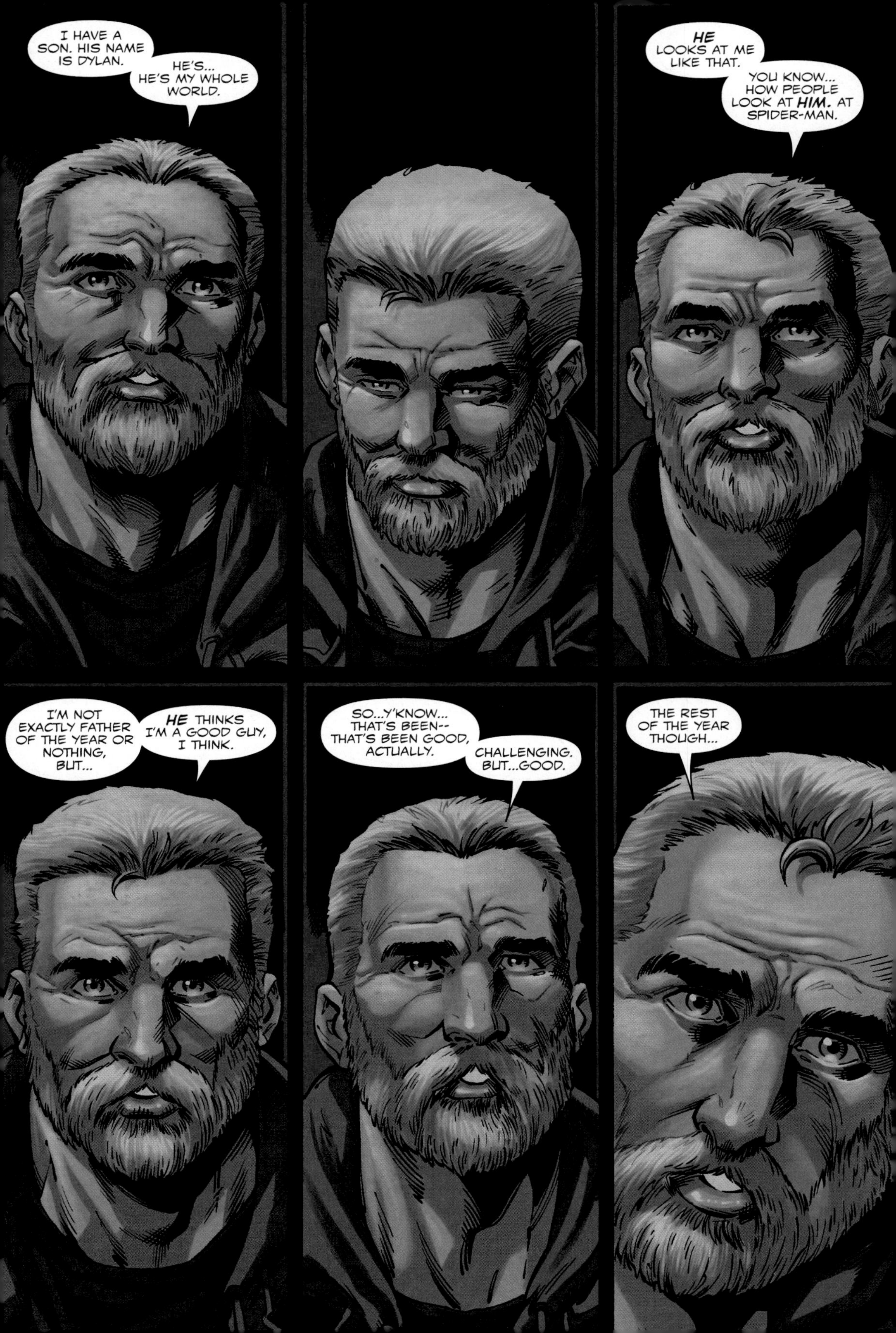
I HAVE A SON. HIS NAME IS DYLAN.
HE'S... HE'S MY WHOLE WORLD.
HE LOOKS AT ME LIKE THAT.
YOU KNOW... HOW PEOPLE LOOK AT HIM. AT SPIDER-MAN.
I'M NOT EXACTLY FATHER OF THE YEAR OR NOTHING, BUT...
HE THINKS I'M A GOOD GUY, I THINK.
SO...Y'KNOW... THAT'S BEEN-- THAT'S BEEN GOOD, ACTUALLY.
CHALLENGING. BUT...GOOD.
THE REST OF THE YEAR THOUGH...

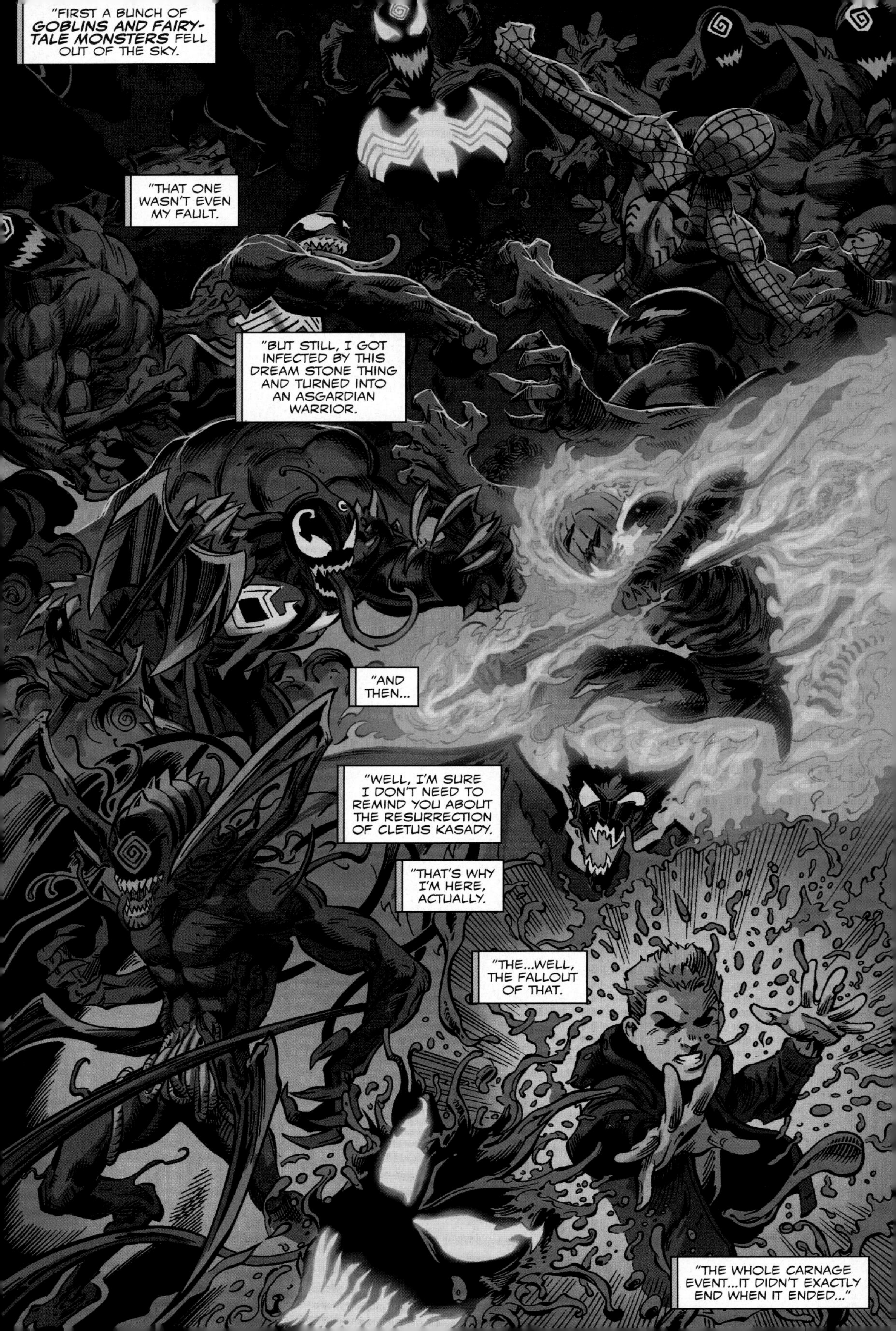
"FIRST A BUNCH OF GOBLINS AND FAIRY-TALE MONSTERS FELL OUT OF THE SKY.
"THAT ONE WASN'T EVEN MY FAULT.
"BUT STILL, I GOT INFECTED BY THIS DREAM STONE THING AND TURNED INTO AN ASGARDIAN WARRIOR.
"AND THEN...
"WELL, I'M SURE I DON'T NEED TO REMIND YOU ABOUT THE RESURRECTION OF CLETUS KASADY.
"THAT'S WHY I'M HERE, ACTUALLY.
"THE...WELL, THE FALLOUT OF THAT.
"THE WHOLE CARNAGE EVENT...IT DIDN'T EXACTLY END WHEN IT ENDED..."

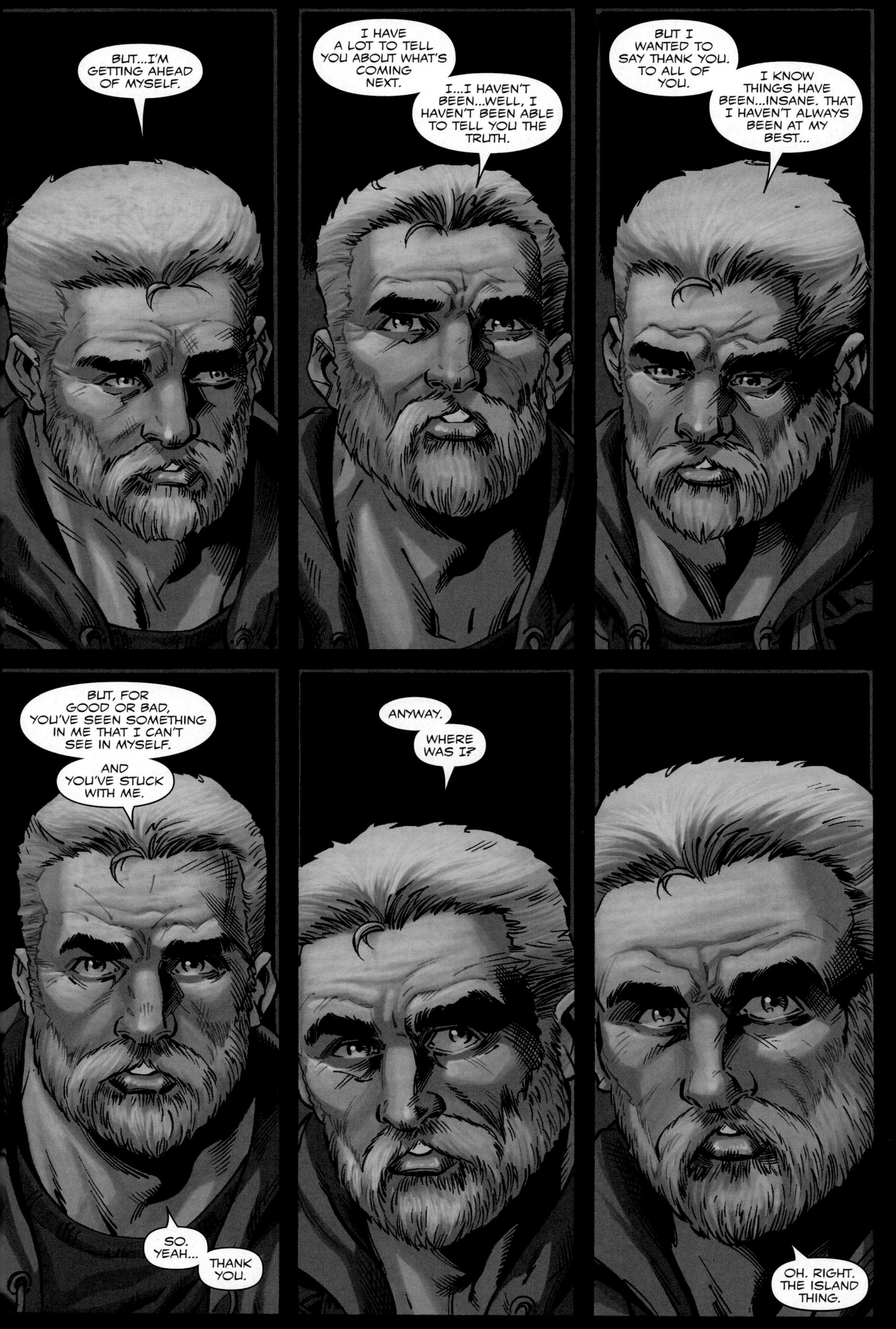
BUT...I'M GETTING AHEAD OF MYSELF.
I HAVE A LOT TO TELL YOU ABOUT WHAT'S COMING NEXT.
I...I HAVEN'T BEEN...WELL, I HAVEN'T BEEN ABLE TO TELL YOU THE TRUTH.
BUT I WANTED TO SAY THANK YOU. TO ALL OF YOU.
I KNOW THINGS HAVE BEEN...INSANE. THAT I HAVEN'T ALWAYS BEEN AT MY BEST...
BUT, FOR GOOD OR BAD, YOU'VE SEEN SOMETHING IN ME THAT I CAN'T SEE IN MYSELF.
AND YOU'VE STUCK WITH ME.
SO. YEAH...
THANK YOU.
ANYWAY.
WHERE WAS I?
OH. RIGHT. THE ISLAND THING.

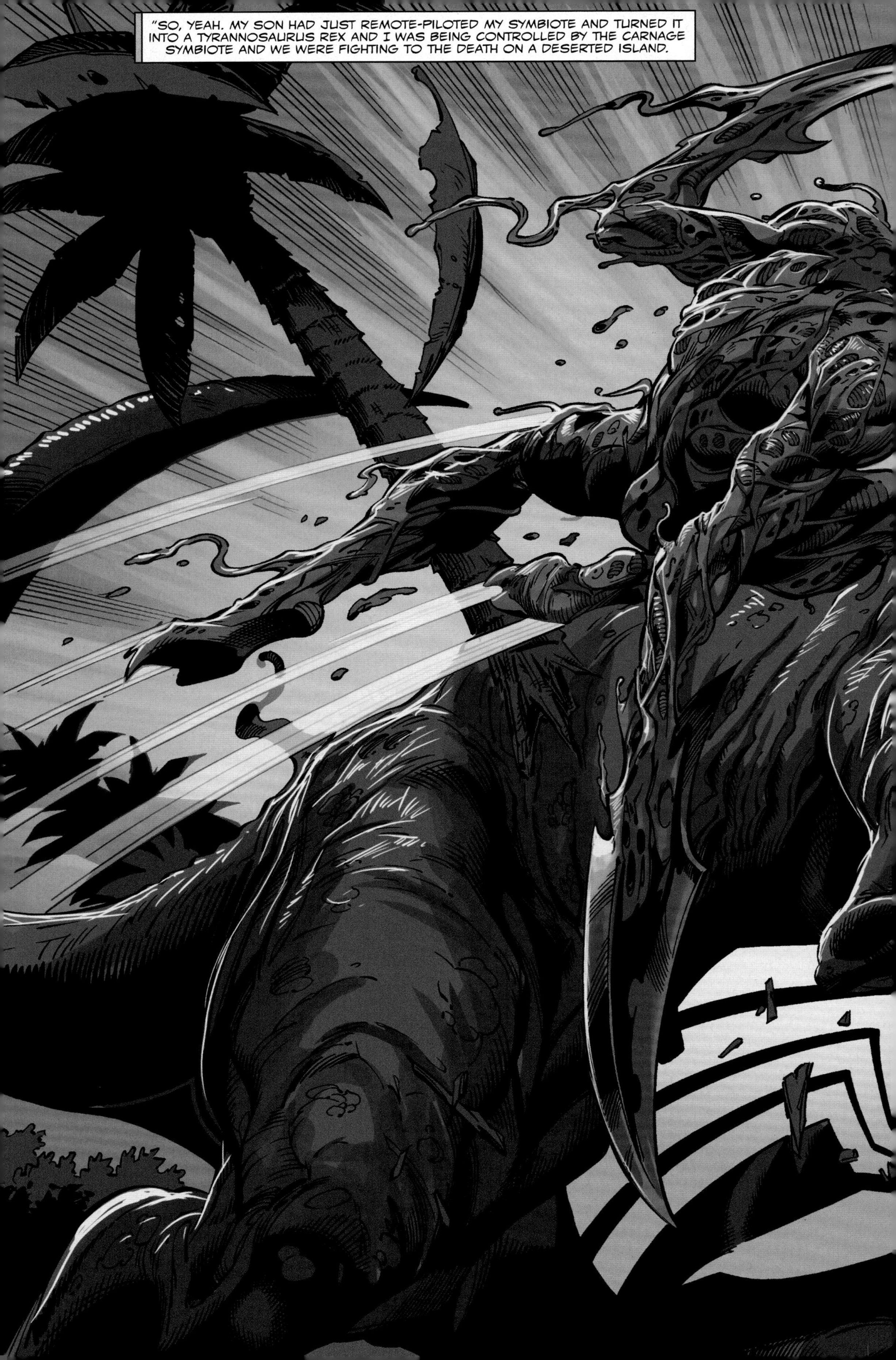
"SO, YEAH. MY SON HAD JUST REMOTE-PILOTED MY SYMBIOTE AND TURNED IT INTO A TYRANNOSAURUS REX AND I WAS BEING CONTROLLED BY THE CARNAGE SYMBIOTE AND WE WERE FIGHTING TO THE DEATH ON A DESERTED ISLAND.

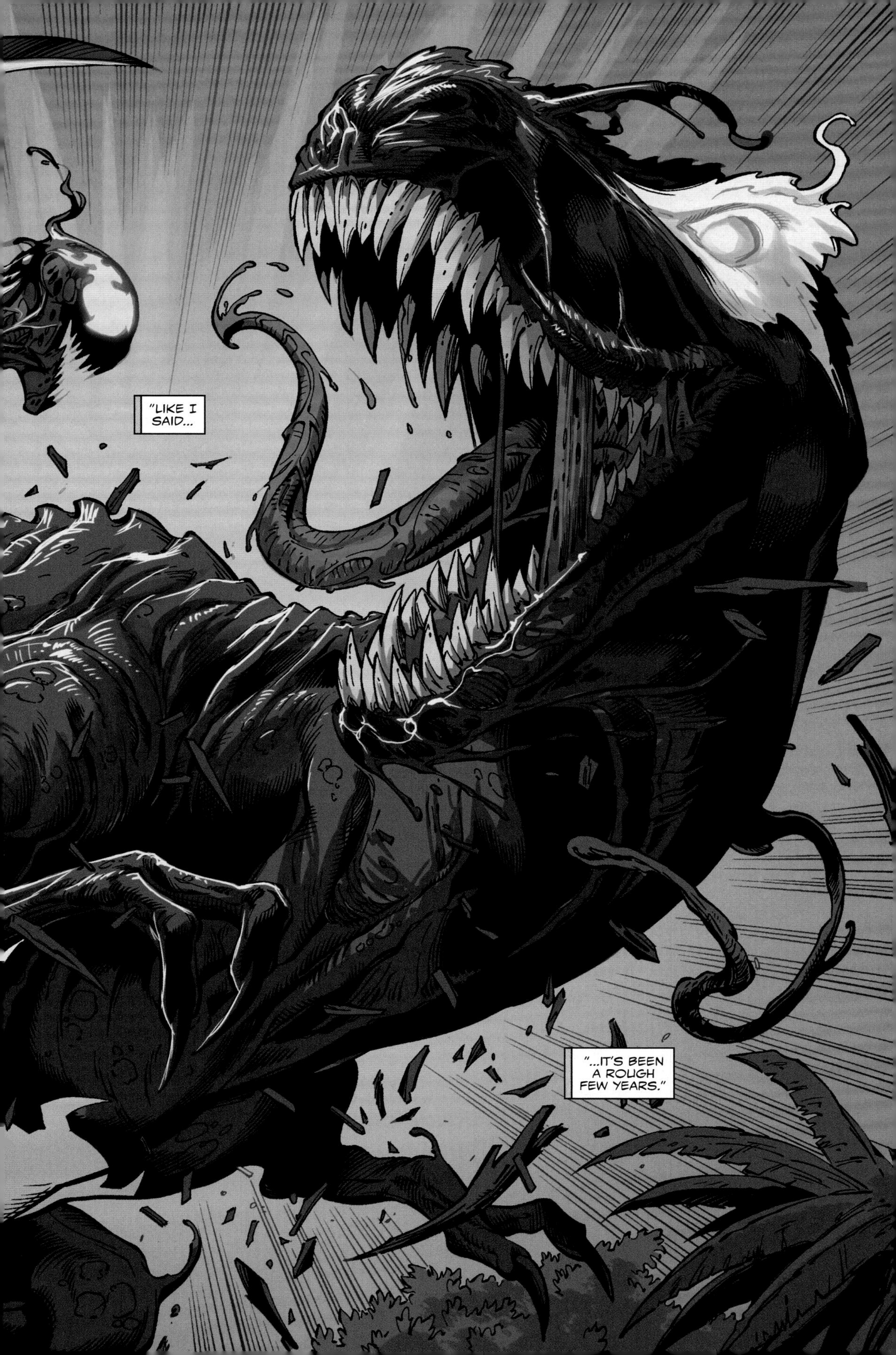
"LIKE I SAID...
"...IT'S BEEN A ROUGH FEW YEARS."

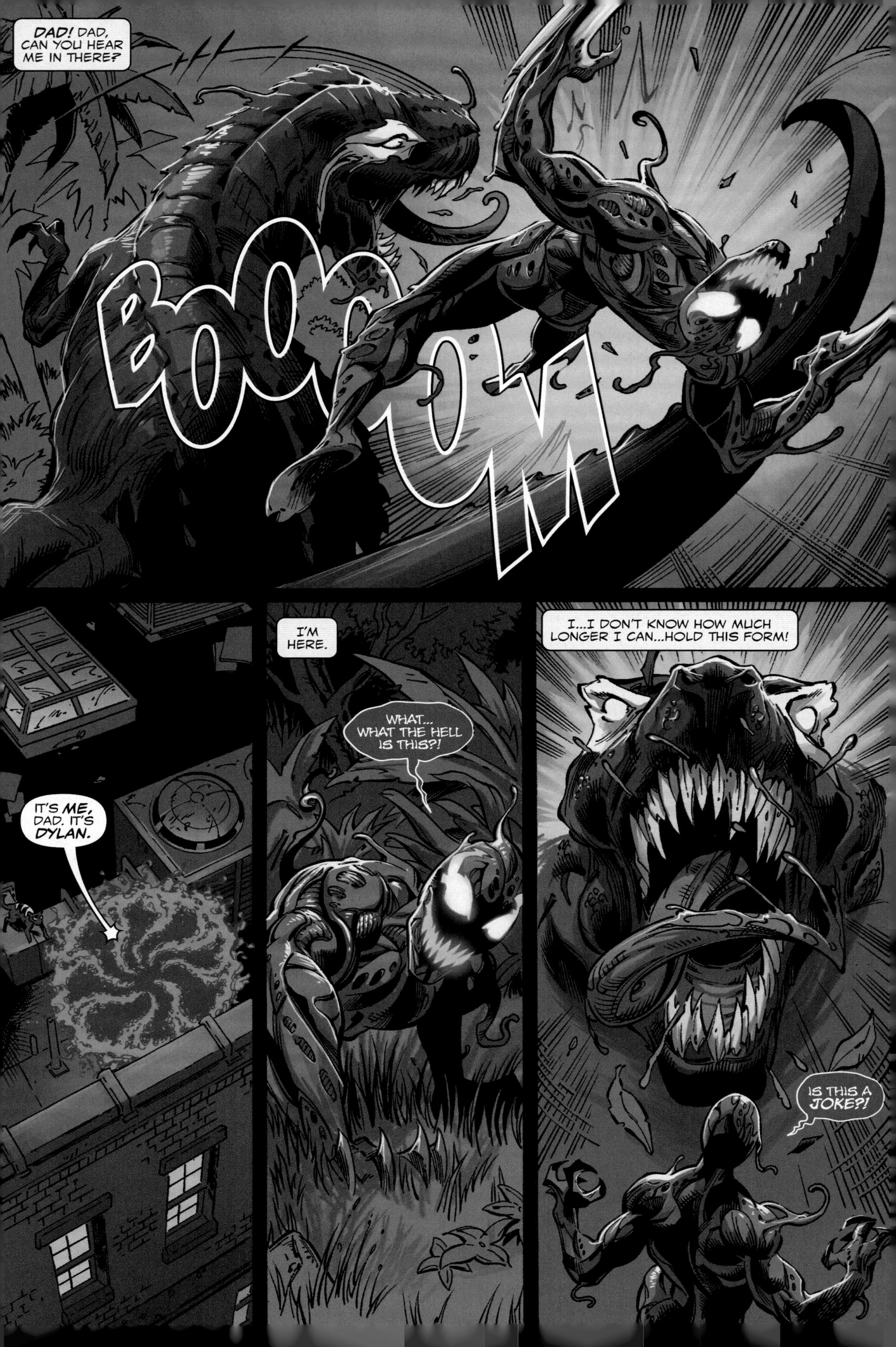
DAD! DAD, CAN YOU HEAR ME IN THERE?
BOOOOM
IT'S ME, DAD. IT'S DYLAN.
I'M HERE.
WHAT... WHAT THE HELL IS THIS?!
I...I DON'T KNOW HOW MUCH LONGER I CAN...HOLD THIS FORM!
IS THIS A JOKE?!

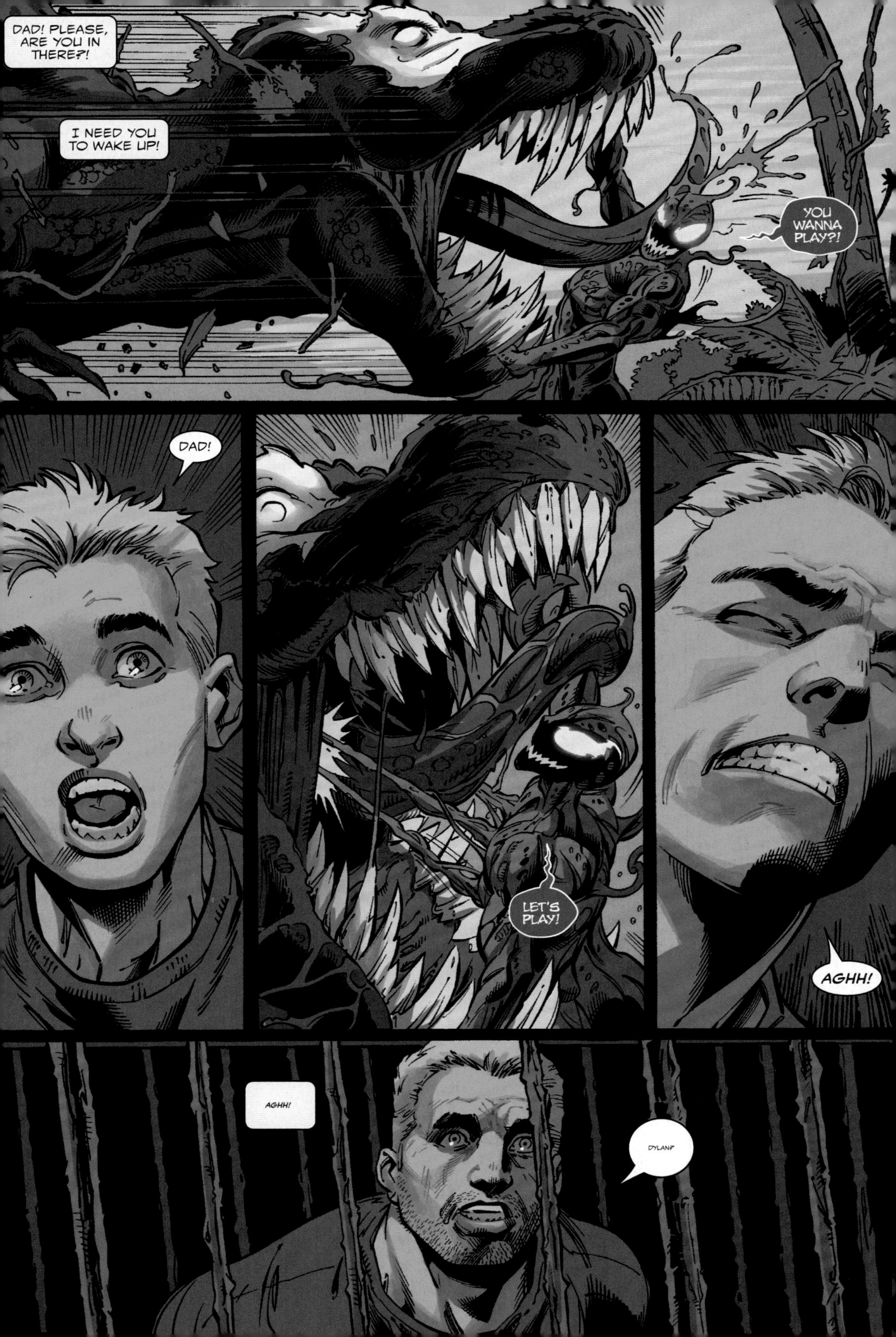
DAD! PLEASE, ARE YOU IN THERE?!
I NEED YOU TO WAKE UP!
YOU WANNA PLAY?!
DAD!
LET'S PLAY!
AGHH!
AGHH!
DYLAN?

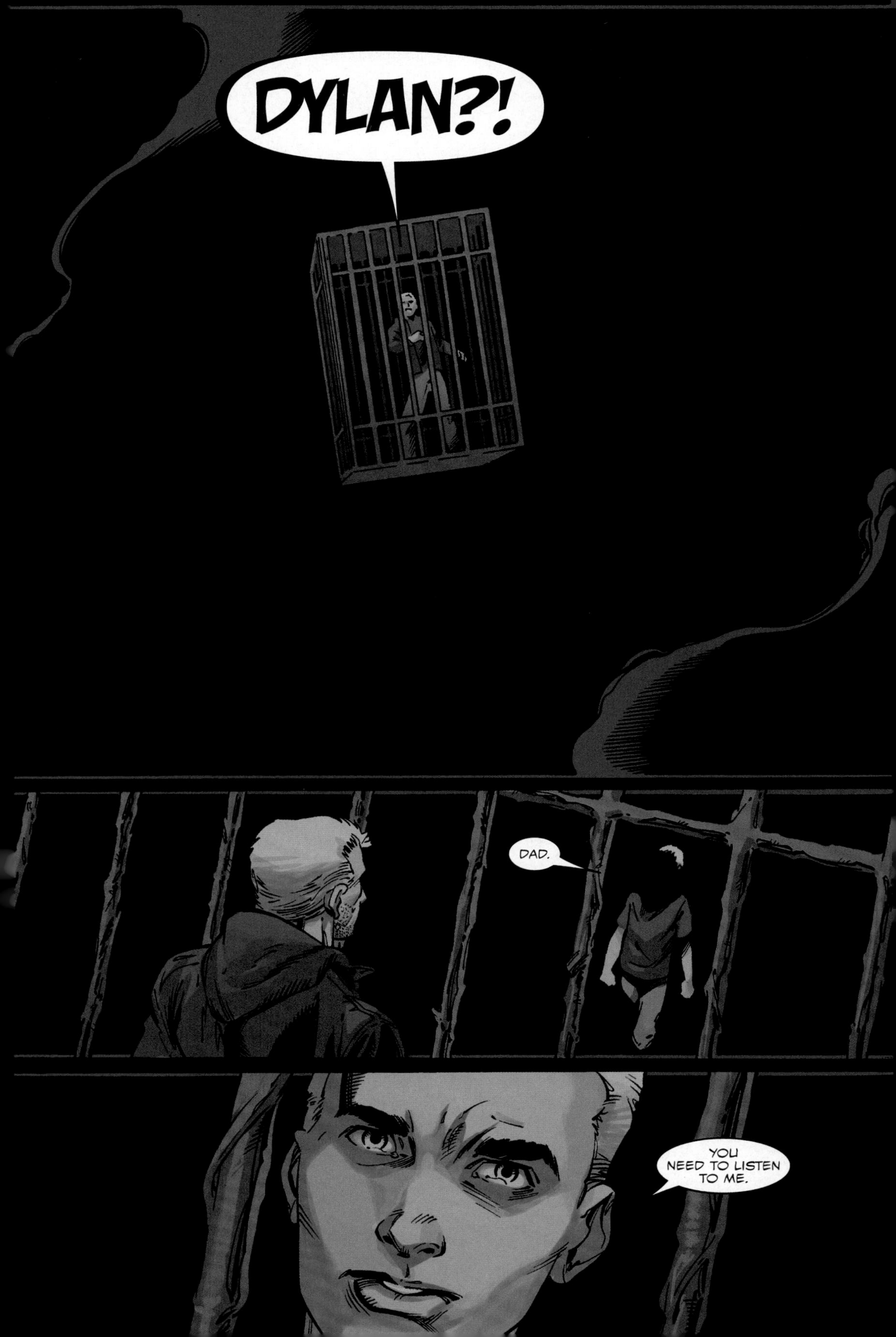
DYLAN?!
DAD.
YOU NEED TO LISTEN TO ME.

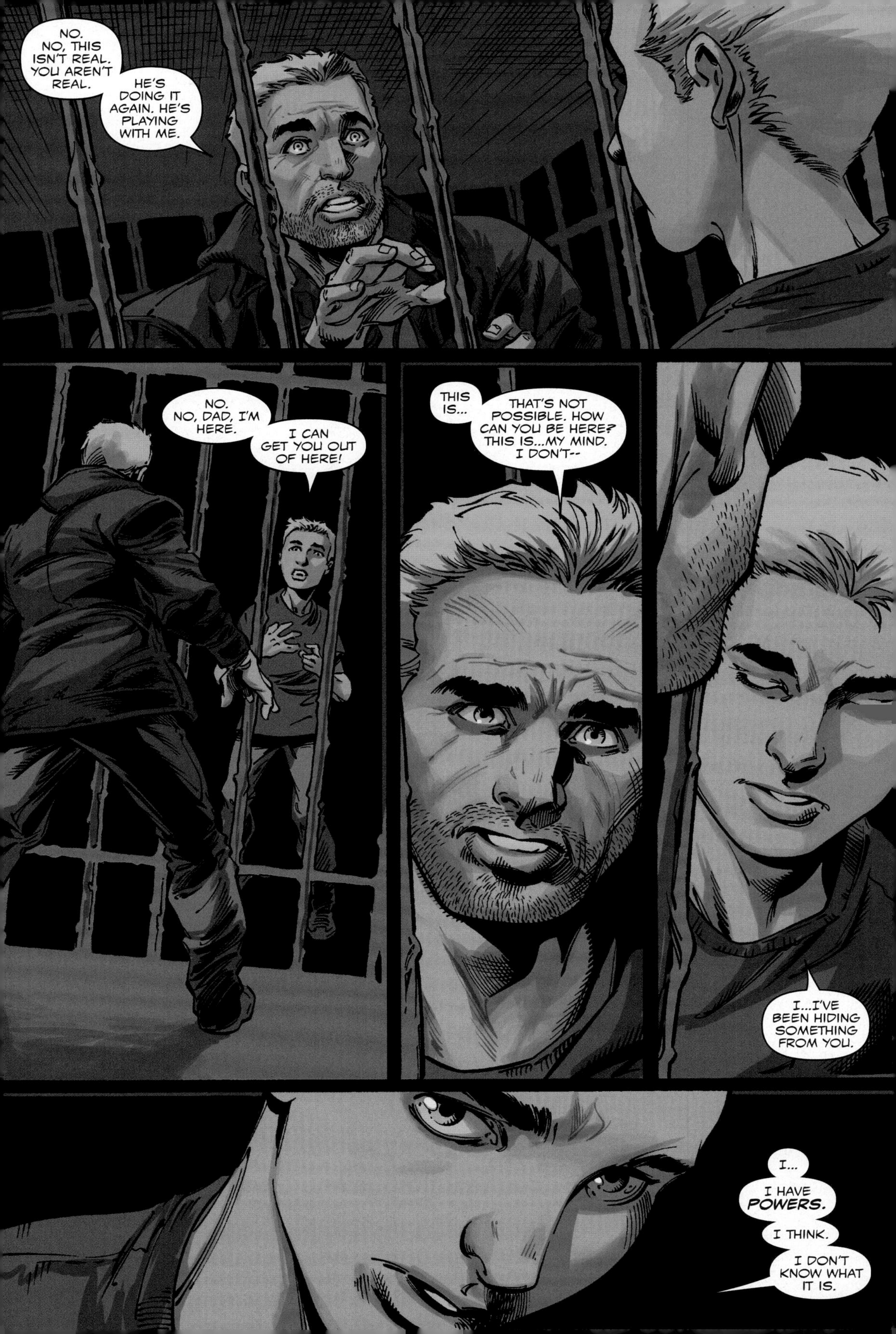
NO. NO, THIS ISN'T REAL. YOU AREN'T REAL.
HE'S DOING IT AGAIN. HE'S PLAYING WITH ME.
NO. NO, DAD, I'M HERE.
I CAN GET YOU OUT OF HERE!
THIS IS...
THAT'S NOT POSSIBLE. HOW CAN YOU BE HERE? THIS IS...MY MIND. I DON'T--
I...I'VE BEEN HIDING SOMETHING FROM YOU.
I...
I HAVE POWERS.
I THINK.
I DON'T KNOW WHAT IT IS.

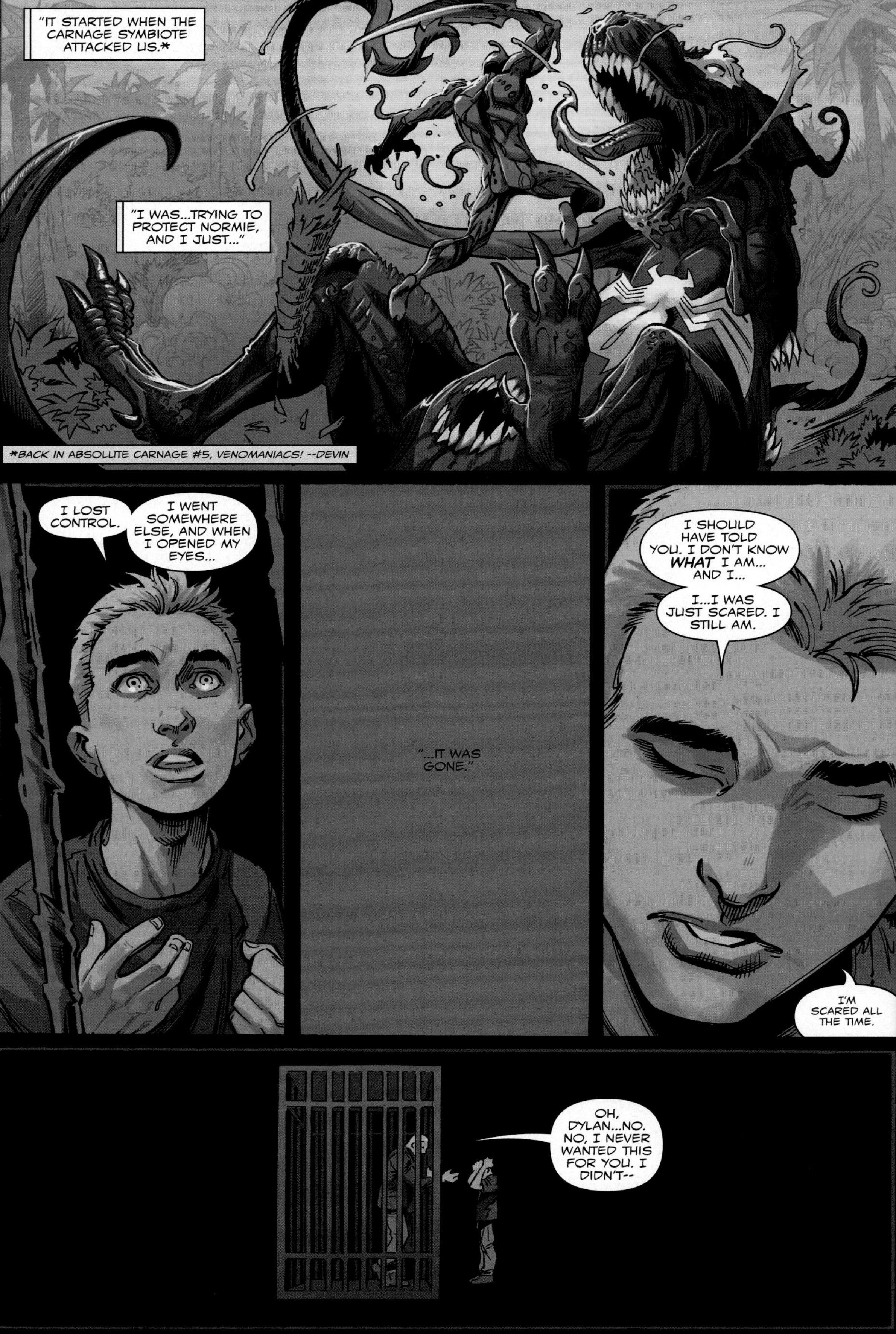
"IT STARTED WHEN THE CARNAGE SYMBIOTE ATTACKED US.*
"I WAS...TRYING TO PROTECT NORMIE, AND I JUST..."
*BACK IN ABSOLUTE CARNAGE #5, VENOMANIACS! --DEVIN
I LOST CONTROL.
I WENT SOMEWHERE ELSE, AND WHEN I OPENED MY EYES...
"...IT WAS GONE."
I SHOULD HAVE TOLD YOU. I DON'T KNOW **WHAT** I AM... AND I...
I...I WAS JUST SCARED. I STILL AM.
I'M SCARED ALL THE TIME.
OH, DYLAN...NO. NO, I NEVER WANTED THIS FOR YOU. I DIDN'T--

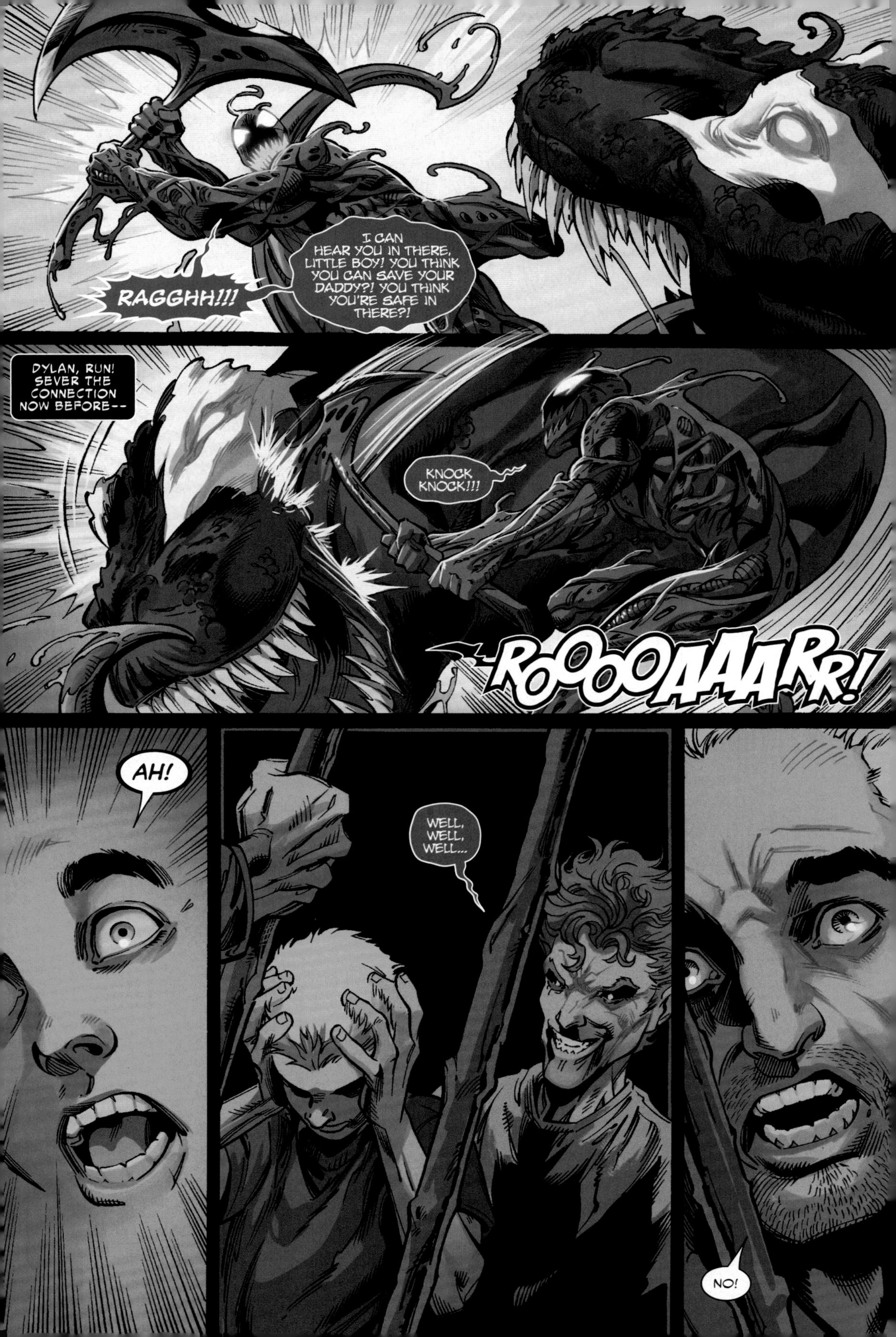
RAGGHH!!!
I CAN HEAR YOU IN THERE, LITTLE BOY! YOU THINK YOU CAN SAVE YOUR DADDY?! YOU THINK YOU'RE SAFE IN THERE?!
DYLAN, RUN! SEVER THE CONNECTION NOW BEFORE--
KNOCK KNOCK!!!
ROOOOOAAARRR!
AH!
WELL, WELL, WELL...
NO!

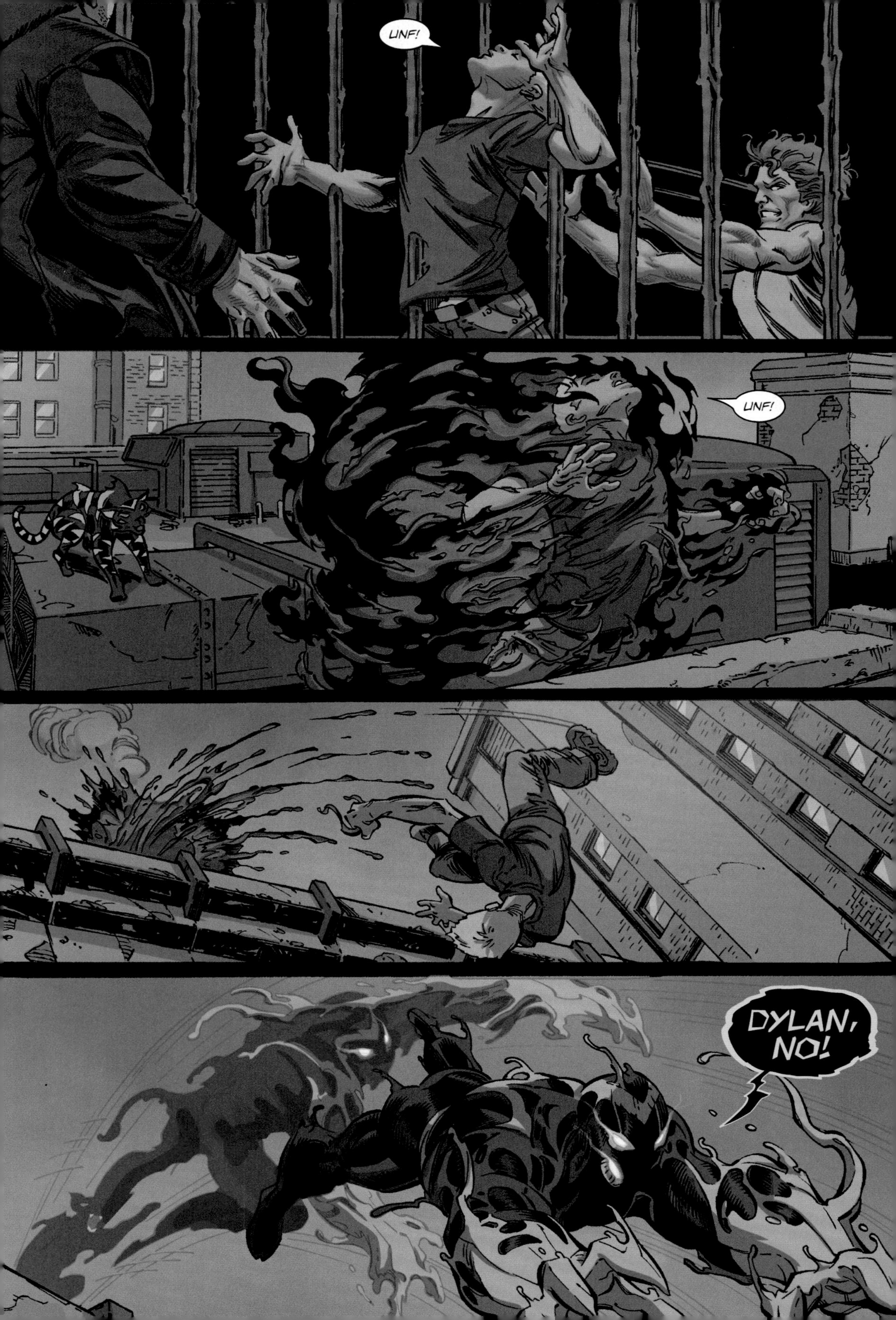
UNF!
UNF!
DYLAN, NO!

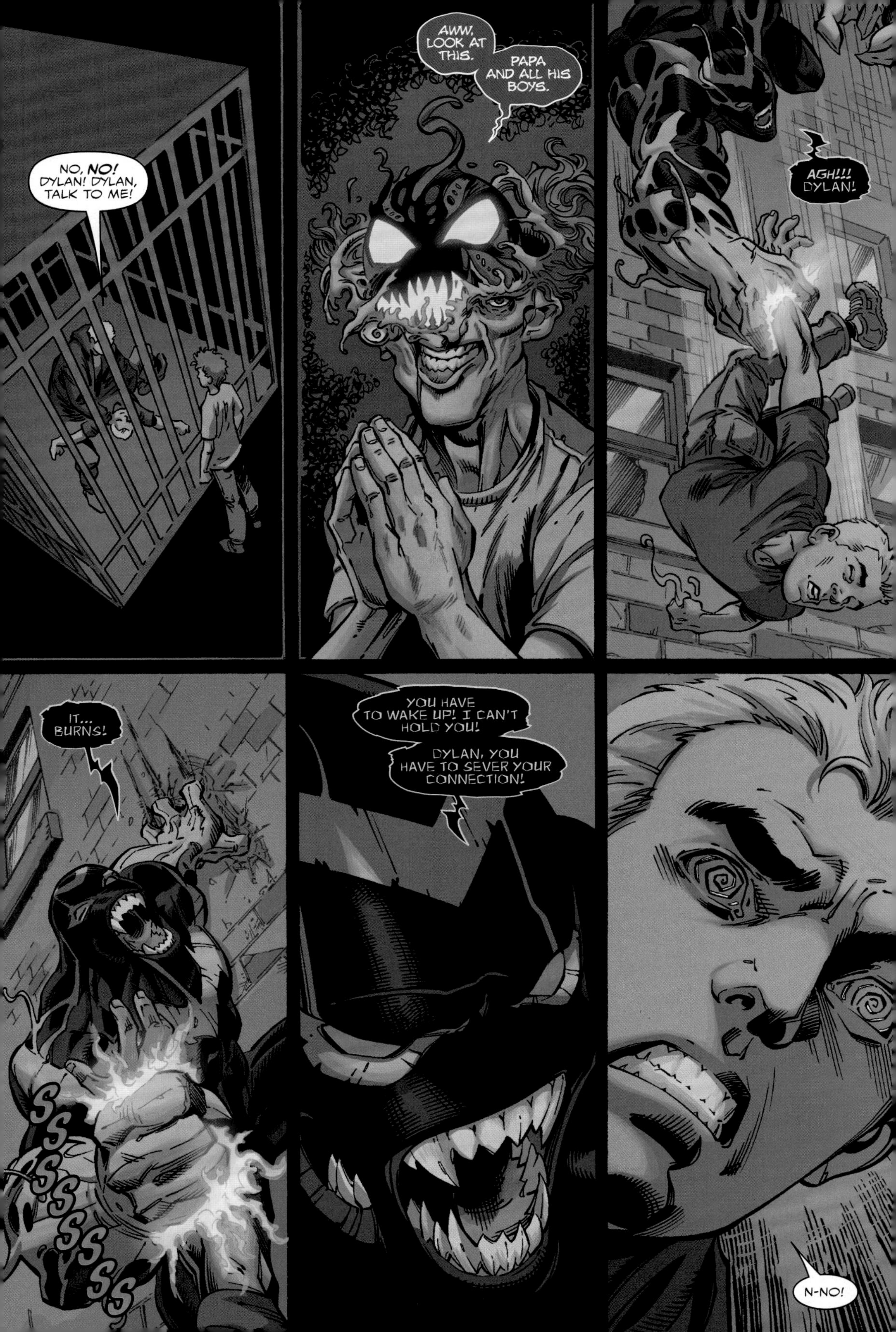
NO, NO! DYLAN! DYLAN, TALK TO ME!
AWW, LOOK AT THIS.
PAPA AND ALL HIS BOYS.
AGH!!! DYLAN!
IT... BURNS!
SSSSSSSSS
YOU HAVE TO WAKE UP! I CAN'T HOLD YOU!
DYLAN, YOU HAVE TO SEVER YOUR CONNECTION!
N-NO!

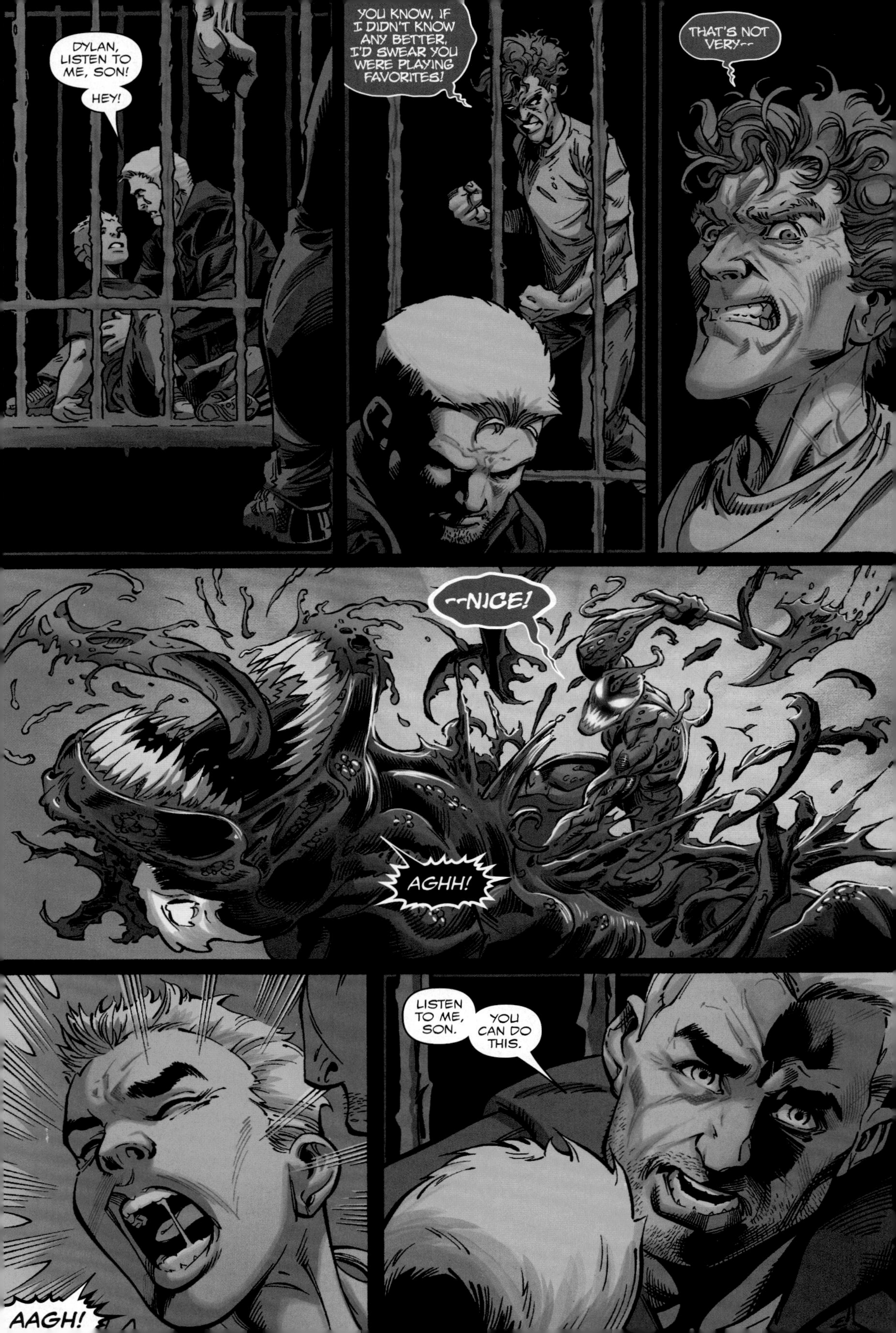
DYLAN, LISTEN TO ME, SON!
HEY!
YOU KNOW, IF I DIDN'T KNOW ANY BETTER, I'D SWEAR YOU WERE PLAYING FAVORITES!
THAT'S NOT VERY--
--NICE!
AGHH!
AAGH!
LISTEN TO ME, SON.
YOU CAN DO THIS.

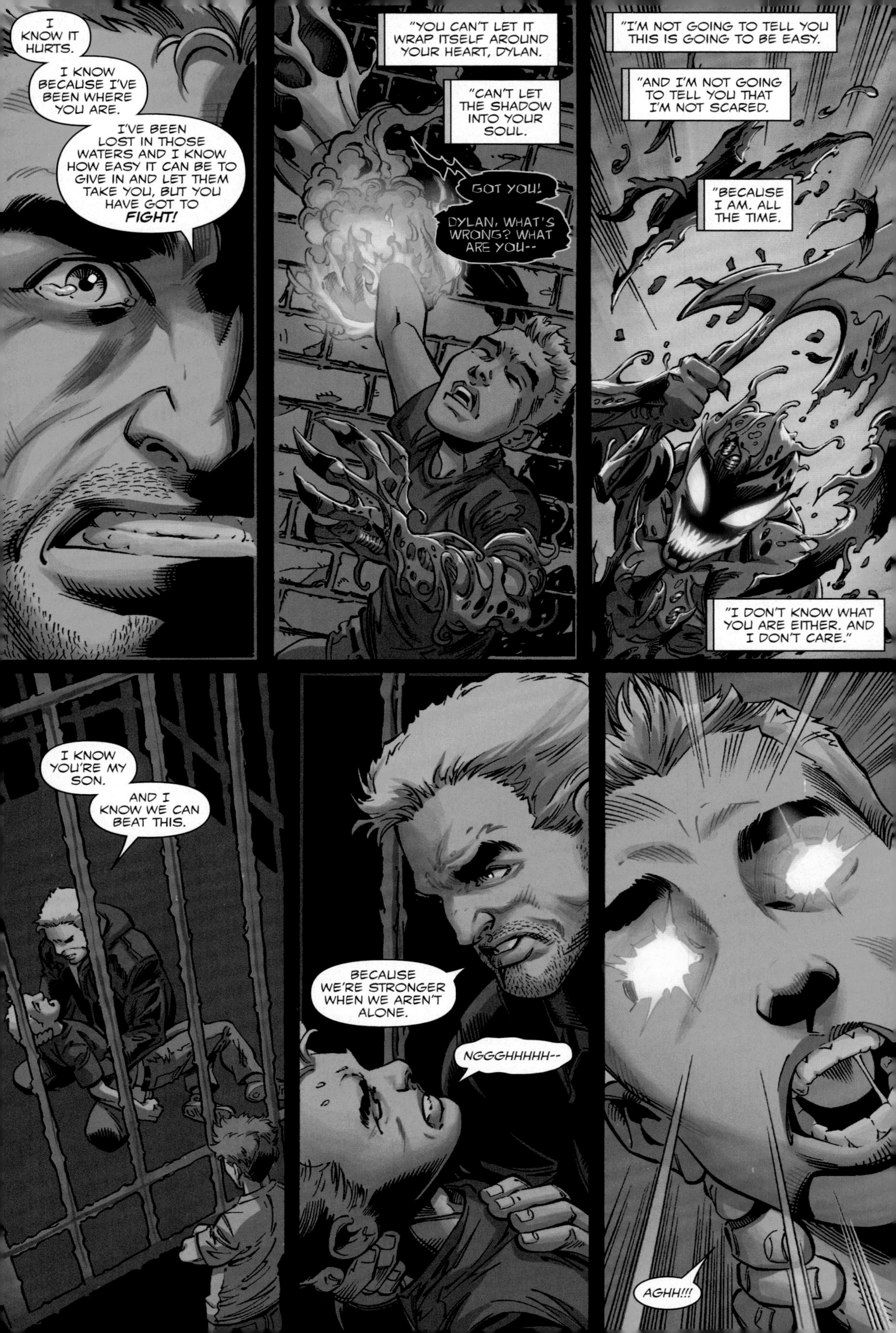
I KNOW IT HURTS.
I KNOW BECAUSE I'VE BEEN WHERE YOU ARE.
I'VE BEEN LOST IN THOSE WATERS AND I KNOW HOW EASY IT CAN BE TO GIVE IN AND LET THEM TAKE YOU, BUT YOU HAVE GOT TO *FIGHT!*
"YOU CAN'T LET IT WRAP ITSELF AROUND YOUR HEART, DYLAN.
"CAN'T LET THE SHADOW INTO YOUR SOUL.
GOT YOU!
DYLAN, WHAT'S WRONG? WHAT ARE YOU--
"I'M NOT GOING TO TELL YOU THIS IS GOING TO BE EASY.
"AND I'M NOT GOING TO TELL YOU THAT I'M NOT SCARED.
"BECAUSE I AM. ALL THE TIME.
"I DON'T KNOW WHAT YOU ARE EITHER. AND I DON'T CARE."
I KNOW YOU'RE MY SON.
AND I KNOW WE CAN BEAT THIS.
BECAUSE WE'RE STRONGER WHEN WE AREN'T ALONE.
NGGGHHHHH--
AGHH!!!

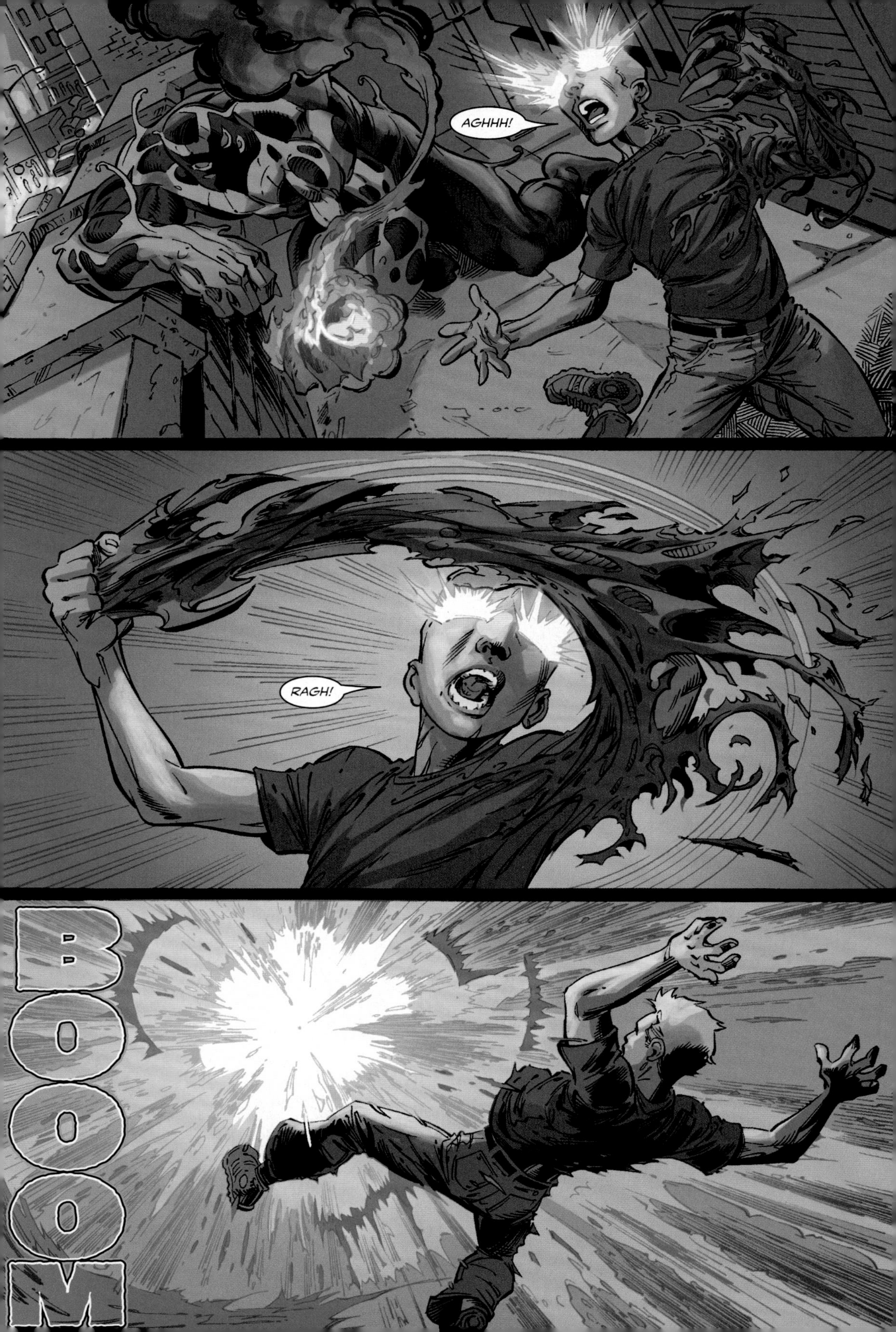
AGHHH!
RAGH!
BOOOM

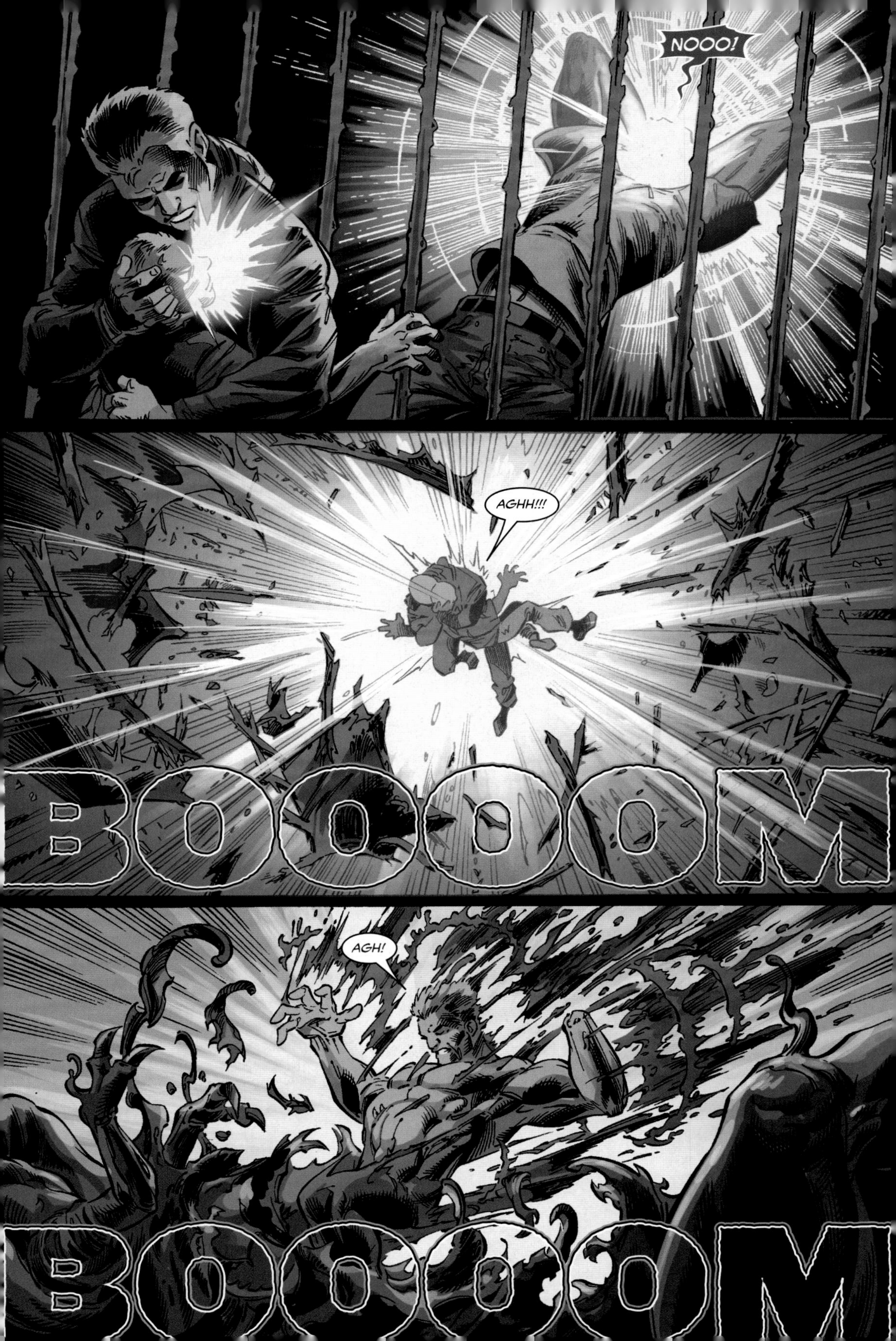
NOOO!
AGHH!!!
BOOOOM
AGH!
BOOOOM

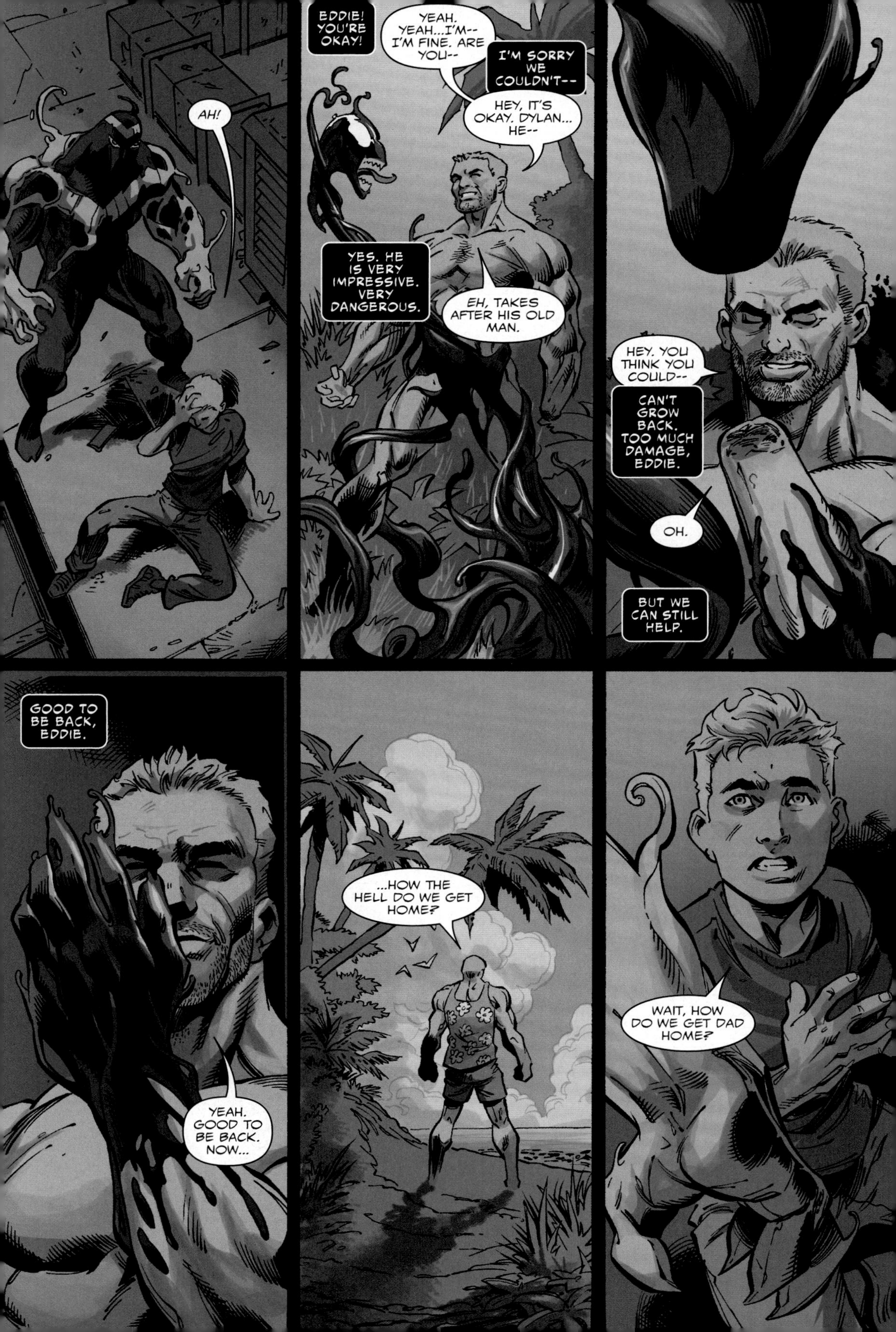
AH!
EDDIE! YOU'RE OKAY!
YEAH. YEAH...I'M-- I'M FINE. ARE YOU--
I'M SORRY WE COULDN'T--
HEY, IT'S OKAY. DYLAN... HE--
YES. HE IS VERY IMPRESSIVE. VERY DANGEROUS.
EH, TAKES AFTER HIS OLD MAN.
HEY. YOU THINK YOU COULD--
CAN'T GROW BACK. TOO MUCH DAMAGE, EDDIE.
OH.
BUT WE CAN STILL HELP.
GOOD TO BE BACK, EDDIE.
YEAH. GOOD TO BE BACK. NOW...
...HOW THE HELL DO WE GET HOME?
WAIT, HOW DO WE GET DAD HOME?

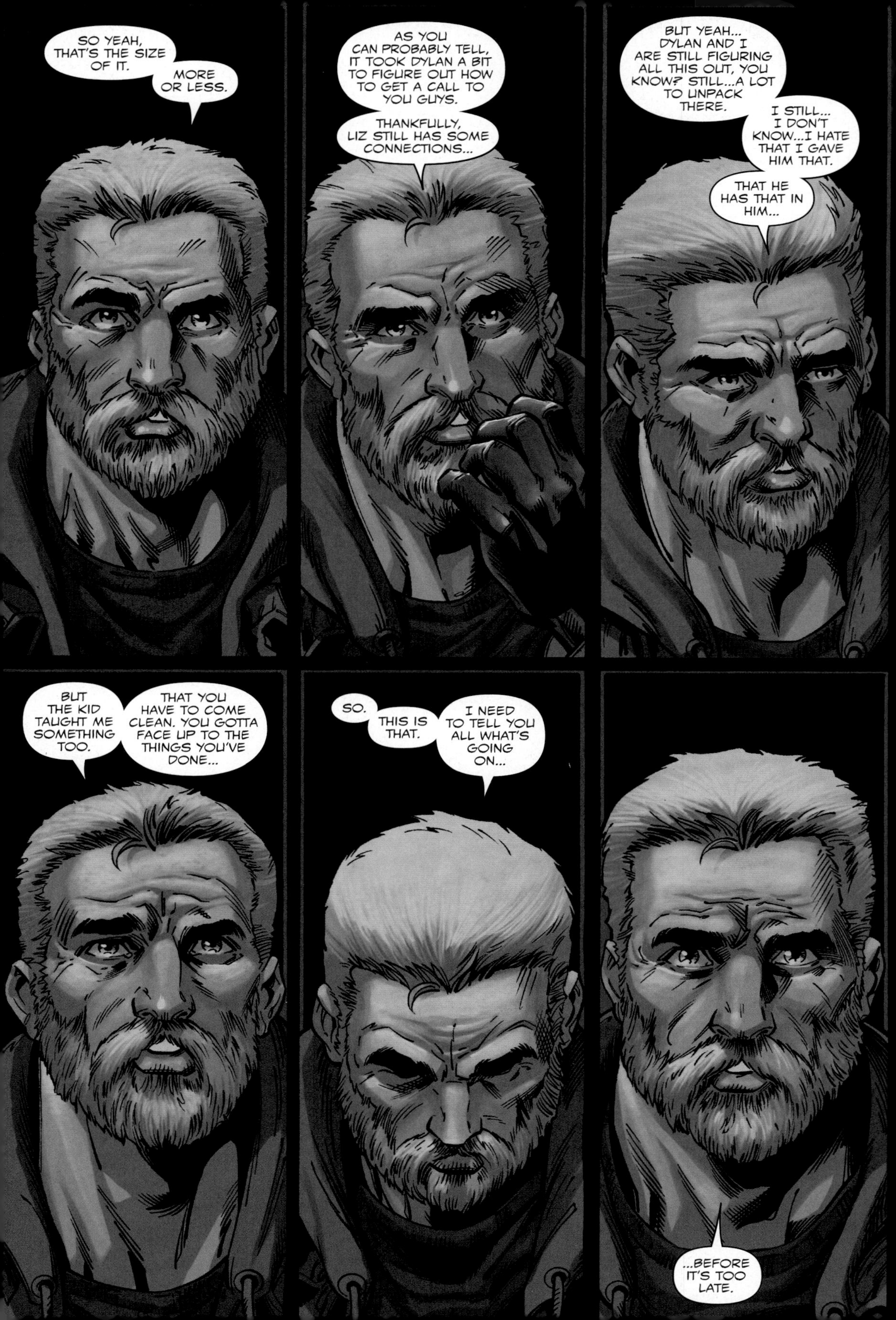
SO YEAH, THAT'S THE SIZE OF IT.
MORE OR LESS.
AS YOU CAN PROBABLY TELL, IT TOOK DYLAN A BIT TO FIGURE OUT HOW TO GET A CALL TO YOU GUYS.
THANKFULLY, LIZ STILL HAS SOME CONNECTIONS...
BUT YEAH... DYLAN AND I ARE STILL FIGURING ALL THIS OUT, YOU KNOW? STILL...A LOT TO UNPACK THERE.
I STILL... I DON'T KNOW...I HATE THAT I GAVE HIM THAT.
THAT HE HAS THAT IN HIM...
BUT THE KID TAUGHT ME SOMETHING TOO.
THAT YOU HAVE TO COME CLEAN. YOU GOTTA FACE UP TO THE THINGS YOU'VE DONE...
SO.
THIS IS THAT.
I NEED TO TELL YOU ALL WHAT'S GOING ON...
...BEFORE IT'S TOO LATE.

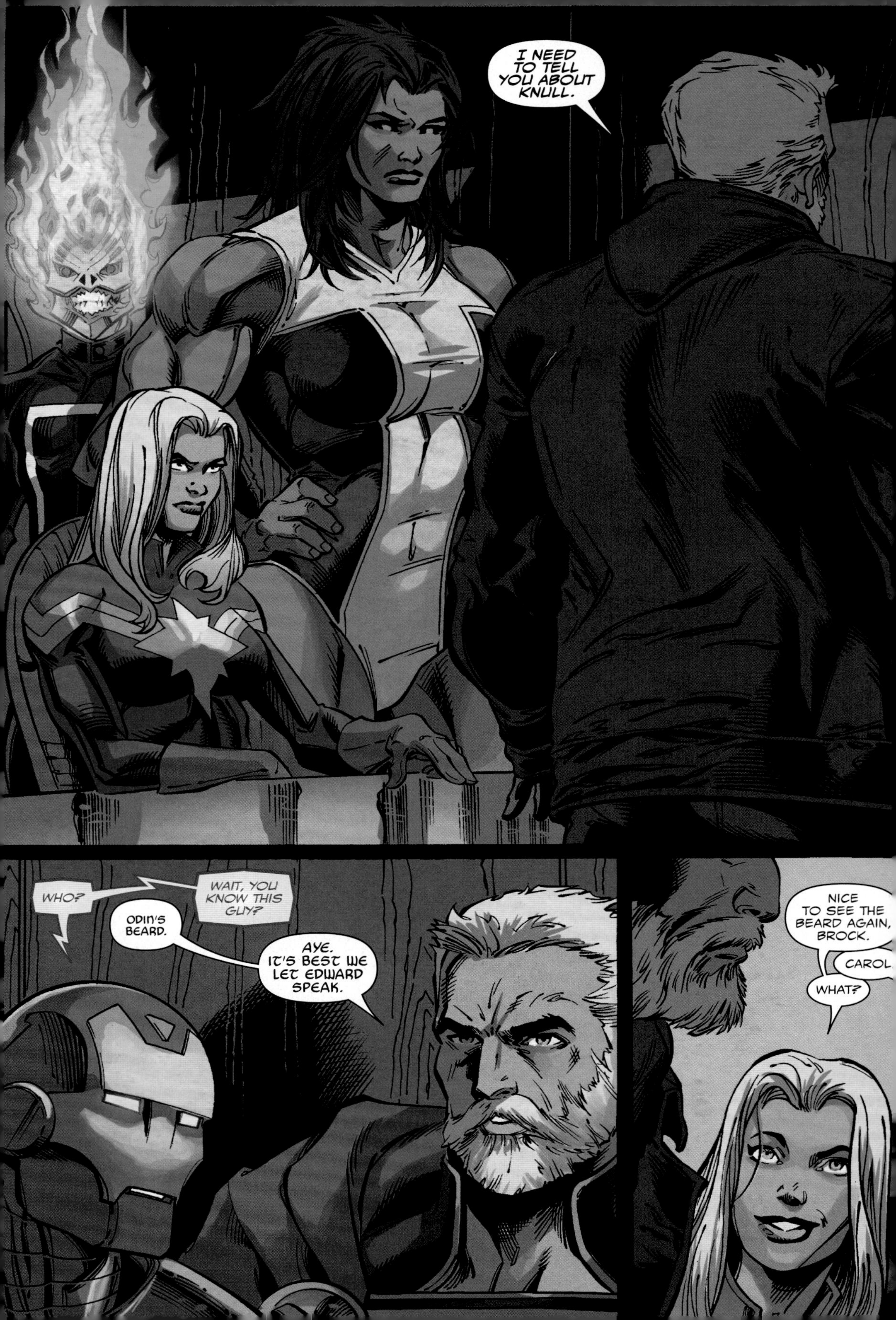

I NEED TO TELL YOU ABOUT KNULL.
WHO?
WAIT, YOU KNOW THIS GUY?
ODIN'S BEARD.
AYE. IT'S BEST WE LET EDWARD SPEAK.
NICE TO SEE THE BEARD AGAIN, BROCK.
CAROL
WHAT?

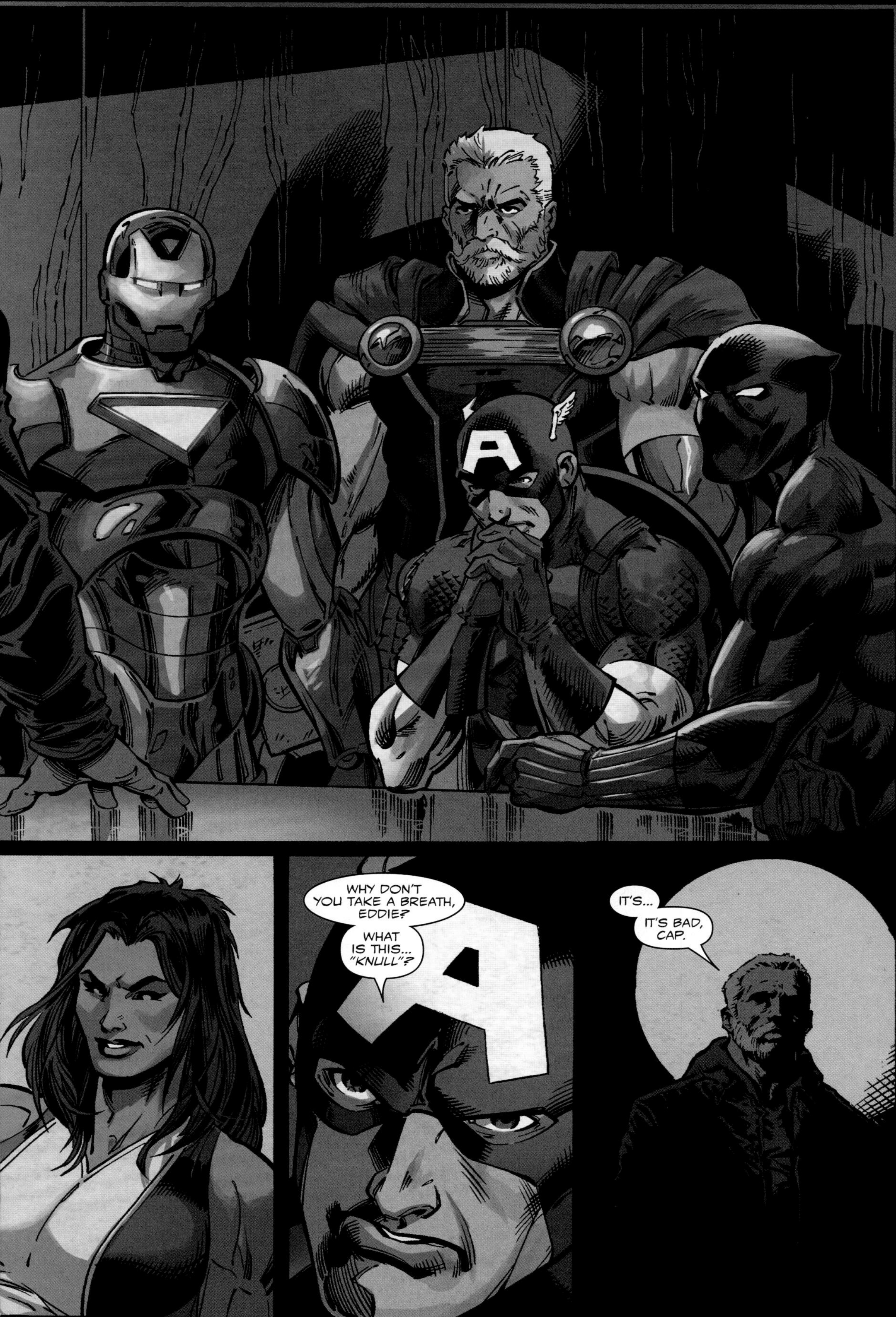
WHY DON'T YOU TAKE A BREATH, EDDIE?
WHAT IS THIS... "KNULL"?
IT'S...
IT'S BAD, CAP.

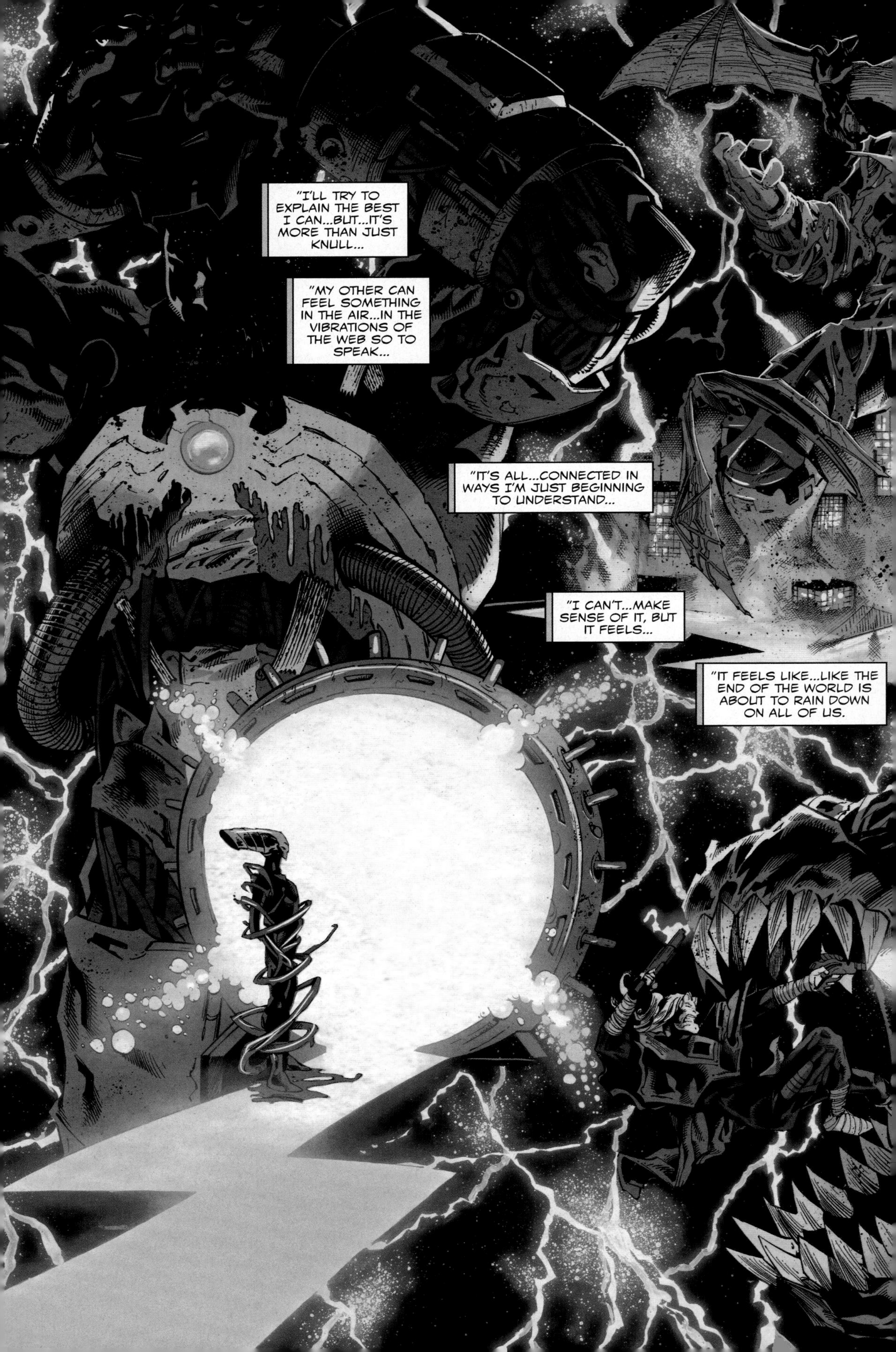
"I'LL TRY TO EXPLAIN THE BEST I CAN...BUT...IT'S MORE THAN JUST KNULL...
"MY OTHER CAN FEEL SOMETHING IN THE AIR...IN THE VIBRATIONS OF THE WEB SO TO SPEAK...
"IT'S ALL...CONNECTED IN WAYS I'M JUST BEGINNING TO UNDERSTAND...
"I CAN'T...MAKE SENSE OF IT, BUT IT FEELS...
"IT FEELS LIKE...LIKE THE END OF THE WORLD IS ABOUT TO RAIN DOWN ON ALL OF US.

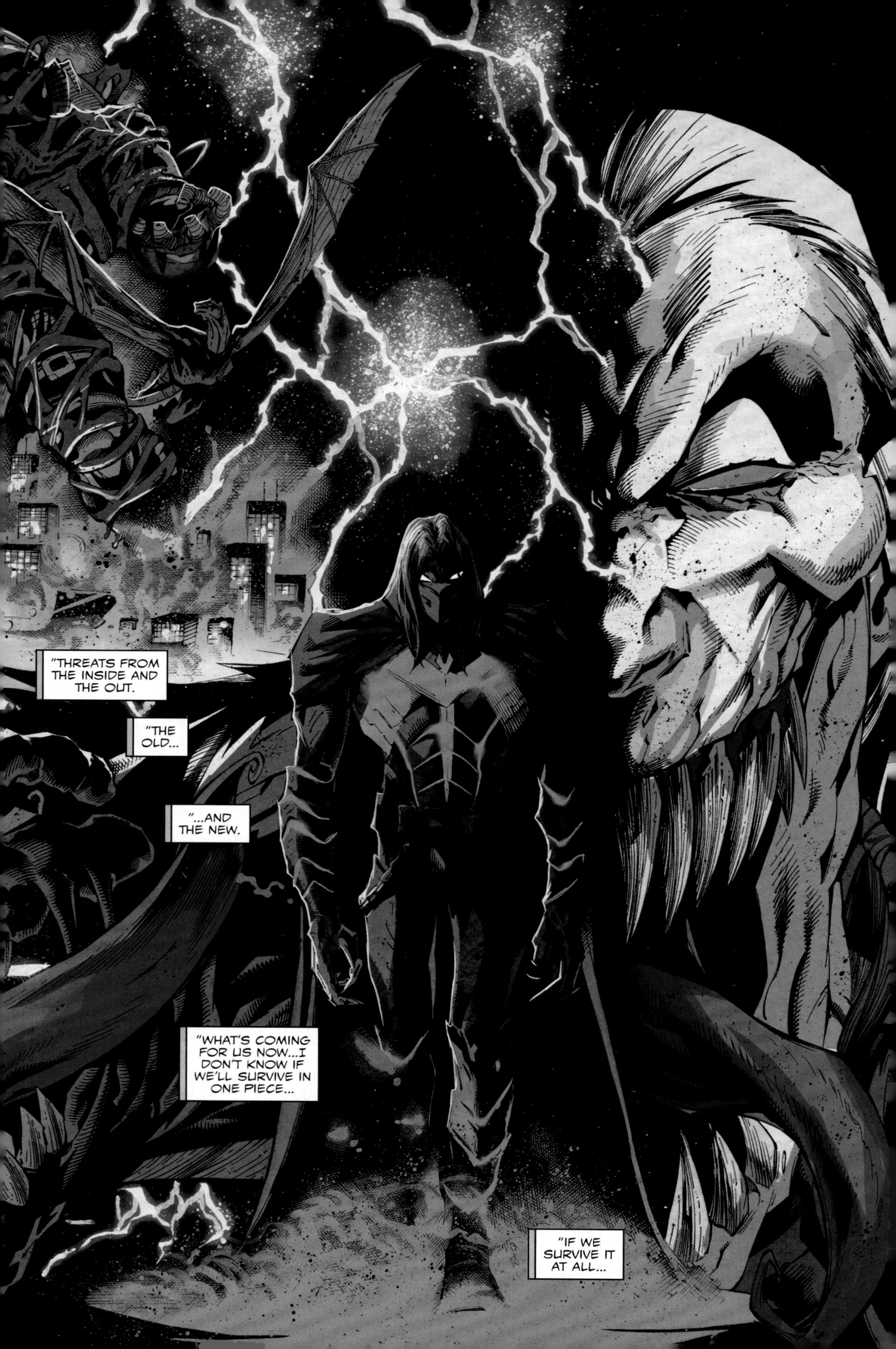
"THREATS FROM THE INSIDE AND THE OUT.
"THE OLD...
"...AND THE NEW.
"WHAT'S COMING FOR US NOW...I DON'T KNOW IF WE'LL SURVIVE IN ONE PIECE...
"IF WE SURVIVE IT AT ALL...

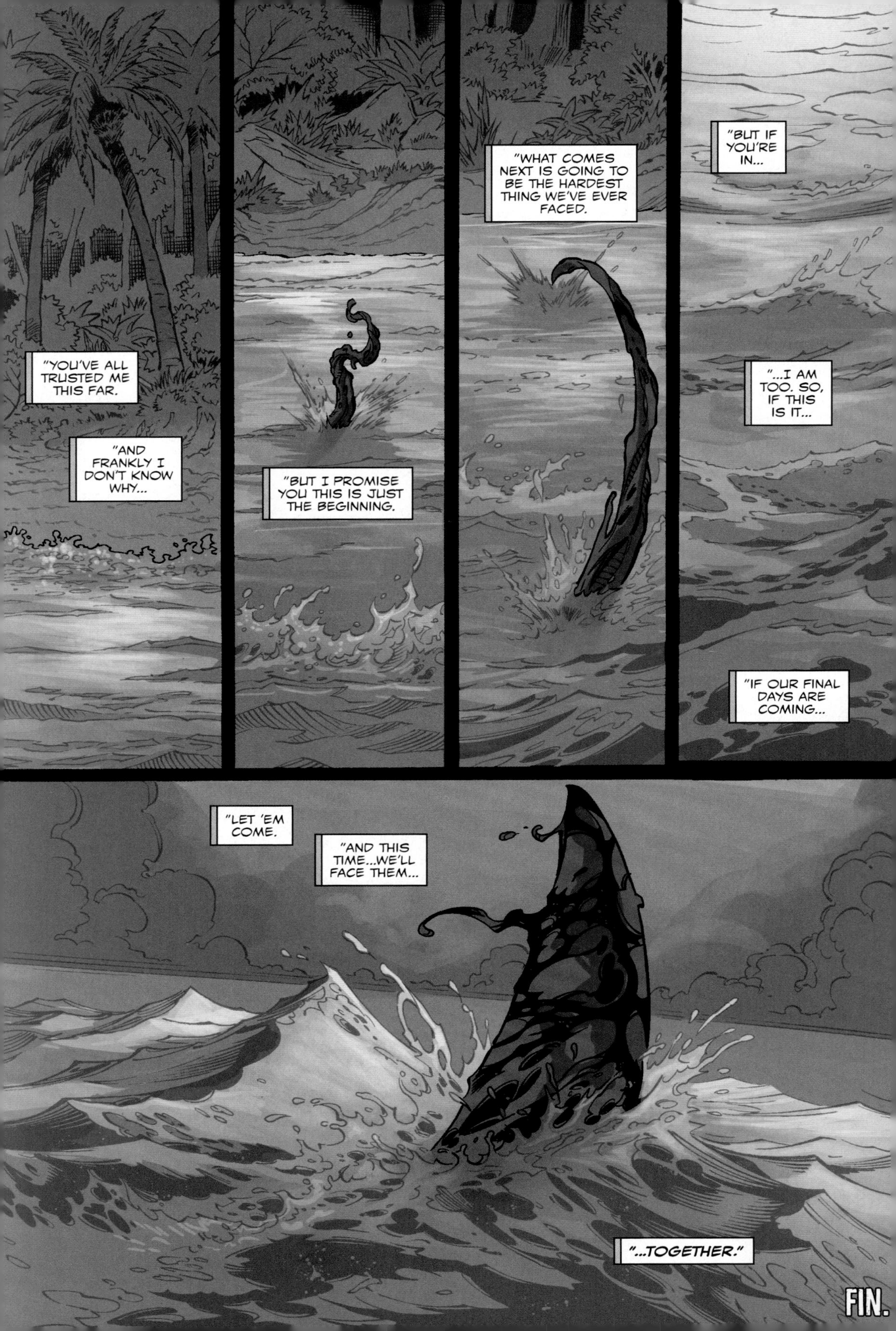
"YOU'VE ALL TRUSTED ME THIS FAR.
"AND FRANKLY I DON'T KNOW WHY...
"BUT I PROMISE YOU THIS IS JUST THE BEGINNING.
"WHAT COMES NEXT IS GOING TO BE THE HARDEST THING WE'VE EVER FACED.
"BUT IF YOU'RE IN...
"...I AM TOO. SO, IF THIS IS IT...
"IF OUR FINAL DAYS ARE COMING...
"LET 'EM COME.
"AND THIS TIME...WE'LL FACE THEM...
"...TOGETHER."
FIN.

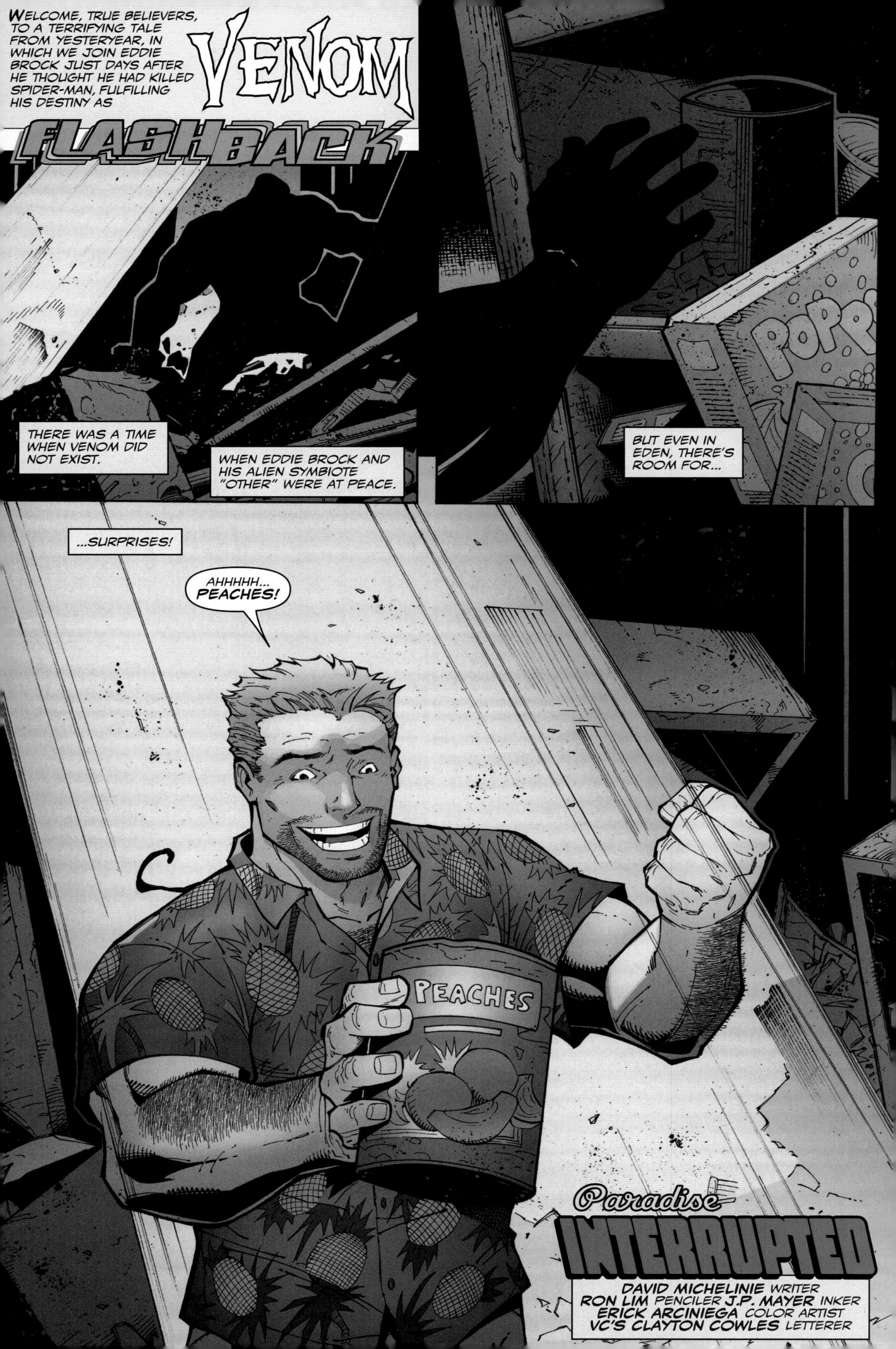
WELCOME, TRUE BELIEVERS, TO A TERRIFYING TALE FROM YESTERYEAR, IN WHICH WE JOIN EDDIE BROCK JUST DAYS AFTER HE THOUGHT HE HAD KILLED SPIDER-MAN, FULFILLING HIS DESTINY AS
VENOM
FLASHBACK
THERE WAS A TIME WHEN VENOM DID NOT EXIST.
WHEN EDDIE BROCK AND HIS ALIEN SYMBIOTE "OTHER" WERE AT PEACE.
BUT EVEN IN EDEN, THERE'S ROOM FOR...
...SURPRISES!
AHHHHH... PEACHES!
PEACHES
Paradise
INTERRUPTED
DAVID MICHELINIE WRITER
RON LIM PENCILER J.P. MAYER INKER
ERICK ARCINIEGA COLOR ARTIST
VC'S CLAYTON COWLES LETTERER

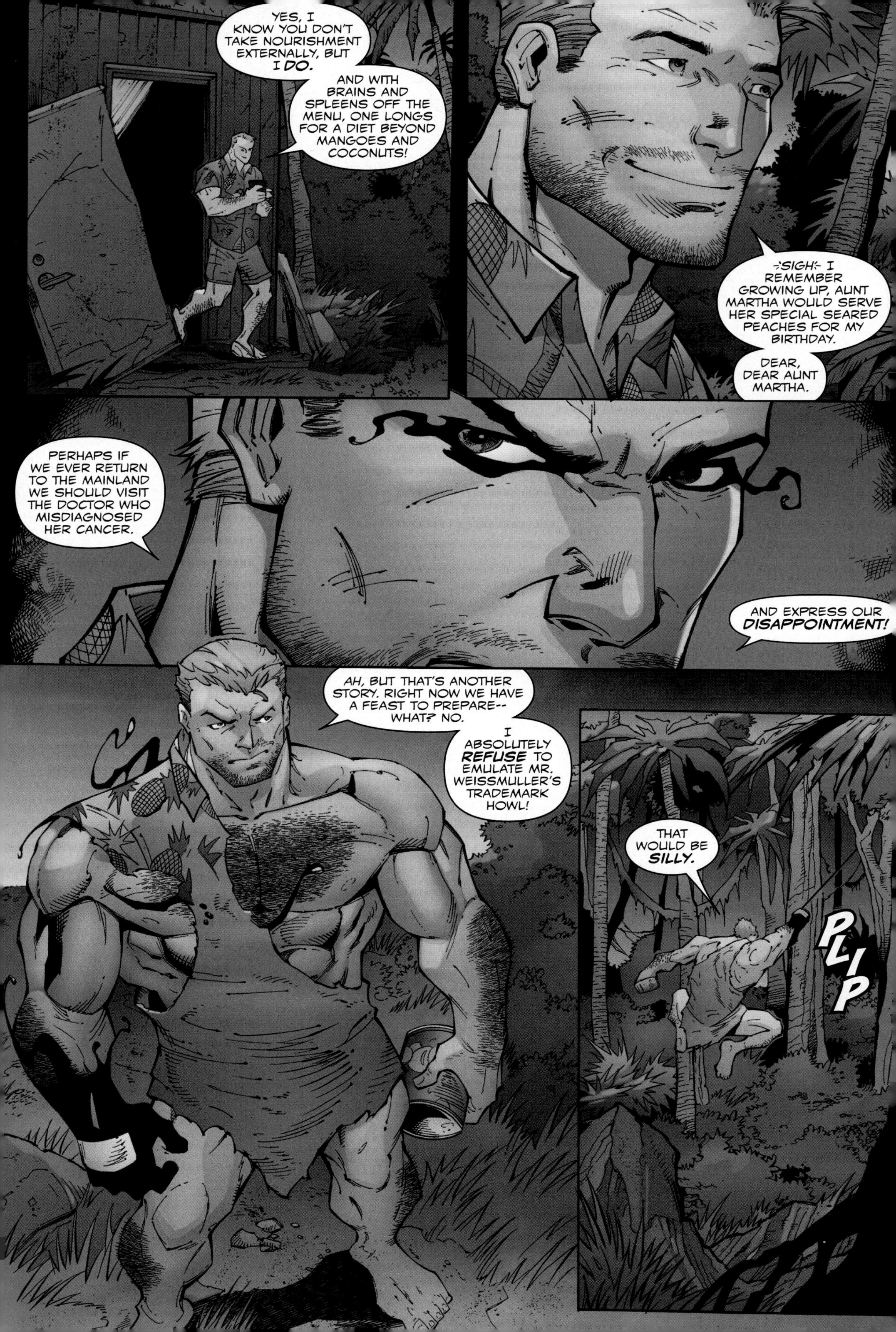
YES, I KNOW YOU DON'T TAKE NOURISHMENT EXTERNALLY, BUT I DO.
AND WITH BRAINS AND SPLEENS OFF THE MENU, ONE LONGS FOR A DIET BEYOND MANGOES AND COCONUTS!
-SIGH- I REMEMBER GROWING UP, AUNT MARTHA WOULD SERVE HER SPECIAL SEARED PEACHES FOR MY BIRTHDAY.
DEAR, DEAR AUNT MARTHA.
PERHAPS IF WE EVER RETURN TO THE MAINLAND WE SHOULD VISIT THE DOCTOR WHO MISDIAGNOSED HER CANCER.
AND EXPRESS OUR DISAPPOINTMENT!
AH, BUT THAT'S ANOTHER STORY. RIGHT NOW WE HAVE A FEAST TO PREPARE-- WHAT? NO.
I ABSOLUTELY REFUSE TO EMULATE MR. WEISSMULLER'S TRADEMARK HOWL!
THAT WOULD BE SILLY.
PLIP

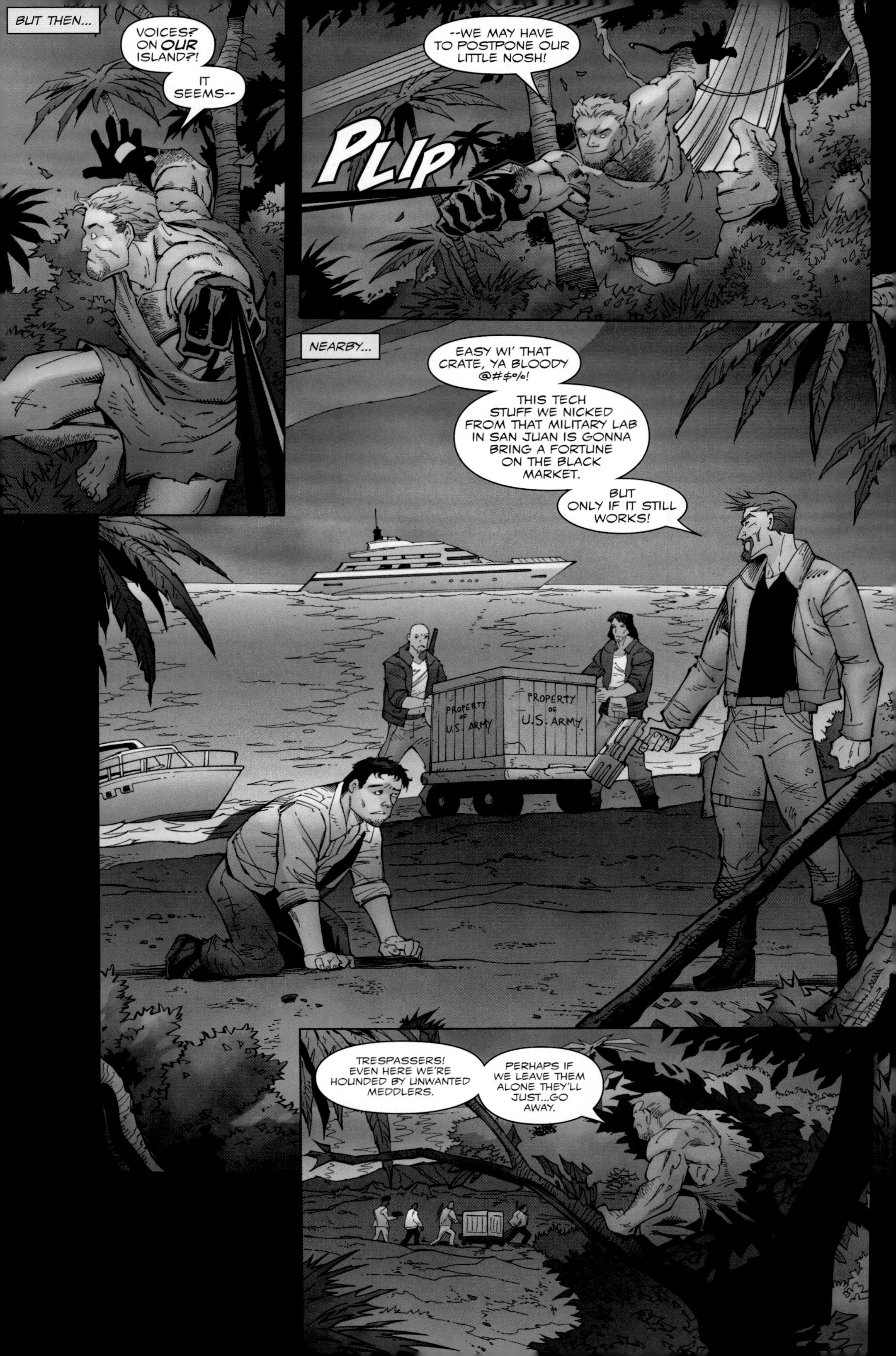
BUT THEN...
VOICES? ON OUR ISLAND?!
IT SEEMS--
--WE MAY HAVE TO POSTPONE OUR LITTLE NOSH!
PLIP
NEARBY...
EASY WI' THAT CRATE, YA BLOODY @#$%!
THIS TECH STUFF WE NICKED FROM THAT MILITARY LAB IN SAN JUAN IS GONNA BRING A FORTUNE ON THE BLACK MARKET.
BUT ONLY IF IT STILL WORKS!
PROPERTY OF U.S. ARMY
PROPERTY OF U.S. ARMY
TRESPASSERS! EVEN HERE WE'RE HOUNDED BY UNWANTED MEDDLERS.
PERHAPS IF WE LEAVE THEM ALONE THEY'LL JUST...GO AWAY.

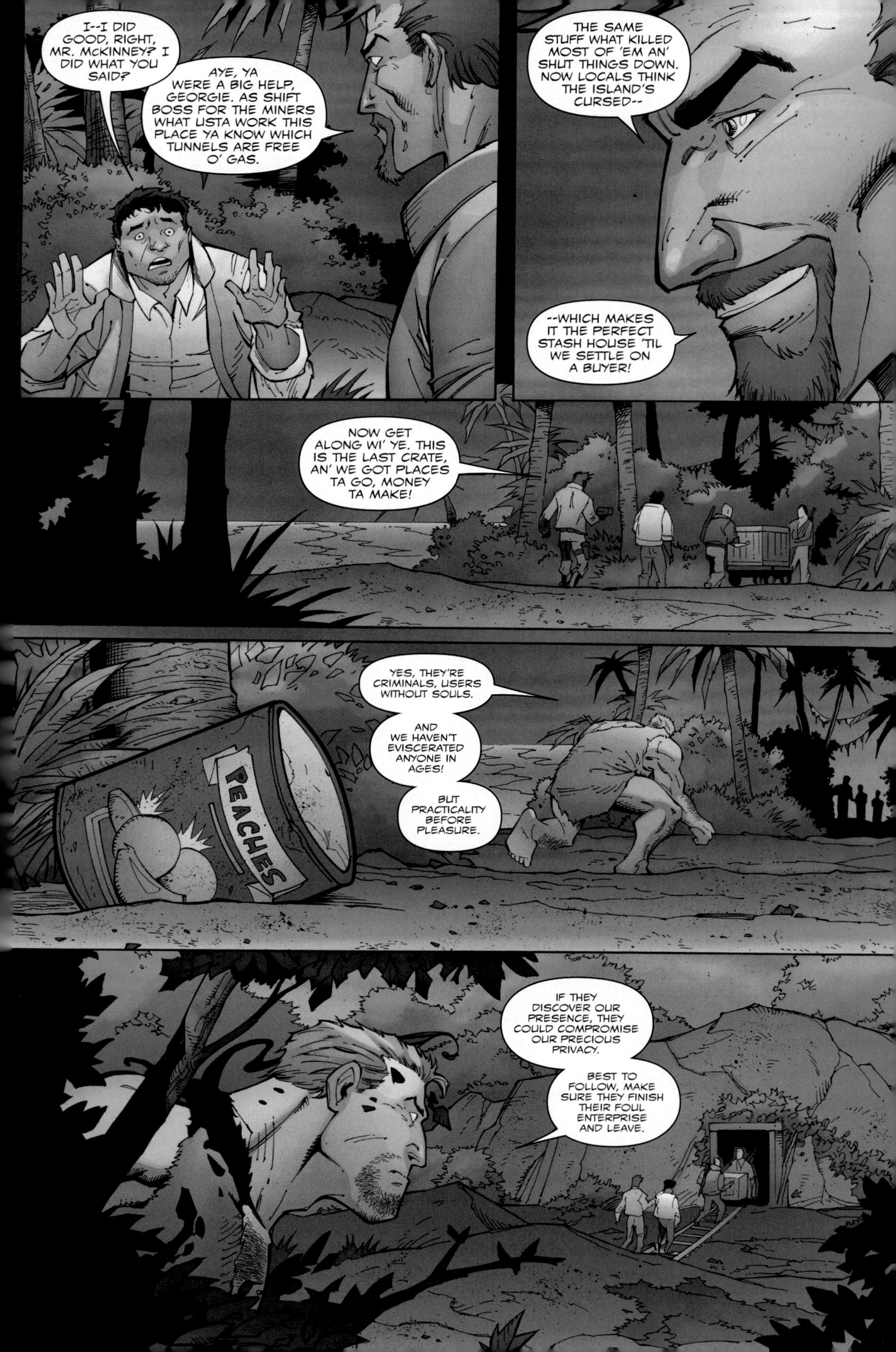
I--I DID GOOD, RIGHT, MR. MCKINNEY? I DID WHAT YOU SAID?
AYE, YA WERE A BIG HELP, GEORGIE. AS SHIFT BOSS FOR THE MINERS WHAT USTA WORK THIS PLACE YA KNOW WHICH TUNNELS ARE FREE O' GAS.
THE SAME STUFF WHAT KILLED MOST OF 'EM AN' SHUT THINGS DOWN. NOW LOCALS THINK THE ISLAND'S CURSED--
--WHICH MAKES IT THE PERFECT STASH HOUSE 'TIL WE SETTLE ON A BUYER!
NOW GET ALONG WI' YE. THIS IS THE LAST CRATE, AN' WE GOT PLACES TA GO, MONEY TA MAKE!
YES, THEY'RE CRIMINALS, USERS WITHOUT SOULS.
AND WE HAVEN'T EVISCERATED ANYONE IN AGES!
BUT PRACTICALITY BEFORE PLEASURE.
PEACHES
IF THEY DISCOVER OUR PRESENCE, THEY COULD COMPROMISE OUR PRECIOUS PRIVACY.
BEST TO FOLLOW, MAKE SURE THEY FINISH THEIR FOUL ENTERPRISE AND LEAVE.

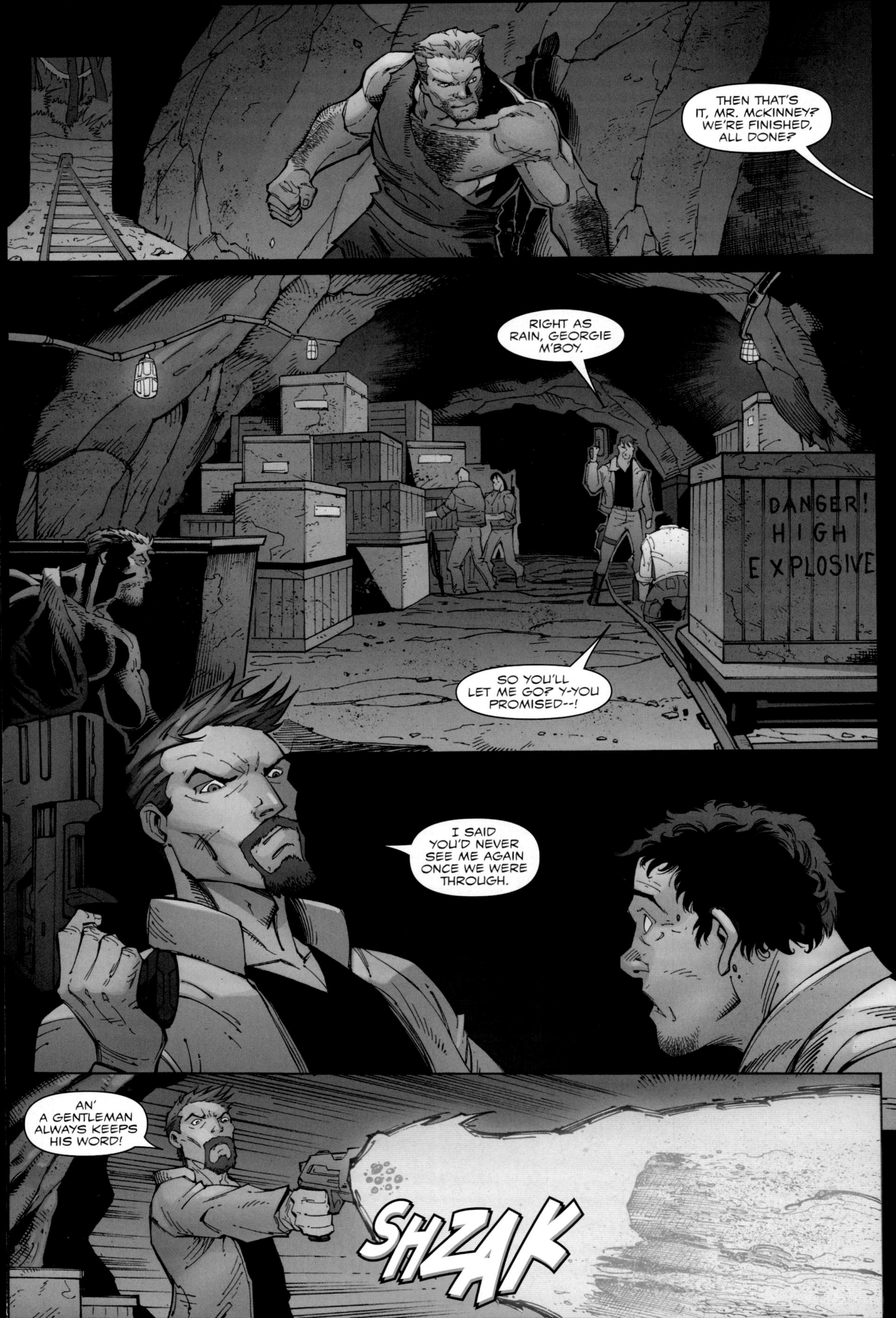
THEN THAT'S IT, MR. McKINNEY? WE'RE FINISHED, ALL DONE?
RIGHT AS RAIN, GEORGIE M'BOY.
DANGER! HIGH EXPLOSIVE
SO YOU'LL LET ME GO? Y-YOU PROMISED--!
I SAID YOU'D NEVER SEE ME AGAIN ONCE WE WERE THROUGH.
AN' A GENTLEMAN ALWAYS KEEPS HIS WORD!
SHZAK

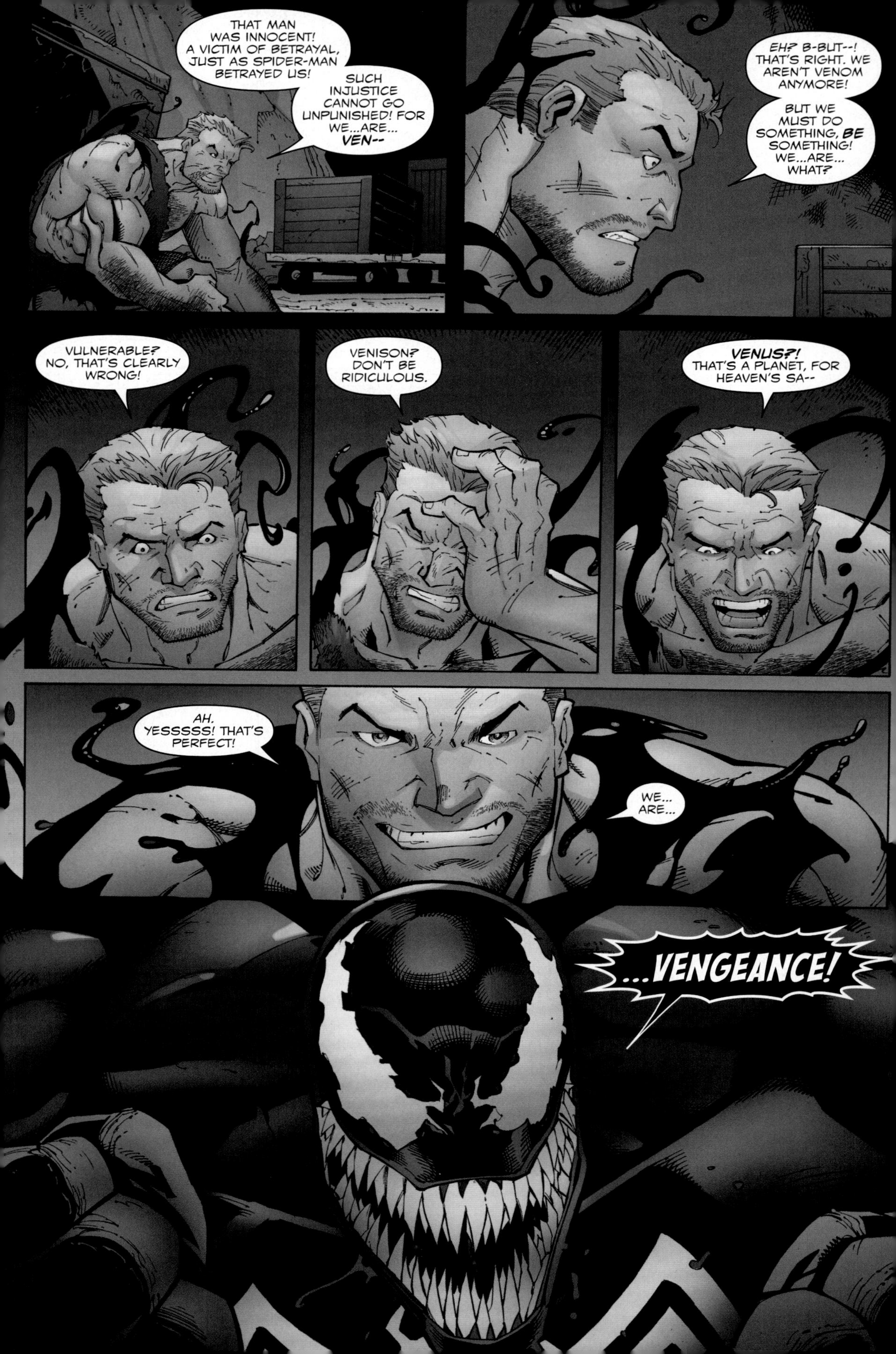

THAT MAN WAS INNOCENT! A VICTIM OF BETRAYAL, JUST AS SPIDER-MAN BETRAYED US!
SUCH INJUSTICE CANNOT GO UNPUNISHED! FOR WE...ARE... VEN--
EH? B-BUT--! THAT'S RIGHT. WE AREN'T VENOM ANYMORE!
BUT WE MUST DO SOMETHING, BE SOMETHING! WE...ARE... WHAT?
VULNERABLE? NO, THAT'S CLEARLY WRONG!
VENISON? DON'T BE RIDICULOUS.
VENUS?! THAT'S A PLANET, FOR HEAVEN'S SA--
AH. YESSSSS! THAT'S PERFECT!
WE... ARE...
...VENGEANCE!

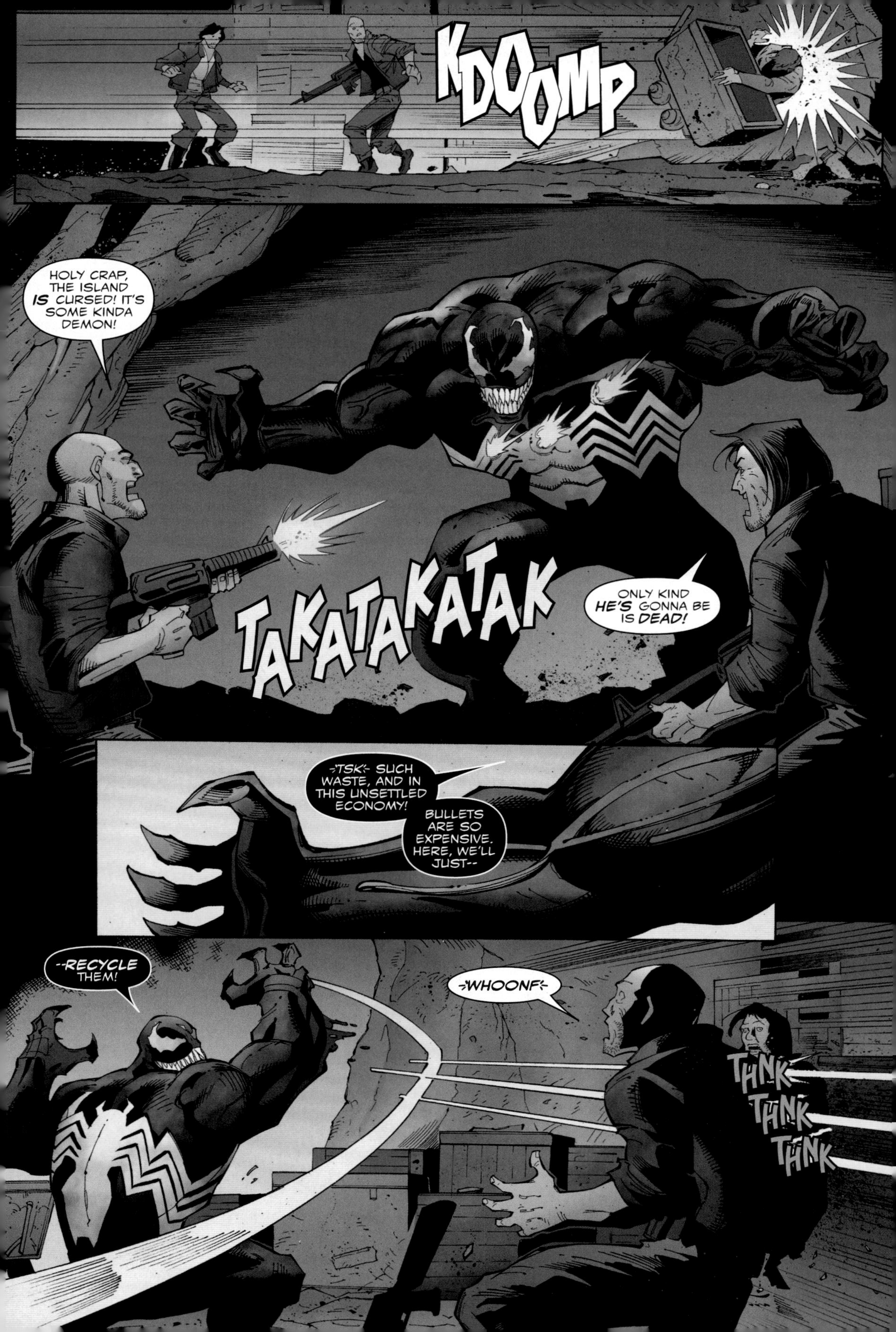
KDOOMP
HOLY CRAP, THE ISLAND IS CURSED! IT'S SOME KINDA DEMON!
TAKATAKATAK
ONLY KIND HE'S GONNA BE IS DEAD!
-TSK- SUCH WASTE, AND IN THIS UNSETTLED ECONOMY!
BULLETS ARE SO EXPENSIVE. HERE, WE'LL JUST--
--RECYCLE THEM!
-WHOONF-
THNK
THNK
THNK

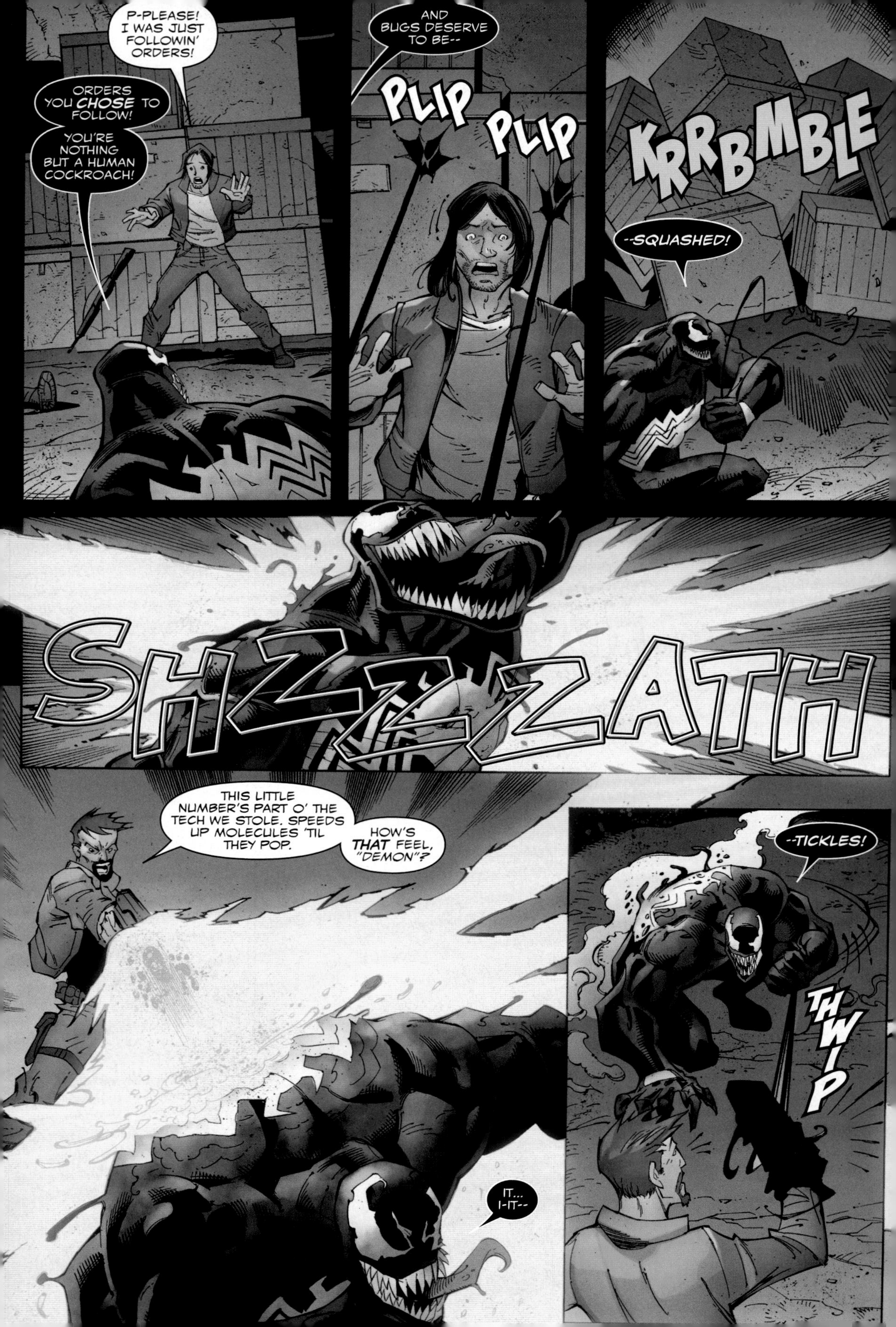
P-PLEASE! I WAS JUST FOLLOWIN' ORDERS!
ORDERS YOU CHOSE TO FOLLOW!
YOU'RE NOTHING BUT A HUMAN COCKROACH!
AND BUGS DESERVE TO BE--
PLIP
PLIP
KRRBMBLE
--SQUASHED!
SHZZZATH
THIS LITTLE NUMBER'S PART O' THE TECH WE STOLE. SPEEDS UP MOLECULES 'TIL THEY POP.
HOW'S THAT FEEL, "DEMON"?
--TICKLES!
THWIP
IT... I-IT--

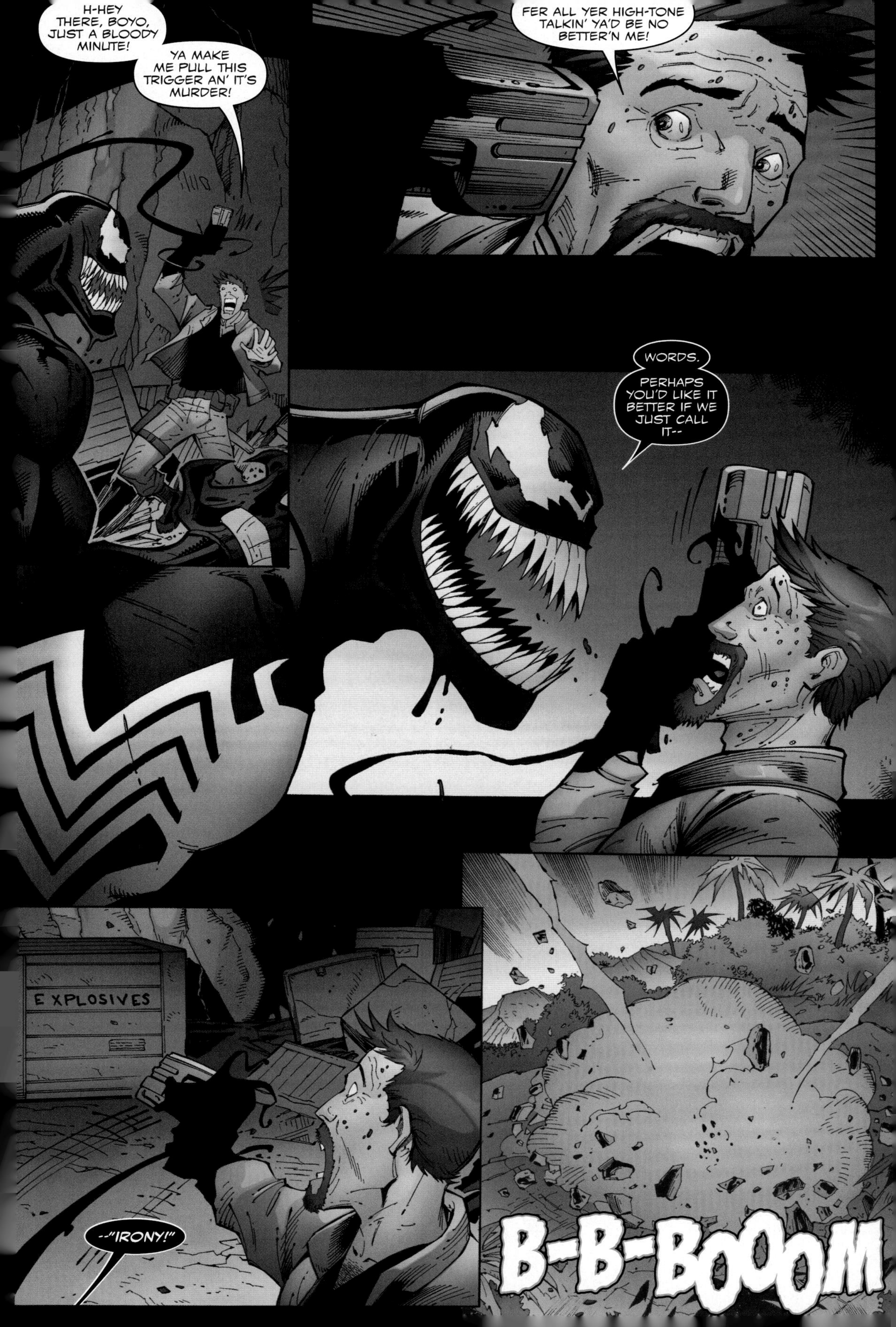
H-HEY THERE, BOYO, JUST A BLOODY MINUTE!
YA MAKE ME PULL THIS TRIGGER AN' IT'S MURDER!
FER ALL YER HIGH-TONE TALKIN' YA'D BE NO BETTER'N ME!
WORDS.
PERHAPS YOU'D LIKE IT BETTER IF WE JUST CALL IT--
EXPLOSIVES
--"IRONY!"
B-B-BOOOOM

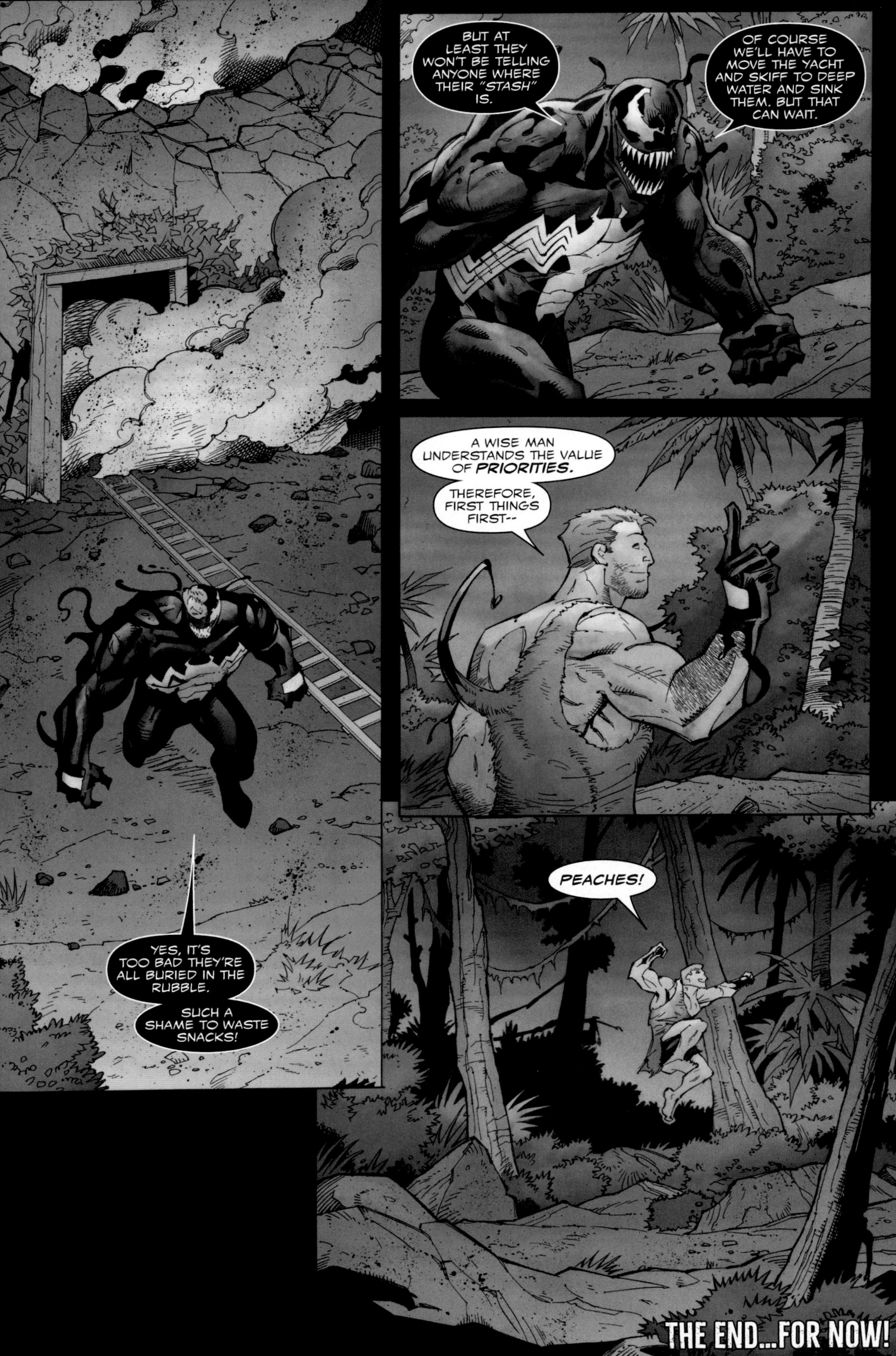

BUT AT LEAST THEY WON'T BE TELLING ANYONE WHERE THEIR "STASH" IS.
OF COURSE WE'LL HAVE TO MOVE THE YACHT AND SKIFF TO DEEP WATER AND SINK THEM. BUT THAT CAN WAIT.
YES, IT'S TOO BAD THEY'RE ALL BURIED IN THE RUBBLE.
SUCH A SHAME TO WASTE SNACKS!
A WISE MAN UNDERSTANDS THE VALUE OF PRIORITIES.
THEREFORE, FIRST THINGS FIRST--
PEACHES!
THE END...FOR NOW!

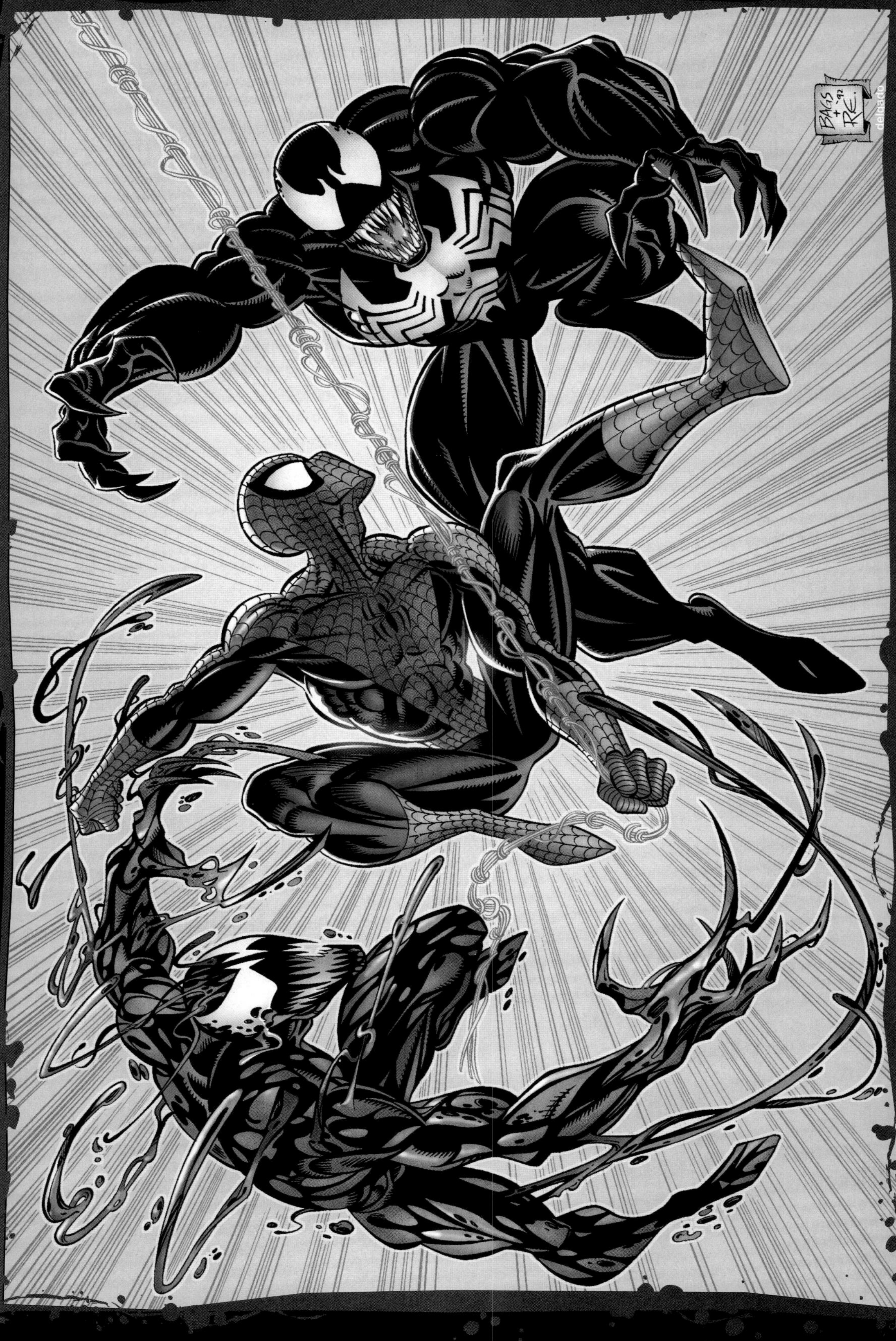

#25 HIDDEN GEM VARIANT BY **MARK BAGLEY** & **EDGAR DELGADO**

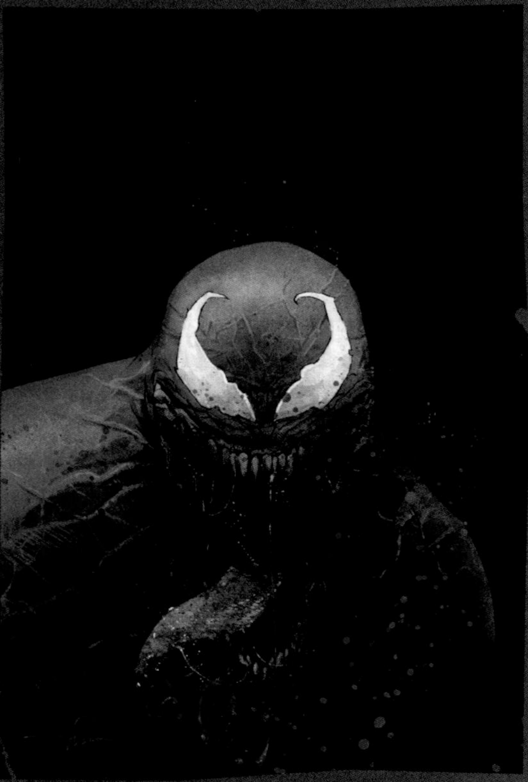

#25 VARIANT
BY **GERARDO ZAFFINO**

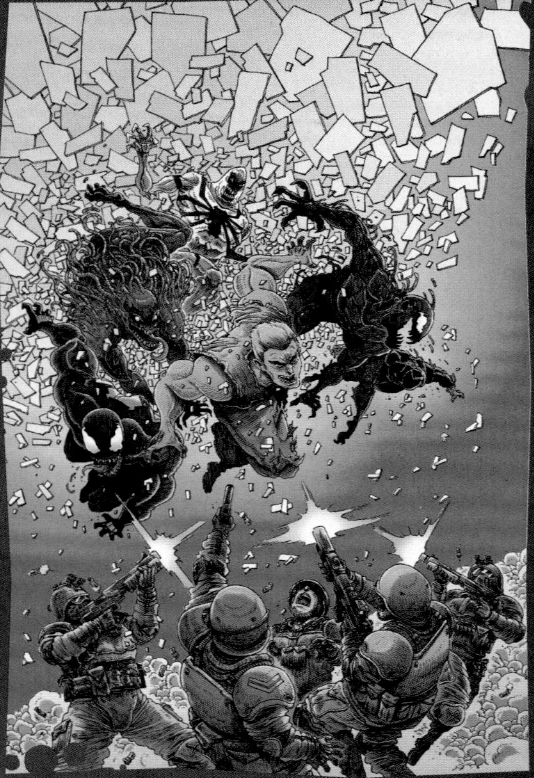

#25 VARIANT
BY **JAMES STOKOE**

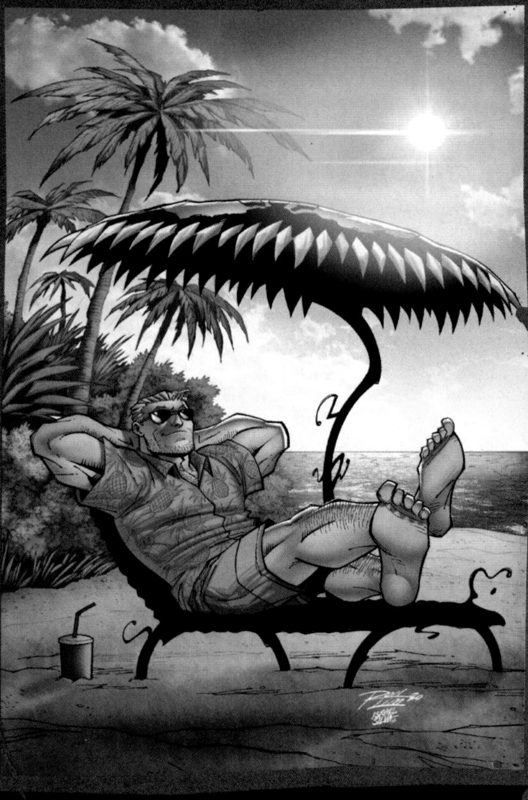

#25 VARIANT
BY **RON LIM** & **ISRAEL SILVA**

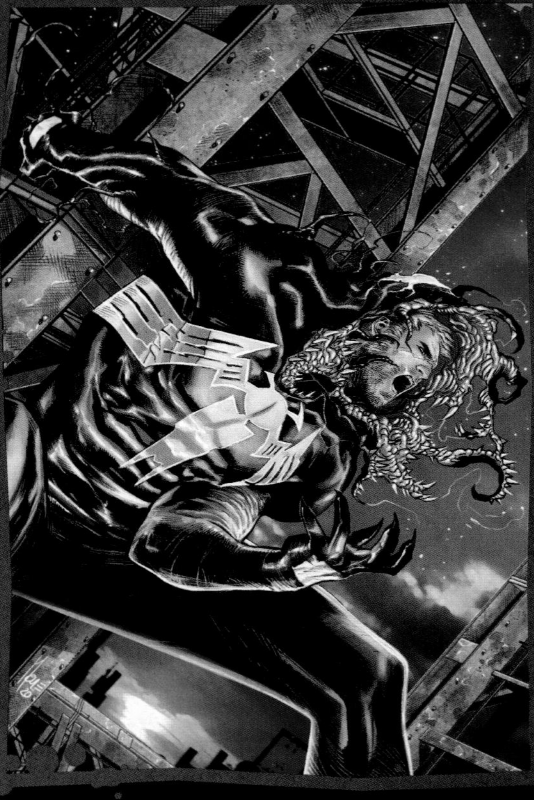

#25 VARIANT
BY **MARCO CHECCHETTO**

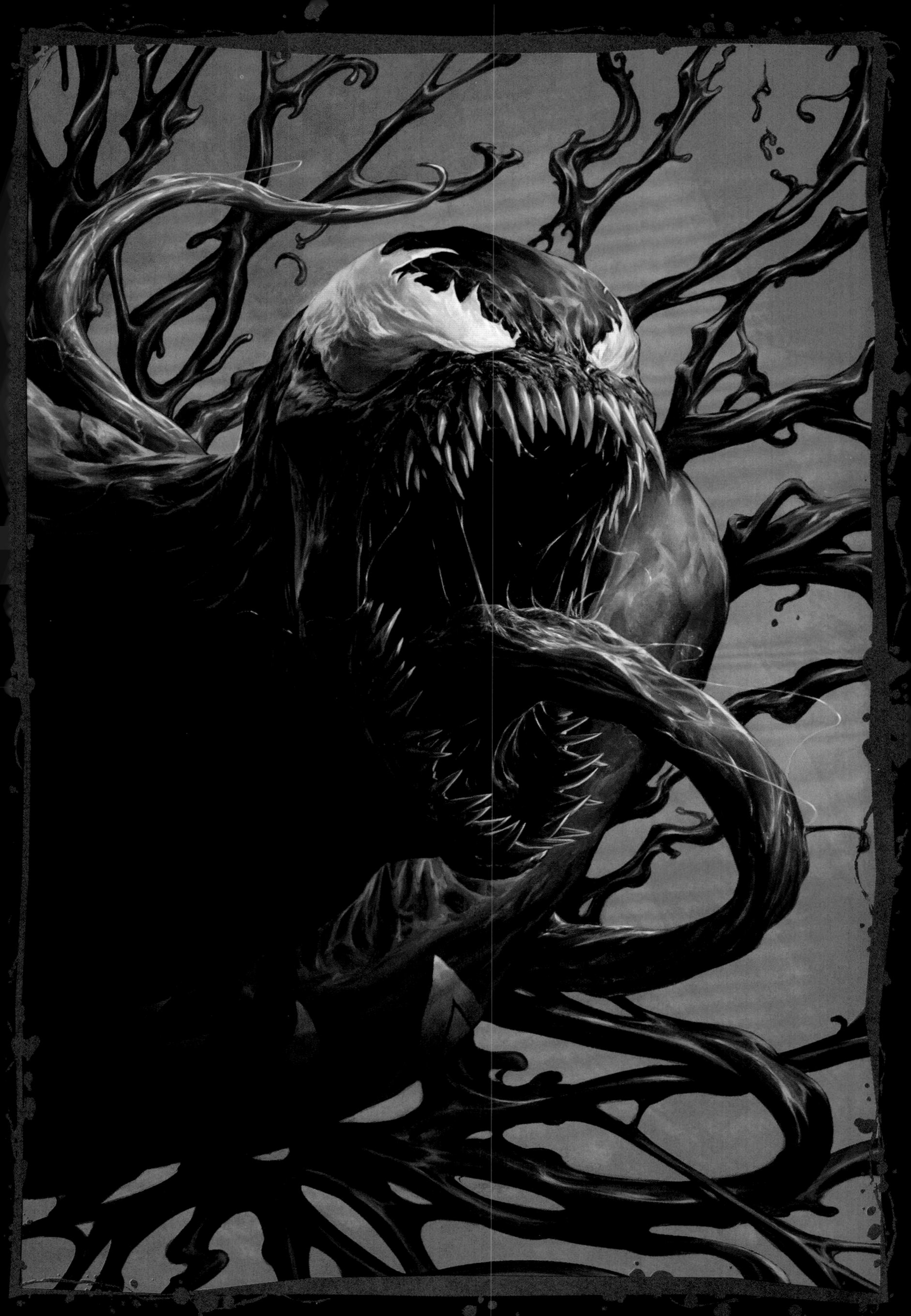

#25 VARIANT BY **DAVE RAPOZA**

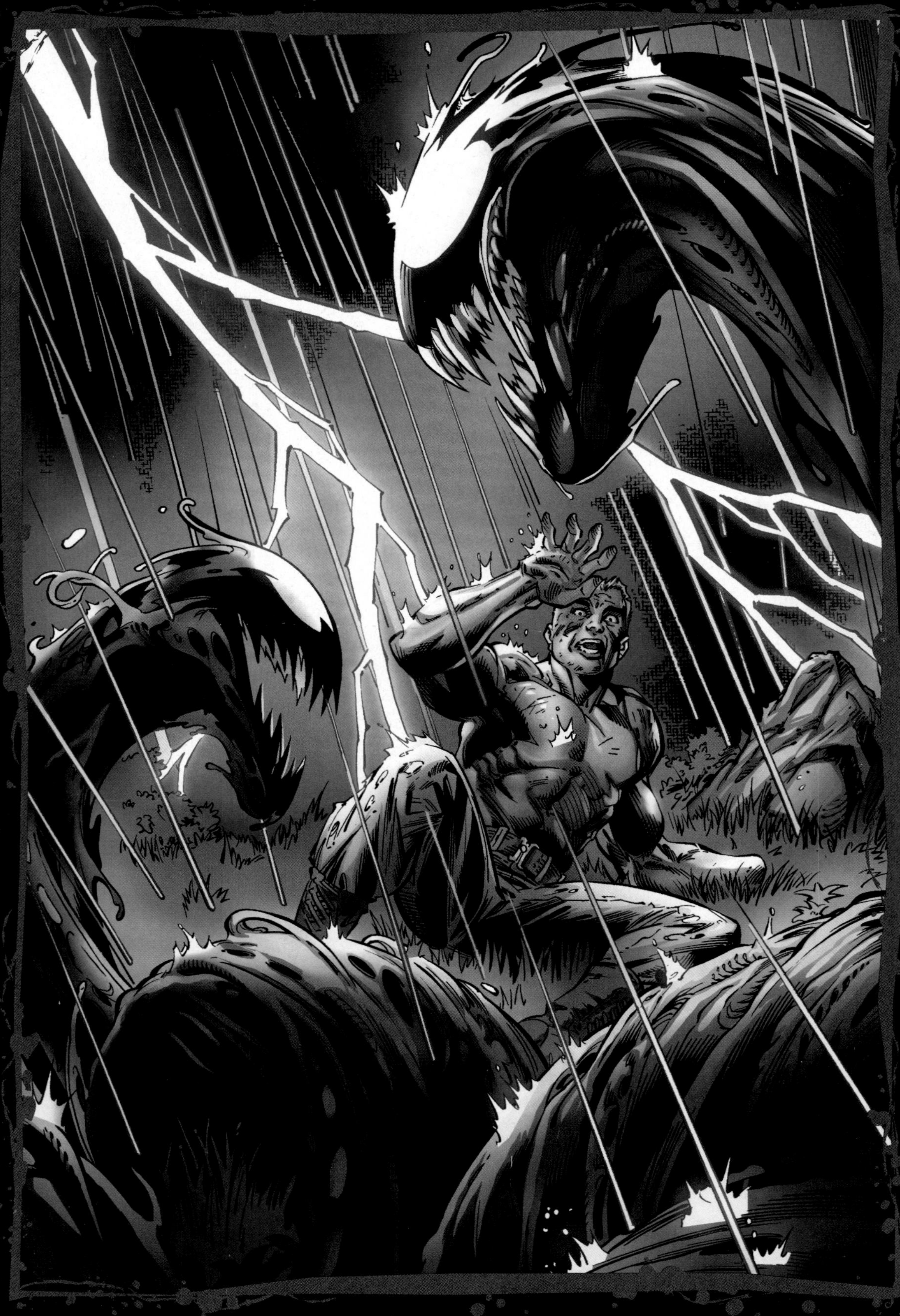

#25 VARIANT BY **MARK BAGLEY, ANDY OWENS** & **JASON KEITH**